46.8

Soviet and Post-Soviet Politics and Society (SPPS) Vol. 100

ISSN 1614-3515

General Editor: Andreas Umland, *The Catholic University of Eichstaett-Ingolstadt*, umland@stanfordalumni.org

Editorial Assistant: Olena Sivuda, *Drahomanov Pedagogical University of Kyiv*, SLS6255@ku-eichstaett.de

D1705159

Soviet and Post-Soviet Politics and Society (SPPS)

ISSN 1614-3515

Founded in 2004 and refereed since 2007, SPPS makes available affordable English-, German- and Russian-language studies on the history of the countries of the former Soviet bloc from the late Tsarist period to today. It publishes approximately 15-20 volumes per year, and focuses on issues in transitions to and from democracy such as economic crisis, identity formation, civil society development, and constitutional reform in CEE and the NIS. SPPS also aims to highlight so far understudied themes in East European studies such as right-wing radicalism, religious life, higher education, or human rights protection. The authors and titles of all previously published manuscripts are listed at the end of this book. For a full description of the series and reviews of its books, see www.ibidem-verlag.de/red/spps.

Note for authors (as of 2009): After successful review, fully formatted and carefully edited electronic master copies of up to 250 pages will be published as b/w A5 paperbacks and marketed in Germany (e.g. vlb.de, buchkatalog.de, amazon.de) and internationally (e.g. amazon. com). For longer books, formatting/editorial assistance, different binding, oversize maps, coloured illustrations and other special arrangements, authors' fees between €100 and €1500 apply. Publication of German doctoral dissertations follows a separate procedure. Authors are asked to provide a high-quality electronic picture on the object of their study for the book's front-cover. Younger authors may add a foreword from an established scholar. Monograph authors and collected volume editors receive two free as well as further copies for a reduced authors' price, and will be asked to contribute to marketing their book as well as finding reviewers and review journals for them. These conditions are subject to yearly review, and to be modified, in the future. Further details at www.ibidem-verlag.de/red/spps-authors.

Editorial correspondence & manuscripts should, until 2011, be sent to: Dr. Andreas Umland, ZIMOS, Ostenstr. 27, 85072 Eichstätt, Germany; e-mail: umland@stanfordalumni.org

Business correspondence & review copy requests should be sent to: *ibidem*-Verlag, Julius-Leber-Weg 11, D-30457 Hannover, Germany; tel.: +49(0)511-2622200; fax: +49(0)511-2622201; spps@ibidem-verlag.de.

Book orders & payments should be made via the publisher's electronic book shop at: www.ibidem-verlag.de/red/SPPS_EN/

Authors, reviewers, referees, and editors for (as well as all other persons sympathetic to) SPPS are invited to join its networks at www.facebook.com/group.php?gid=52638198614 www.linkedin.com/groups?about=&gid=103012 www.xing.com/net/spps-ibidem-verlag/

Recent Volumes

91   Christopher Gilley
     The 'Change of Signposts' in the Ukrainian Emigration
     A Contribution to the History of Sovietophilism in the 1920s
     With a foreword by Frank Golczewski
     ISBN 978-3-89821-965-5

92   Philipp Casula, Jeronim Perovic (Eds.)
     Identities and Politics During the Putin Presidency
     The Discursive Foundations of Russia's Stability
     With a foreword by Heiko Haumann
     ISBN 978-3-8382-0015-6

93   Marcel Viëtor
     Europa und die Frage nach seinen Grenzen im Osten
     Zur Konstruktion 'europäischer Identität' in Geschichte und Gegenwart
     Mit einem Vorwort von Albrecht Lehmann
     ISBN 978-3-8382-0045-3

94   Ben Hellman, Andrei Rogachevskii
     Filming the Unfilmable
     Casper Wrede's 'One Day in the Life of Ivan Denisovich'
     ISBN 978-3-8382-0044-6

95   Eva Fuchslocher
     Vaterland, Sprache, Glaube
     Orthodoxie und Nationenbildung am Beispiel Georgiens
     Mit einem Vorwort von Christina von Braun
     ISBN 978-3-89821-884-9

96   Vladimir Kantor
     Das Westlertum und der Weg Russlands
     Zur Entwicklung der russischen Literatur und Philosophie
     Ediert von Dagmar Herrmann
     Mit einem Beitrag von Nikolaus Lobkowicz
     ISBN 978-3-8382-0102-3

97   Kamran Musayev
     Die postsowjetische Transformation im Baltikum und Südkaukasus
     Eine vergleichende Untersuchung der politischen Entwicklung Lettlands und Aserbaidschans 1985-2009
     Mit einem Vorwort von Leonid Luks
     Ediert von Sandro Henschel
     ISBN 978-3-8382-0103-0

98   Tatiana Zhurzhenko
     Borderlands into Bordered Lands
     Geopolitics of Identity in Post-Soviet Ukraine
     With a foreword by Dieter Segert
     ISBN 978-3-8382-0042-2

99   Кирилл Галушко, Лидия Смола (ред.)
     Пределы падения – варианты украинского будущего
     Аналитико-прогностические исследования
     ISBN 978-3-8382-0148-1

Michael Minkenberg (ed.)

HISTORICAL LEGACIES AND THE RADICAL RIGHT IN POST-COLD WAR CENTRAL AND EASTERN EUROPE

With an afterword by Sabrina P. Ramet

ibidem-Verlag
Stuttgart

Bibliografische Information der Deutschen Nationalbibliothek
Die Deutsche Nationalbibliothek verzeichnet diese Publikation in der
Deutschen Nationalbibliografie; detaillierte bibliografische Daten sind im
Internet über http://dnb.d-nb.de abrufbar.

Bibliographic information published by the Deutsche Nationalbibliothek
Die Deutsche Nationalbibliothek lists this publication in the Deutsche Nationalbibliografie;
detailed bibliographic data are available in the Internet at http://dnb.d-nb.de.

First published in: *Communist and Post-Communist Studies* 42:4 (2009), pp. 445-572.
Reprinted with kind permission by the editors.

Front cover collage: © Michael Minkenberg 2010.
Picture with Russian demonstrator on front cover: © Galina Kozhevnikova 2009.

∞

Gedruckt auf alterungsbeständigem, säurefreien Papier
Printed on acid-free paper

ISSN: 1614-3515

ISBN-10: 3-8382-0124-8
ISBN-13: 978-3-8382-0124-5

© *ibidem*-Verlag
Stuttgart 2010

Contents

List of Contributors

Timm Beichelt, Faculty of Social and Cultural Sciences, European University Viadrina Frankfurt (Oder), Germany.

Lenka Bustikova, Department of Political Science, Duke University, Durham, North Carolina.

James Frusetta, Department of History, Hampden-Sydney College, Hampden-Sydney, Virginia.

Simona Guerra, School of Politics and International Relations, University of Nottingham, United Kingdom.

Anca Glont, Department of History, University of Illinois Urbana, Urbana, Illinois.

John Ishiyama, Department of Political Science, University of North Texas, Denton, Texas.

Herbert Kitschelt, Department of Political Science, Duke University, Durham, North Carolina.

Sarah L. de Lange, Department of Political Science, University of Amsterdam, Amsterdam, The Netherlands.

Michael Minkenberg, Max Weber Chair of German and European Studies, New York University, and Faculty of Social and Cultural Sciences, European University Viadrina Frankfurt (Oder), Germany.

Sabrina P. Ramet, Department of Political Science, Norwegian University of Science and Technology, Trondheim, and Centre for the Study of Civil War, Peace Research Institute Oslo, Norway.

Acknowledgments

This book is a reprint of a special issue "Legacies and the Radical Right in Post-1989 Central and Eastern Europe", which I edited as guest editor in *Communist and Post-Communist Studies* (vol. 42, no. 4, December 2009). I gratefully acknowledge the journal's permission to reprint the special issue in book format. Both book and special issue result from a workshop "The Radical Right in Post-1989 Central and Eastern Europe – the Role of Legacies" which took place from April 24 – 26, 2008, at the Center of European and Mediterranean Studies at New York University (see www.cems.as.nyu.edu/docs/CP/1041/2008AnnualReport.pdf, pp. 15-17).

Many helpful hands and resourceful supporters have made workshop and publications possible. I want to thank Alisa Shadrin who was my graduate assitant at NYU in 2007/08 and without whose help and skills in organizing the workshop none of the events would have taken place. I thank NYU's staff and colleagues, especially Kathrin DiPaola, director of Deutsches Haus at NYU for organizational and moral support. Thanks also to New York University and the New York Office of the German Academic Exchange Service (DAAD) for providing the funds necessary to turn this project idea from possibility to reality. And very special thanks to my assistant Dominika Kowszewicz at the Center for European and Mediterranean Studies at NYU for helping me to edit the text and prepare it for the publisher, and also for providing some ideas for the book's cover page.

Michael Minkenberg
Berlin/New York
June 17, 2010

Leninist beneficiaries? Pre-1989 legacies and the radical right in post-1989 Central and Eastern Europe
Some introductory observations

Michael Minkenberg

ABSTRACT: A central topos in the study of Central and Eastern European contemporary politics in general, and of its radical right politics in particular is the emphasis on the extraordinary relevance of history and geography. In fact, the entire transformation process after 1989 is often clothed in terms of historical and geographical categories, either as "return of history" or a "return to Europe", or both. In these various scenarios, the radical right claims a prominent place in this politics of return, and the study of this current echoes the more general concern, in the analysis of the region, with historical analogies and the role of legacies. Sometimes analogies are drawn between the post-1989 radical right and interwar fascism, in terms of "Weimarization" of the transformation countries and the return of the pre-socialist, ultranationalist or even fascist past – "the return of history". Others argue that since some Central and Eastern European party systems increasingly resemble their Western European counterparts, so does the radical right, at least where it is electorally successful – the "return to Europe". According to yet another line of thought, the radical right in the region is a phenomenon sui generis, inherently shaped by the historical forces of state socialism and the transformation process and, as a result and in contrast to Western Europe, ideologically more extreme and anti-democratic while organizationally more a movement than a party phenomenon. In all these approaches, the key concept "legacies" and the radical right are often underspecified. This volume takes a closer look at the intersection of history or particular legacies, and the mobilization of the radical right in the post-1989 world of the region, while attempting to provide a sharper focus on key concepts. Regardless of the different approaches, all contributions show that with the radical right, a peculiar "syncretic construct" (Tismaneanu) has emerged in Central and Eastern Europe after 1989, which is derived from both pre-communist and communist legacies.

"The ideological extinction of Leninist formations left behind a vacuum that has been filled by syncretic constructs drawing from the region's pre-communist and communist heritage" (Tismaneanu, 2007, p. 35). Such is a recent assessment of the political trajectory in Central and Eastern Europe by one of the experts of the region. Among these "syncretic constructs" Vladimir Tismaneanu lists "nationalism in both its civic and ethnic incarnations, liberalism, democratic socialism, conservatism, populism, neo-Leninism, and even more or less refurbished fascism" (*ibid.*). This seems more or less the inventory of Western party politics minus the Green movement, plus a somewhat reconstructed Leninism. However, the emphasis is not on the equivalence of the situation with "the West" but with "the past", the region's heritage. And equally important, almost half of the phenomena identified as filling the post-Leninist vacuum constitute what can be summarily described as the radical right (see below). Here, in a nutshell, lies a central topos in the study of the region's contemporary politics in general, and of its radical right politics in particular: the emphasis on the extraordinary relevance of history and geography. It is this intersection of history or particular legacies, and the mobilization of the radical right in the post-1989 world of the region, which constitutes the core of this publication.

The entire transformation process after 1989 is often clothed in terms of historical and geographical categories, either as a "return of history" or a "return to Europe", or both. On the one hand, historical analogies are invoked which cast the various countries' development after the fall of communism in light of the remapping of the region in the wake of World War I and the 1919 peace treaties. Some authors see it even as the belated conclusion of the Wilsonian project of state and nation making after that war (Judt, 2005, pp. 637-638). As is well known, Europe's Wilsonian order after World War I ended in the rise of fascism and a period of totalitarian politics and wartime destruction, and yet, the "legacy" of 1919 seemed to persist until and well beyond the 1989 upheavals. On the other hand, post-1989 Central and Eastern Europe are characterized as a region catching up with its Western counterpart – the "return to Europe" – while still being identified in terms of a distinct "otherness" which often includes notions of backwardness (Wolff, 1994; Kopstein, 2003). Whether this return can ever be completed under such a conceptual premise, remains an open question.

Either way, the radical right in contemporary Central and Eastern Europe claims a prominent place in this politics of return, and the study of this current echoes the more general concern, in the analyses of the region, with historical analogies and the role of legacies. Sometimes analogies are drawn between the post-1989 radical right and interwar fascism, in terms of a "Weimarization" of the transformation countries and the return of the pre-socialist, ultranationalist or even fascist past – the "return of history". Another interpretation argues that since some Central and East European party systems increasingly resemble their West European counterparts, so does the radical right, at least where it is electorally successful – the "return to Europe". A third line of thought states that the radical right in the region is a phenomenon *sui generis*, inherently shaped by the historical forces of state socialism and the transformation process and, as a result and in contrast to Western Europe, ideologically more extreme and anti-democratic while organizationally more a movement than a party phenomenon (Minkenberg, 2002; Mudde, 2000, 2007).

But while these historical arguments or the reference to legacies are widespread in the comparative analysis of the radical right in Central and Eastern Europe (not to mention the single-case country studies which all too readily explain the radical right's features and mobilization by the respective country's particular past and heritage), there remains a fuzziness how this past is operationalized in such explanations, and what kind of legacies are held relevant. Therefore, a few general remarks about the legacy approach in the study of Central and Eastern European politics after 1989, its variants and its limits, seem appropriate. A first distinction to be made is that between the more sweeping claims that "history matters" and a narrow focus on a particular legacy, such as the experience of Leninism.

In his programmatic essay "why and how history matters", Charles Tilly provides a number of reasons why explanations in political science cannot do without careful historical analysis (Tilly, 2006). The usefulness of historical analysis ranges from large-scale political processes, such as the effects of the so-called system of Westphalia on the patterns of war and international relations from its inception in the 17th century until the present, to the more narrow phenomenon of the modularity of one particular political process or outcome for subsequent political action and programs, for example the French revolution or the nation building processes, from macro-processes of state formation to micro-processes of social movement formation (Anderson, 1983). Tilly acknowledges that in these processes spatial variation – due to the incorporation of locally prevalent and diverging culture (language, beliefs,

social categories) – is bounded by path dependency "such that events occur-
ring at one state in a sequence contain the range of events that is possible at
later stages" (Tilly, 2006, p. 421; Mahoney and Schensul, 2006). These categories seem quite useful in the explanation of the rise and performance of the
radical right in Central and Eastern Europe. They have also been applied to
the study of regime change and democratization in post-communist Europe,
in the context of which the legacy approach was first developed.

In his seminal essay, Kenneth Jowitt argued that Leninist legacies
which all former East Bloc countries in Europe share, favor an authoritarian
rather than liberal, democratic and capitalist way of life (Jowitt, 1992a, p.
293). Leninism as an institutional arrangement (or political regime) and ac-
companying cultural traits (or cultural regime), consisted of a traditional culture and a sharp distinction between private and public realms and virtues,
the institutionalization of charisma through the rule of "the Party", the fragmentation of society, lack of established elites, and mutual distrust among
members of society. Jowitt anticipated troubling effects of this system of rule
on the prospects for democracy in the region: "The Leninist legacy in Eastern
Europe consists largely – not exclusively – of fragmented, mutually suspicious, societies with little religio-cultural support for tolerant and individually
self-reliant behaviour, and of a fragmented region made up of countries that
view each other with animosity. The way Leninists ruled and the way Leninism collapsed contributed to this inheritance" (*ibid.*, p. 304). As the only effective way out of this situation, Jowitt hoped for a massive intervention of Western Europe and the United States.[1]

The debate which followed Jowitt's article shall not be recounted here
(for an appraisal see Tismaneanu et al., 2006). But it is important to note how
this legacy concept in the study of Central and East European politics after
1989 developed over time. On the one hand, a number of scholars, though at
times quite critical of Jowitt's own approach and pessimism, followed the logic
of his argument and focused on the communist era as the independent variable in studying the prospects of liberalization, capitalism and democracy in
the region (Ekiert and Hanson, 2003; Tismaneanu et al., 2006). Here, the
variation of post-communist outcomes, such as successful or unsuccessful
regime change, is related to the nature of post-communist regimes. A particularly instructive application of this approach is the comparative analysis of

---

1   Although Jowitt's pessimistic prediction did not come true, his emphasis on the cru-
     cial role of the West was seen by some as one of the accomplishments of his
     analysis (Howard, 2006, p. 41).

party competition in selected countries, relating the degree of structured party systems to the role of bureaucracy and rationality in the old regime (Kitschelt et al. 1999). However, in a critical essay, Herbert Kitschelt (2003) warns of two "excesses" in the explanation of post-communist regime diversity: that of deep explanations, that is, going back far into history and accounting for a variety of causes next to Leninist legacies, such as religion, geographic location and others, and that of shallow explanations, that is, focusing on the patterns set by the transformation process itself, by bargaining dynamics etc. In his conclusion, Kitschelt seems to follow Tilly's recommendation to focus on both macro and micro processes, on path dependency and agency, to combine causal mechanism with causal depth, including cultural mechanisms (*ibid.*, p. 80).

A rather different approach is taken by those who widen the concept of legacies to various dimensions and layers. For example, in the introduction to their book on "Liberalization and Leninist Legacies", Crawford and Lijphart (1997) identify and explore six key legacies (*ibid.*, pp. 11-12): (a) the cultural legacy: the history of backwardness, victimization, and intolerance; (b) the social legacy: the absence of an established successor elite; (c) the political legacy: weak party systems with shallow roots in society; (d) the national legacy: the interrupted process of nation-building; (e) the institutional legacy: the survival of Leninist institutions; and (f) the administrative and economic legacy: centralized states and command economies. At the end of their survey of the legacies and relevant literature, the two authors conclude that if the goal is to trace the impact of these legacies, it makes little sense to study them in isolation from the immediate context of the transformation process. Rather, they argue that this context is salient for any such analysis because it provides the conditions under which past legacies will or will not play a role in shaping the direction of regime change. In their own words:

> New institutions shaped by these forces have the power to create a competitive political system where once there was none, and in doing so, to weaken the past legacies of political intolerance and inability to negotiate and compromise. They also can provide incentives for the rise of oppositional elites ... New institutions also provide society with incentives to participate in the political process. But their norms, rules and procedures do not always tell us which social divisions will become politically central" (*ibid.* p. 34).

However, their enumeration of legacy types betrays Jowitt's rather narrow focus on Leninism: at least two of the six legacies can be attributed to the pre-communist past. Hence, these legacies should not be studied in isolation of their immediate context of pre- and post-1989 developments, they should also be studied in their interaction with each other if one is interested in their effects on post-1989 politics.

That the concept of legacy is rather slippery, has been observed many times. As the introductory quote by Tismaneanu illustrates, it may encompass anything that precedes the post-communist regime change. But "if the weight of the past affects the present, at a minimum it is necessary to specify which past" (Kopstein, 2003, p. 233). With regard to Central and Eastern Europe, the relevant past comprises three basic layers: that of 1989-1992 or the immediate context of transformation; that of 1949-1989, or the experience of Leninism as a political and cultural regime; and that of 1919-1949, or the Wilsonian order after World War I and the experience of interwar regimes which, in the region of interest, have been predominantly non-democratic and non-communist. The exception to that are Czechoslovakia at one extreme, that is, a democratic regime, and the Soviet Union on the other, that is, a communist regime. The question here is: "how can a legacy be recognized? How far back in the past is it necessary to go before theoretical traction is lost?" (*ibid.*).

This question becomes particularly important for the analysis of the radical right in the region. Clearly, this is a shift in the application of the legacy approach which, in all its variety, was conceptualized for explanations of regime change, not for a particular movement or party family. Yet, measures of successful regime change often include the indicator of support for anti-democratic, or anti-system parties or movements (Auer, 2000; Beichelt, 2001). Already Jowitt himself identified – as one of the outcomes of the "Leninist extinction" – nativist and violent reactions to the costs of the transformation process (Jowitt, 1992b, p. 275; Howard, 2006, p. 39). But the conceptual links and causal connections warrant further specification.

Regardless of its particular historical positioning, the radical right is, almost by definition, a prime agent, as well as target, in the business of reinventing or instrumentalizing a country's past. In any of these interpretations, history – in its more recent (state-socialist and regime transformative) and more distant (pre-socialist) manifestations – can be accredited with a crucial role in the shape and development of the radical right. It seems that in contrast to its Western European counterpart, whether it is catching up or not, the Central and Eastern European radical right is particularly conditioned by the force of history, that the histories of state socialism and of pre-socialist (non-democratic) experiences can be seen as major factors in shaping both the contents and the opportunities of the radical right in these new or emerging democracies.

The argument that the Central and East European radical right is particularly susceptible to historical legacies is related to both the region's and the radical right's characteristics. Most experts agree that the radical right can be defined as a radically exclusionist political force, which, more than other political currents and movements, employs rigid historical references in the imagination of the community it claims to fight for. In this vein, the core political program or ideology of the radical right is a populist and romantic ultranationalism. More specifically, the radical right is involved in an effort to construct an idea of nation and national belonging by radicalizing ethnic, religious, lingual, other cultural and political criteria of inclusion and exclusion, that is to condense the idea of nation into an image of extreme collective homogeneity and to bring about a congruence between the state and the nation in these exclusionary terms (Minkenberg, 1998, pp. 29-47; *idem*, 2000; 2008; Carter, 2005, pp. 14-20; Kitschelt and McGann, 1995, chap.1; Kitschelt, 2007, p. 1179; Mudde, 2007, pp. 15-26). As the main criterion is not the opposition to democracy, this concept of the radical right is rather inclusive in that it covers more extreme variants of openly anti-democratic or fascist movements and parties, as well as the more vaguely defined currents of right-wing populism, or religiously based nationalism (Minkenberg, 2008, pp. 12-15; Mudde, 2007, pp. 138-157).

The comparative literature on the radical right in post-1989 Central and Eastern Europe employs some or most of these definitional characteristics and combines them with the region's experience of regime change and transformation and its particular state-socialist or Leninist past (Minkenberg, 2002; Mudde, 2000; Ost, 2005; Ramet, 1999). But while the importance of history or particular legacies for the trajectory of the radical right in the region is regularly emphasized in the literature, there is both a fuzziness in the application of the legacy concept and the lack of a more conceptually grounded analysis or a systematic testing of its effects (or absence thereof). Such research is still in its infancy (Tismaneanu, 1998). If at all, the role of the past is typically operationalized in sequential terms, as historical reference points, such as when some experts suggest to create new typologies of right-wing radical parties in Central and Eastern Europe by classifying them according to the (historical) origins of their ideological identity. For example, Cas Mudde proposes to distinguish pre-communist radical right parties which are rooted in the political culture and ideas of the period before communism (such as the Russian Pamyat or Polish PWN-PSN), communist radical right parties that are characterized by a combination of nationalism and nostalgia for the communist past (like the Romanian PRM and PUNR), and post-communist radical right parties which are newly established and focus on current issues (like the Serbian Radical Party or the Russian LDPR) (Mudde, 2000; Shafir, 2000).

While it is plausible to characterize such parties according to their *historical* origins (except for most cases of the pre-communist radical right), it makes less sense *ideologically*. Radical right parties which emerged in Eastern Europe after 1989 may or may not nurture a strong longing for a particular part of the country's past, they may focus on current issues *and* cultivate the (re-invented) nationalist image of some part of the country's non-democratic past. That is, the categories of pre- and post-communist radical right seem ideologically unspecified. In his more recent study on the radical right in Europe, Mudde (2007) not only drops this typology but refrains altogether from testing regional effects on, or the relevance of the East-West divide for, the radical right – let alone distinct legacy effects, which could be subsumed under regional effects. The regional particularities of post-socialist Europe are only marginally identified, as when Mudde compares levels of democratic support and ethnic diversity in the region's aspiring democracies during the 1990s and finds only little evidence for a causal effect on electoral success of the radical right (Mudde, 2007, pp. 205-216). And the argument of the effect of an authoritarian or Leninist legacy on the radical right is settled with a few remarks and a broad brushstroke: "The obvious problem with this general thesis is that it cannot account for the striking absence of populist radical right success in most of the post-communist world or for the intra-regional differences" (*ibid.*, p. 217).

Indeed, when held at such an abstract and general level, the legacy argument evaporates. But the obvious next step would be to ask if different "pasts" or legacies account for variation of radical right success, or of radical right formations, in light of the legacy approaches which strive to explain variations of regimes (as the systemic equivalent to types of radical right groups) and success of democratization (equivalent to the electoral success of the radical right). One such effort was suggested by Timm Beichelt and Michael Minkenberg. Based on earlier work by the present author (Minkenberg, 2000, 2002), they identified a number of region-specific legacies as part of the opportunity structures for the radical right and sought to explain both variation in electoral support and ideological type of the dominant radical right actor in the respective country (Beichelt and Minkenberg, 2002; see also discussion in Ishiyama, in this volume). Among these were the type of nation: civic, cultural, or ethnic (Minkenberg, 1998; Hobsbawm, 1990), the existence of external homelands, the presence of a national minority (Brubaker, 1997; Smith, 2001), and the nature of the regime conflict in the early transition (Beichelt, 2001; Linz and Stepan, 1996). They also included the more current variables of social and cultural costs of transformation to their analysis. The following table summarizes the results of the analysis for a number of transition countries in the 1990s (Table 1).

The empirical overview revealed some patterns while allowing also for striking peculiarities. In general, in cases with more than two facilitating variables the radical right could count on higher levels of electoral support, and *vice versa*. This was true for the Czech Republic and Hungary on the one hand, where right-wing radical parties played only a minor role, and for Romania and Russia on the other, where strong right-wing radical groups coexist with communist-nationalist parties. Here a striking role of particular legacies appeared: countries with a strong pre-1989 communist-nationalist tradition seemed to produce the fascist-autocratic variant of right-wing radicalism as the major party type, and the radical right had a problematic effect on the development of democracy. Due to the interplay of the radical right and the post-communist left, a "Weimarization" of these regimes remains a possible path for further development. In Russia the election of Putin slowed down this process but right-wing radicalism continued to obscure the chances of democracy (Beichelt, in this volume). The Romanian presidential elections of 2000, with the former Ceauşescu ally Iliescu and the fascist-autocratic Tudor taking a large share of the votes, confirmed the trend, but in subsequent elections until EU accession in 2007, it faded (Frusetta and Glont, in this volume). Thirdly, racist or ethnocentrist types of right-wing radical parties dominate the scene in the cases where democracy has taken root.

Table 1.   Legacies, opportunity structures and right-wing radical electoral potential in post-socialist Europe (1990s)

		Legacies and opportunity structures				Electoral potential			
	Nation type	Existence of external homelands	Existence of a strong national minority	Regime conflict: Regime contested by major political forces	Transformation costs	Non reformed post-communist parties with "communist-nationalist" predecessors (pre-1989) (a)(b)	Nationalist parties (a)(c)	Sum	Dominant party type (e)
Bulgaria (1990-2000)	Culture	No	Yes	Yes	Very high	0	0	0	
Estonia (1992-2000)	Ethnic	No	Yes	No	Very high	0	0	0	
Hungary (1990-2000)	Ethnic	Yes	Yes	No	High	0	3.6	3.6	Racist
Czech Rep. (1992-2000)	Ethnic	No	No	No	(Very) high	0	6.0	6.0	Racist
Slovakia (1992-2000)	In flux	No	Yes	Yes	High	0	7.2	7.2	Racist
Poland (1991-2000)	Culture	No	No	No	High	0	9.0 (d)	9.0	Racist, fundamentalist
Russia (1993-2000)	Culture	Yes	Yes	Yes	Very high	23.3	8.6	31.9	Fascist-autocratic
Romania (1990-2000)	Ethnic	Yes	Yes	Yes	High	29.1	14.4	43.5	Fascist-autocratic

(a) Average result of the last two elections until end of 2000 in national parliamentary elections.

(b) Parties included: Romania: PDSR, Russia: KPRF.

(c) Parties included: Czech Republic: SPR-RSC, Hungary: MIÉP; Poland: KPN, ZChN, Slovakia: SNS, Romania: PUNR, PRM, Russia: LDPR.

(d) Difficult to determine because in 1997 right-wing radicals ran on the AWS ticket which cannot be characterized as a radical party altogether.

(e) For classification see Minkenberg (2002).

Source: Beichelt and Minkenberg (2002, p. 16).

This points to the possibility that these parties are "catching up" with Western European cases (Bustikova and Kitschelt, de Lange and Guerra, in this volume). But unlike most Western European cases, these parties' leaders and platforms advocate more backwards-looking ideologies, notably with regard to "lost territories", open anti-Semitism or racism, and anti-democratic sentiments (Minkenberg, 2002).

In light of these general patterns, the cases of Estonia and especially Bulgaria were striking in that they contained rather favorable opportunity structures but obviously no right-wing radical electoral potential. Clearly, Bulgaria was the odd case in this sample. Based on the analytical model, there should have been a large electoral potential for the radical right, but the findings pointed to the opposite. One reason could be that the political bloc of the right still exhibited characteristics of a movement organization with low levels of programmatic coherence, and the electoral as well as the party system were rather fluid. This has not changed much until EU accession in 2007, but in the meantime, a strong radical right has emerged (Frusetta and Glont, in this volume). The absence of any right-wing radical party in Estonia (and the other Baltic states), despite the highly publicized discrimination of the Russian ethnic minority, must be attributed to the precarious situation of the country vis-à-vis its Russian neighbor. Any open right-wing radical political activities were bound to provoke Russian counter-action the threat of which pushes even nationalists towards embracing Western ideas and integration. In the meantime, with EU accession of the Baltic states in 2004, sizable nationalist currents have emerged in this region as well (Minkenberg and Perrineau, 2007). Contrary to these two cases, the Polish situation appeared reversed in that comparatively unfavorable opportunity structures have allowed for a rather sizable, and after 2000 growing, support for the radical right. Here, low levels of formal structuring of the political right and in particular the ambiguous role of Catholicism played into the hands of ultranationalist political entrepreneurs (de Lange and Guerra, in this volume).

Obviously, this conceptualization of legacies for the explanation of variation in both ideological type and electoral success in the 1990s is only the sketch of an ambitious program and not a sufficient operationalization. These and other deficits, such as the reduction of non-legacy factors to only one dimension of transformation-induced costs cannot be easily overcome. Moreover, this model is subject to Kitschelt's and Tilly's warnings that causal depth/structures should not be employed at the expense of causal analysis/processes. It does, however, put the analysis of the radical right in Central and Eastern Europe in a larger historical-institutional context and points out some of the steps and the general direction future research may take. Against this backdrop, this publication aims to provide some of these steps and add a few more insights. For the contributions which follow, legacies were understood in two major ways. On the one hand, they constitute a contextual factor and, in that sense, a part of structural and cultural opportunities for new movements and parties in the region, along with particular "post-socialist pathways" which individual countries have taken on the road to democracy. On the other, legacies are seen as textual factors, as part of the ideological baggage of the past which is revived – and reinterpreted – by the radical right. The articles can roughly grouped into these two categories of legacies. The pieces by Bustikova and Kitschelt as well as the one by Ishiyama employ the role of legacies as context, whereas the contributions by Beichelt, de Lange and Guerra and Frusetta and Glont treat legacies as text.

The analysis by Lenka Bustikova and Herbert Kitschelt addresses a wide range of phenomena, both in terms of country cases included in their comparative investigation as well as the variables they test as causal factors for the electoral success of the radical right. The article follows Kitschelt's earlier work on post-communist party competition and the type of communist regimes (see above) and suggests a political-economic perspective, rather than one based on cultural and identity politics, for the explanation of voting for the radical right. Their argument is that in countries with a legacy of national-accommodative communism which provide a welfare state safety net for the losers of regime change, the radical right receives only limited support. The opposite is true for countries with a patrimonial communist legacy. Here, "red-brown" authoritarian and exclusionary programs resonate in significant segments of the public, mixed with anti-capitalist positions. Bustikova and Kitschelt test these propositions for 17 countries and find that these legacies cast a shadow over the processes after 1989 and account for the general patterns of radical right mobilization. As the authors readily admit, their analysis is restricted to the demand side of the radical right and warrants a complementary study of the strategic moves of these parties and how they are constrained by the respective legacies in the electoral arena.

The "red-brown" alliance in a number of post-communist countries is at the heart of the article by John Ishiyama. He does not ask how historical legacies shape the mobilization of the radical right but, more narrowly, how they affect the emergence of "red-brown" or "national bolshevik" tendencies in Central and Eastern Europe. Ishiyama employs a rather deep level of causality and aspires to test the proposition that pre-communist national identities as well as the legacy of the communist regime itself can explain the emergence of national communism and the red-brown politics in the post-communist era. This is measured by the size of the red-brown vote, conceptualized as those voters for communist successor parties who exhibit strong levels of nationalism and xenophobia. With nine country cases, the number of countries under consideration is smaller than in the Bustikova and Kitschelt piece. But similar to the work by Kitschelt, Ishiyama argues that red-brown voting is facilitated by the retarding effects on party competition, that is, the delayed or under development of cleavages, by the institutional legacy of the previous communist regime. He shows this by comparing this particular type of legacy with others in the literature, that is, the role of empire, nation type, presence of minorities, external homelands and organizational transition (see also above). In this light, pre-communist legacies account for rather little variation.

In Timm Beichelt's contribution, however, pre-communist legacies in Russia, such as the Russian empire, anti-Western national identity, and Orthodox Christianity, take center stage in the explanation of the radical right. However, his focus is on legacy as the ingredient into the political currents, not as part of the opportunity structures. In other words, contrary to the pieces by Bustikova/Kitschelt and Ishiyama, Beichelt shifts the focus from demand side to supply side. He demonstrates that the Russian radical right employs two major strands, imperial nationalism – the LDPR – and social nationalism – the CPRF (the communist successor party) – , both fueled by anti-modernist radicalism, and, thus, provides an in-depth analysis of the red-brown phenomenon in Russia. Beichelt shows that the difference between red and brown nationalists does not rest in the nationalist elements of their ideologies, but rather in their different degree of "oppositionalism" to the new regime, with Zhirinovsky's LDPR showing more willingness to cooperate with the new power that be. Finally the paper shows, through its detailed analysis of party programs and rhetoric, that the concept of Leninism is undergoing significant change, that the "Leninist label" has transcended its original meaning. This points to a growing salience of pre-communist elements of the Russian heritage and demands more careful analysis of the different layers of the past, as they reappear in the post-communist political struggles.

A similarly insightful in-depth look is provided by Sarah de Lange and Simone Guerra who study the trajectory of the Polish radical right party League of Polish Families (LPR). By analyzing both demand and supply side in the Polish electoral arena, the two authors highlight the particular role of religion, in this case Polish Catholicism, both as a marker of Polish national identity and a hallmark of right-wing politics. They can demonstrate a high level of congruence between the LPR voters' concerns with key issues such as abortion, the role of the Church, and the settlement of foreigners in Poland, and the party's programmatic repertoire. The LPR has tapped into deep Catholic conservative and nationalist sentiments the roots of which pre-date the era of communism in Poland. The communist regime – and the opposition to it – seem less significant in explaining the rise of the LPR after 2000 than their competitive advantage in construing an agenda which combines Catholic values and ultra-nationalism with salient issues such as the fight against the remnants of the communist era and European integration.

The final paper also takes a deeper look into the pre-communist past. James Frusetta and Anca Glont compare the adaptation of interwar fascist discourse into the contemporary radical right in Bulgaria and Romania. By carefully re-constructing the respective discourses in the interwar period and in the post-1989 era and by comparing them, the authors show that the key element for the adaptation of the fascist discourse is not the "copying" of the interwar movement styles and ideologies. Rather, they argue, it is the legacy of the communist era which matters, more specifically the legacy of the communists' own approaches to interwar fascism which functions as a "useable past" for the contemporary radical right. This is demonstrated by highlighting that in both Bulgaria and Romania the radical right presents itself as the heir to interwar fascism while in fact sharing little in common as far as their ideology is concerned. The dual legacies of fascist ideology and communism are merged into a new ultranationalist agenda, suitable for the post-communist arena of competitive politics.

All contributions show that with the radical right, a peculiar "syncretic construct" (Tismaneanu) has emerged in Central and Eastern Europe after 1989. It is derived from both pre-communist and communist legacies. However, except for Poland, the radical right seems to be less a true executor of the "Leninist extinction" (Jowitt), but a beneficiary of Leninism in that it is able to profitably carry on some of the Leninist legacies – or is facilitated by them – in a post-dictatorial setting.

This overall finding, along with more specific insights provided by the individual contributions to this publication, may only be a little piece in the larger puzzle of the role of legacies in the post-1989 political transformation. Clearly, the publication has not settled – and could not hope to settle – the debate whether communist legacies are more important than pre-communist ones in the political trajectory of Central and East European democracies, or whether cultural legacies are more relevant than social or economic ones. It points, however, to a particular role of the cultural dimension and of the appropriation and re-interpretation of a country's past in right-wing radical politics. Future studies of the phenomenon may want to pay closer attention to the multidimensionality of legacies and tackle the issue of the respective relevance of the various dimensions more systematically. They may also want to compare the role and relevance of legacies for the radical right in a post-communist setting with that in other (earlier) post-dictatorial circumstances.

References

Anderson, B., 1983. Imagined Communities. Verso, London.

Auer, S., 2000. Nationalism in Central Europe – a chance or a threat for the emerging liberal democratic order? East European Politics and Societies 14 (2), 213-245.

Beichelt, T., 2001. Demokratische Konsolidierung im Postsozialistischen Europa. Die Rolle der politischen Institutionen. Leske + Budrich, Opladen.

Beichelt, T., Minkenberg, M., 2002. Explaining the Radical Right in Transition: Theories of Right-wing Radicalism and Opportunity Structures in Post-socialist Europe FIT Paper 3/2002. Frankfurter Institut für Transformationsstudien, Frankfurt (Oder).

Brubaker, R., 1997. Nationalism Reframed. Nationhood and the National Question in the New Europe. Cambridge University Press, Cambridge.

Carter, E., 2005. The Extreme Right in Western Europe. Success or Failure? Manchester University Press, Manchester.

Crawford, B., Lijphart, A., 1997. Old legacies new institutions. Explaining political and economic trajectories in post-communist regimes. In: idem. (Ed.), Liberalization and Leninist Legacies. Comparative Perspectives on Democratic Transitions. The Regents of the University of California Berkeley, Berkeley, pp. 1-39.

Ekiert, G., Hanson S.E. (Eds.), 2003. Capitalism and Democracy in Central and Eastern Europe. Assessing the Legacy of Communist Rule. Cambridge University Press, Cambridge.

Hobsbawm, E., 1990. Nations and Nationalism Since 1780. Programme, Myth, Reality. Cambridge University Press, Cambridge.

Howard, M.M., 2006. The Leninist legacy revisited. In: Tismaneanu, V., Howard, M.M., Sil, R. (Eds.), World Order After Leninism. University of Washington Press, Seattle and London, pp. 34-46.

Jowitt, K., 1992a. The Leninist legacy. In: idem, (Ed.), New World Disorder. The Leninist Extinction. The University of California Press, Cambridge, 284-305.

Jowitt, K., 1992b. The Leninist extinction. In: idem, (Ed.), New World Disorder. The Leninist Extinction. The University of California Press, Cambridge, pp. 249-283.

Judt, T., 2005. Postwar. A History of Europe since 1945. Penguin, London.

Kitschelt, H., 2003. Accounting for postcommunist regime diversity. What counts as a good cause? In: Ekiert, G., Hanson, S. (Eds.) Capitalism and Democracy in Central and Eastern Europe. Cambridge University Press, Cambridge, pp. 49-86.

Kitschelt, H., 2007. Growth and persistence of the radical right in postindustrial democracies. Advances and challenges in comparative research. West European Politics 30 (5), 1176-1207.

Kitschelt, H., McGann, A., 1995. The Radical Right in Western Europe. A Comparative Analysis. University of Michigan Press, Ann Arbor.

Kitschelt, H., Mansfeldova, Z., Markowski, R., Tóka, G., 1999. Post-communist Party Systems: Competition, Representation, and Inter-party Co-operation. Cambridge University Press, Cambridge.

Kopstein, J., 2003. Postcommunist Democracy. Legacies and Outcomes. Comparative Politics, January, 231-250.

Linz, J., Stepan, A., 1996. Problems of Democratic Transition and Consolidation. Johns Hopkins University Press, Baltimore.

Mahoney, J., Schensul, D., 2006. Historical context and path dependence. In: Goodin, R., Tilly, C. (Eds.), The Oxford Handbook of Contextual Political Analysis. Oxford University Press, Oxford, pp. 454-471.

Minkenberg, M., 1998. Die neue radikale Rechte im Vergleich. USA, Frankreich, Deutschland. Westdeutscher Verlag, Opladen/Wiesbaden.

Minkenberg, M., 2000. The renewal of the radical right: between modernity and anti-modernity. Government and Opposition 35 (2), 170-188.

Minkenberg, M., 2002. The radical right in post-socialist Central and Eastern Europe.: comparative observations and interpretations. East European Politics and Societies 16 (2), 335-362.

Minkenberg, M., 2008. The Radical Right in Europe. An Overview. Verlag Bertelsmann Stiftung, Gütersloh.

Minkenberg, M., Perrineau, P., 2007. The radical right in the European elections 2004. International Political Science Review 28 (1), 29-55.

Mudde, C., 2000. Extreme-right parties in Eastern Europe. Patterns of Prejudice 34 (1), 5-27.

Mudde, C., 2007. Populist Radical Right Parties in Europe. Cambridge University Press, Cambridge.

Ost, D., 2005. The Defeat of Solidarity. Anger and Politics in Postcommunist Europe. Cornell University Press, Ithaca.

Ramet, S. (Ed.), 1999. The Radical Right in Central and Eastern Europe Since 1989. The Pennsylvania State University Press, University Park.

Shafir, M. 2000. Marginalization or mainstream? The extreme right in post-communist Romania. In: Hainsworth, P. (Ed.), The Politics of the Extreme Right: From the Margins to the Mainstream. Pinter, London, pp. 247-267.

Smith, A., 2001. Nationalism. Theory, Ideology, History. Polity Press, Cambridge.

Tilly, C., 2006. Why and how history matters. In: Goodin, R., Tilly, C. (Eds.), The Oxford Handbook of Contextual Political Analysis. Oxford University Press, Oxford, pp. 417-437.

Tismaneanu, V., 1998. Fantasies of Salvation: Democracy, Nationalism, and Myth in Post-Communist Europe. Princeton University Press, Princeton.

Tismaneanu, V., 2007. Is East-Central Europe backsliding? Leninist legacies, pluralist dilemmas. Journal of Democracy 18 (4), 33-39.

Tismaneanu, V., Howard, M.M., Sil, R. (Eds.), 2006. World Order after Leninism. University of Washington Press, Seattle and London.

Wolff, L., 1994. Inventing Eastern Europe. The Map of Civilization on the Mind of the Enlightenment. Stanford University Press, Stanford.

The radical right in post-communist Europe
Comparative perspectives on legacies and party competition

Lenka Bustikova, Herbert Kitschelt[1]

ABSTRACT: *What role do legacies of past mobilization under late communist rule play in the success of the radical right parties in Eastern Europe? This article considers two major legacies: the legacy of national-accommodative communism and the legacy of patrimonial communism. We investigate the effect of welfare retrenchment on vote support for radical right in 2000s. Social policy reform retrenchment in universalistic welfare systems has a highly incendiary potential for political conflict and radical parties. In countries with a legacy of national accommodative communism, early differentiation of major parties on socio-cultural issues and strategies of social policy compensation kept reform losers at bay, which limited voter success of radical parties. Highly polarized patrimonial regimes, on the contrary, are the most fertile breeding ground for the radical right due to the high levels of inequality and dissatisfaction resulting from a rapid dismantling of the welfare state. The ethnic composition of countries plays an important role in the radical right mobilization as well. Radical right parties benefit from a situation in which the titular majority faces a small ethno-cultural minority.*

Introduction

What role do legacies of past mobilization under late communist rule play in the success of the radical right parties in Eastern Europe? Legacies are deep, durable causes that affect the potential for radical right wing politics across the post-communist region. The distinctive role of these legacies, drawing on the communist and even the pre-communist interwar era, however, tends to become progressively diluted, as post-communist polities move into the 21st century and face new political-economic and socio-cultural challenges. Nev-

---

1   The authors would like to thank participants of „The Radical Right in post-1989 Central and Eastern Europe: The Role of Legacies" 2008 conference, hosted by New York University's Center for European and Mediterranean Studies, organized by Michael Minkenberg, for helpful comments. We also thank two anonymous reviewers.

ertheless, legacies create the baseline for patterns of party competition, shape partisan politics, and thus mold a proximate cause of radical right mobilization. Building on previous research, we consider two major legacies in Eastern Europe: the legacy of national-accommodative communism and the legacy of patrimonial communism.

Contrary to an often-held view of radical right in Eastern Europe based on political culture and identity politics, we suggest that a political-economic perspective is an apt tool for addressing the sources of radical right voters' grievances (Held, 1996; Hockenos, 1993; Kopecky and Mudde, 2003; Minkenberg, 2002; Mudde, 2005; Ost, 2005; Ramet, 1999). We claim that the study of economic grievances, when matched with ethnic and socio-cultural attributes of party competition, is one of the avenues to account for radical right party success and failure over time. In this paper, we take intolerance to socio-cultural "otherness" as given. We assume that politicization of these attitudes occurs during critical events when the "other" becomes a scapegoat for economic misery. Economic resentment stemming from the retrenchment of the welfare state since late 1990s catalyzes exclusionary party appeals to voters.

In countries with a legacy of national-accommodative communism, which have cushioned losers of reforms through their relatively generous welfare states, the potential for distinctive radical right parties has always been limited. Moreover, moderate right-wing parties have incorporated exclusionary appeals into their programmatic agenda, thus further reducing the options for the successful entry and endurance of the radical right.

Regimes with the patrimonial legacy and high political contestation have moved in the opposite direction. The direct successors of communist parties or new right wing entrants have developed 'red-brown' authoritarian and exclusionary appeals that are often mixed with anti-market stances. Highly polarized patrimonial regimes with high levels of inequality resulting from a rapid dismantling of the welfare state are the most fertile breeding ground for the radical right.

Our argument proceeds in several steps. We first define radical right parties and then discuss our theoretical expectations as to how legacies affect radical right party mobilization. We hypothesize that the ethnic composition of countries plays an important role in radical right mobilization, and specifically that radical right parties, particularly those that comply with the democratic rules of game, benefit from a situation in which the titular majority faces a small ethno-cultural minority. Further, we probe the effect of welfare retrenchment on vote support for radical right in 2000s. We argue that social policy reform retrenchment in universalistic, comprehensive insurance and service systems has a highly incendiary potential for political conflict. We conclude with empirical observations that generally support our theoretical claims.

Legacies

We base our definition of the radical right parties on their authoritarian cultural conservatism and exclusionary character. We relate these two dimensions to the grid-group theory (Wildavsky et al., 1990), where the group stands for exclusionary appeals based on group membership, such as nationalism, and the grid stands for socio-culturally conservative appeals that seek to subordinate individual choices to normative constraints, for example, exclusion of gays from public life. Table 2 contains vote shares for radical right parties in the 2000s as well as classification of parties into the radical right and 'nearby' moderate right wing parties.

What are the conditions under which politicians choose strategic actions that facilitate the entry and success of radical right parties in post-communist polities with open electoral competition? In order to answer the question, we build on the earlier analysis of one of the paper authors concerning the "legacies" of communist rule for the articulation of partisan alternatives under post-communism and the choice of political-economic reform trajectories (Kitschelt and McGann, 1995; Kitschelt et al., 1999) and blend this with Timothy Frye's (2002) arguments about the presence of more or less "polarized" party systems. Pop-Eleches defines legacies as "the structural, cultural, and institutional starting points of ex-communist countries at the outset of the transition" (Pop-Eleches, 2007: 910). What we consider here are institutional legacies of the communist rule and we pit against each other two ideal types of non-polarized, consensual "nationally accommodative" democratic post-communism and polarized, conflictual post-communism, that originates in one of two sharply different strands of communist governance, "bureaucratic-authoritarian" or "patrimonial" communism.

While we recognize the important effects of authoritarian pre-communist and religious legacies on the 'return of the radical right' (Held, 1996; Hockenos, 1993; Kopecky and Mudde, 2003; Minkenberg, 2002; Mudde, 2005; Shafir, 2008 and Ramet, 1999), we focus, in this paper, on patterns of party competition and restrict ourselves to the most proximate legacy, the legacy of communism. While we recognize that radical right ideologies are complex and context specific, we focus our classification of radical right parties on two core ideological components: nationalism and cultural conservatism.

Historical legacies shed light on the content and the origins of the ideological positions held by radical parties in the post-communist setting. Such legacies are relevant, for example, when we consider the potential political opportunities to frame 'the other'. As far as the legacies of pre-communist political regimes, we believe that these are largely accounted for in the discussion of the types of Leninist legacies that preceded the fall of the Berlin wall. We distinguish three types of legacies: the legacy of national-accommodative communism, the legacy or patrimonial communism and the legacy of bureaucratic-authoritarian communism. The first two legacies are rooted in non-democratic regimes that preceded the World War II.

We place ourselves in the camp of those who believe that the post-communist radical right is "a phenomenon *sui generis*, inherently shaped by the historical forces of state socialism and the transformation process" (Minkenberg, 2009: *ibid.*) Further, two distinct features differentiate the post-communist radical right from the Western counterparts. First, the post-communist region has a more recent history of contentious state building compared to the West. The concept of 'the other' revolves around ethnicities settled in the post-communist region for centuries and conceptualizations of 'the other' have deep historical roots. By contrast, the West tells a more contemporary narrative of 'the other' which focuses mostly on immigrants.

Second, the legacy of state socialism and the transition to markets and democracy creates a distinct set of initial conditions that affect the mobilization potentials of radical right. Patterns of preservation and dismantlement of the welfare state can be directly traced to state capacity and economic transition processes affecting rising inequalities and the quality of governance immediately after 1989. Whereas the pre-communist legacies of 'the other' have survived communism and remain important, economic communist legacies may wash away with time. As post-communist countries face 'mundane' challenges of political tradeoffs related to economic redistribution and welfare provision, we expect convergence between the East and the West.

We now discuss these communist legacies and their effect on the post-communist radical right.

(1) National-accommodative communism without polarization of parties on economic issues: in a number of countries or constituent republics of large compound republics (Soviet Union, Yugoslavia) by the mid-1980s at the very latest, communist parties had begun to make concessions to anti-communist opposition forces that were still in their formative stages. These concessions expressed themselves in tolerance for free speech, within narrowly circumscribed boundaries, market-oriented economic reforms, and efforts to cultivate national consensus and autonomy as a political value bringing together both communists and non-communists.

After national-accommodative communism, initially all major political forces—former authoritarian regime incumbents and their challengers alike—endorsed and pursued a liberal democratic transformation of society that had as its most salient features the full establishment of capitalist markets and inclusive, universalistic democratic procedures for all residents. At the same time, given the conditions of fierce electoral competition, neither right nor left governments dared to touch the foundations of the socialist quasi-welfare state inherited from the predecessor regime which left little room for polarization between post-communist social democrats and anti-communist liberal-democrats on salient economic policy issues.[2]

Vote-seeking mainstream political parties early on began to seek a differentiation of partisanship along a second dimension of socio-cultural issues that divides those with more restrictive, conservative ethno-cultural grid and nationally exclusionary group conceptions of the polity, often combined with and inspired by appeals to Christian traditionalism, from liberal-secular universalistic, libertarian and cosmopolitan visions.

Strategies of social policy compensation, combined with economic recovery after 1993-1995 kept the intensity of grievances and dissatisfaction with economic liberalization and capitalist institution building at bay. Efforts by conservative parties to open a second dimension of competition and articulate grid/group positions contributed to the success of mainstream parties to keep radical right challengers at bay.

---

2   In fact, post-communist governments expanded the socialist quasi-welfare states in order to compensate the losers of liberalization and capitalist institution building and induced an expansion of social programs, for example, through early retirement schemes for workers who were made redundant by privatization of large companies (Greskovits, 1998; Vanhuysse, 2006).

By the end of the 1990s and in the new millennium, however, fiscal budget strains in the post-communist polities made it increasingly clear that there were limits to the strategy of social policy compensation through ever expanding quasi-socialist welfare states.[3] Faced with these political-economic challenges, how can leaders of conventional center-left and center-right parties defend their turf and stave off radical right and/or left-wing mobilization often with a neo-populist rhetoric that the political elites have betrayed the masses? Post-communist politics appears to offer two potential escape hatches. One is extremely rapid economic growth.[4]

The other escape hatch for established parties is to go into a programmatic political offensive on the second, socio-cultural dimension of ideological differentiation and intensify the incorporation of authoritarian and nationalist exclusionary grid/group appeals in their very own competitive partisan stances, thus increasing the polarization with more secular, libertarian and cosmopolitan programmatic adversaries who are blamed for the social policy reforms and their grievances. Conservative party governments then compensate electoral constituencies not so much by tangible material rewards and benefits, but by appeals to intangible social identities and moral values that invoke restrictive and exclusionary grid/group conceptions. This is a strategy chosen by some of the conservative mainstream parties in countries such as Hungary, Poland, and to a lesser extent Slovenia. Where such grid/group appeals of conventional conservative parties resonate with voters, distinctive radical right parties can be held at bay.

After national-accommodative communism, prospects for the rise of radical right parties were not particularly good in the 1990s. The economic reforms of the 1990s proceeded while compensating losers by maintaining and expanding socialist quasi-welfare states. But after 2000 the compensatory potential of the socialist quasi-welfare state is exhausted and governments cannot avoid reforming social policy through painful restructuring. Given the intensification of socio-cultural ideological polarization between par-

---

3   The share of the population dependent on transfer payments, especially pensions, had grown to or beyond fiscal limits. At the same time, rising prices and wages in the private sector began to compel governments to improve wages in the social service sector (health, education). The cost of social services and pension payments contributed to a financial crisis that could be addressed only by cutbacks, increasing labor productivity in the delivery of services and the introduction or increase of user feeds for social services, especially medical care.

4   Mainstream parties in the Baltic countries and to a lesser extent in Slovakia have pursued such strategies against radical right as well as left populist parties with diverging success.

ties that endorse rather similar economic reform strategies, after 2000s, prospects for the rise of radical right have further dimmed.

Let us indicate a second empirical implication of the interplay between political-economic grievances and party strategies after national-accommodative communism. The deprivations caused by the retrenchment of encompassing, universalist quasi-socialist welfare states pretty comprehensively touched almost every group and stratum in society. If protest and alienation prompted by such policies does cue citizens to opt for radical right wing parties, the supporters of such challengers should have diffuse socio-demographic characteristics. There is not a singular socio-economic category which vulnerability would be so extraordinarily different from that of other categories to give it preponderance in the electorate of radical right wing parties.

> *(2) Bureaucratic-authoritarian or patrimonial communism with post-communist partisan polarization: there are at least two very different constellations of communist legacies that promote the emergence of polarized party competition over economic reform strategies with the advent of democratic politics. In either case, the polarization is between a more or less intransigent former communist ruling party that resists social democratization and an uncompromising anti-communist camp of former regime dissidents. In polities with the first constellation, communist rule was preceded by the rise of a powerful and radical working class movement embedded in a liberal democratic society (Czech Republic 1919-1938; in some ways Germany 1918-1933). After the communist seizure of power, communist leaders never made concessions to non-communist forces, as the strong organization and mass support of socialist politics permitted the construction of tightly controlled, bureaucratic-authoritarian regimes. Unreformed communist parties in the Czech Republic and Germany continue to be successful in elections after 1989.*

In this scenario, economic reform goes through the same sequence as in formerly national-accommodative communist countries, vigorously pushed by the center-right, but it does not involve the same kind of alternation between center-left and center-right governments, because part of the left is unavailable for compromise and policy convergence.[5] But opportunities to rally voters around radical right wing parties remained modest throughout the 1990s and diminished further in the new millennium. The intransigent communist party always remained available to rally voters disappointed with the introduction of the capitalist market regime.[6]

A second constellation resulting in polarized competition around economic reform occurred in post-communist countries with a (3) legacy of "patrimonial" communism. Here communist incumbents always faced highly dispersed, isolated dissidents who had no experience in overcoming collective action problems. The collapse of communism left behind essentially unreformed communist parties set against economic and political liberalization, regardless of whether they kept their communist labels or adopted some other party names. They opposed a highly inexperienced, diffuse, disorganized pro-market and pro-democratic opposition that was in most instances not able to effectively govern a process of political-economic and institutional reform. Where this situation did not yield an outright return to dictatorial rule, like in Belarus, inconsistent, partial economic reforms without capitalist institution building took a heavy toll on the economies. Party polarization, halfhearted reforms, and frequent government turnover scared off investors (Frye, 2002). This situation was exacerbated by the virtual collapse of social security, as pensions devalued, educational and medical services deteriorated, and former state enterprises reneged on their social service provisions. This environment of very widespread social displacement created a political atmosphere where even in the face of polarization between unreconstructed former communist ruling parties and fledgling divided liberal-democratic anticommunists radical right parties could begin to find a space to thrive.

Where communist successor parties presided as new government parties over the deep structural economic crises that unfolded with partial, inconsistent reform in the 1990s, they were eventually forced to adopt social de-

---

5   We are diverging here a bit from the assessment of Vachudova (2005) and Grzymała-Busse (2007) who claim an absence of "robust competition" in the Czech Republic is to be held responsible for a weaker, more inconsistent political-economic reform push, particularly when it comes to the construction of political institutions complementing a capitalist market economy. In the big comparative picture that includes all the Southeast European and post-Soviet polities, however, the reform trajectory of the Czech Republic is much more similar to that of other Central European countries with a prevalent national-accommodative communist legacy.

6   Vaclav Klaus's Czech Civic Party, the major moderately conservative pro-market party in the Czech party system, began to embrace more nationalist and authoritarian positions in the late 1990s.

mocratic reform strategies and begrudgingly to accept the inevitability of the capitalist market economy, for example, in Bulgaria, Romania, Moldova, Serbia. But the same post-communist political-economic trajectory also discredited ineffectual market-liberal reform politicians and their parties, thus creating a political void for dissatisfied citizens to seek out new social-protectionist populist parties. Because communism was finally discredited as a heterodox ideology to fight the political project of capitalist democracy, nothing has become more plausible for political entrepreneurs than to couch their grievances in terms of a radical right exclusionary group and authoritarian grid interpretation. This template both explains the causes of post-communist societal disintegration and offers an alternative vision of political institutionalization to overcome that predicament.

Where communists did not regain power, such as in Russia, it was not liberal democrats who could take advantage of this situation, but non-partisan technocratic government cadres who increasingly manipulated electoral processes through "parties of power." Induced by the government executive's capacity to award material benefits and inflict coercion on politicians, executive elites eventually succeeded in crafting quasi-parties of government that also embrace elements of a nationalist group and authoritarian grid philosophy.

The legacy of patrimonial communism thus fuels radical right political appeals, whether configured around unreconstructed communist-nationalist successor parties or new right wing creations, particularly in the 1990s. In the new millennium, however, both the consolidation of technocratic governing parties that experiment with radical rightist idioms as well as the eventual recovery of post-communist economies propelled by a raw materials boom may hold the growth potential for radical right wing politics in limits. Nevertheless, where radical right partisan groups could establish and entrench themselves in the 1990s, one or both of the following conditions may help them thrive in the new millennium. First, competitors are ineffective in siphoning off potential radical right support. Second, economic recovery is not sufficiently fast and encompassing to lower the temperature of popular dissatisfaction and disgust with politicians.

Table 1 contrasts two legacies and two phases of post-communist economic reform, as sketched on preceding pages. Where national accommodative communism prevailed, the potential for distinctive radical right parties has always been limited. As a consequence, major political parties began to incorporate a non-economic dimension into their "product differentiation" that built on distinctive grid/group appeals. When the challenge of social policy reform broadens disaffection with economic reform and distrust of politicians in the most recent phase of economic restructuring, strategic politicians have even more incentives to appeal to voters based on grid/group programs, something that is all the more plausible if such parties have already established a track record of politicizing this dimension. In this strategic configuration, distinctive radical right parties have few electoral opportunities. At the same time, radical right appeals gain prominence in the competitive struggle among mainline political parties.

By contrast, in countries with patrimonial communist legacies, the lingering massive political-economic problems of the 1990s created a much greater radical right wing potential from the very beginning, albeit one that on the supply side was partially absorbed by unreconstructed, intransigent communist successor parties who also invoked exclusionary group and authoritarian grid conceptions of social order. Nevertheless, given the often-observed weakness of the liberal democratic party camps to overcome their collective action problems and build parties that could attract broad mass support, this supply side configuration still left plenty of supporters available for radical right wing partisan efforts.

After 2000, patrimonial post-communist parties either partially gave up their opposition to market reforms or lost support because even the opponents of post-communist reforms wanted more than a return to the status quo ante. This created more space for radical right wing mobilization. At the same time, as post-communist countries with partial market reform finally began to experience economic recovery after a decade of precipitous decline, in part helped by the exogenous force of a resource boom, the new economic developments may contain the growth of radical right mass support and allow incumbents to consolidate power around more technocratic formula.

Table 1.   Political economy, historical legacies and party systems

		Phase 1: 1989-1999	Phase 2: 2000-
East Central Europe Inheritance of national- accommodative communism	Political-economic trajectory	• Liberalization + capitalist institution building, extension of a quasi-socialist welfare state • Macro-economic stabilization crisis and gradual recovery (1994+)	• Reform/retrenchment of social protection • Macro-economic fiscal crisis and pressure to reduce social protection constrain economic growth
	Market liberal democratic center-left and center-right?	• Strong market-liberals • Reformist former socialist ruling parties as new social democrats	• Market-liberal democrats shrink; • Social democratic center-left; • Strengthening nationalist market-protectionist right
	Anti-capitalist left?	Insignificant	Insignificant
	Radical right?	• Small separate parties: RR (nationalist, ethnic exclusion, often social protectionist)	• RR parties fail, in as much as center-right parties embrace some of their appeal
South-Eastern European and Soviet Inheritance of patrimonial communism	Political-economic trajectory	• Partial liberalization and failed institution building • Prolonged economic depression with very deep turning point • Collapse of social protection and sky-rocketing inequality	• Incremental liberalization and some institution building; • Raw materials rentier economies grow rapidly • Sharp macro-economic recovery from a very low level of economic activity
	Market liberal democratic center-left and center-right?	• Weak and divided market liberal parties and national-conservative parties	• Weak, volatile and divided liberal democrats + national-conservatives • Social democratizing left (some of the former communists) • "parties of power"
	Anti-capitalist left?	• (Post)-communists as anti-liberal anti-democrats	• Residues of authoritarian socialism
	Radical right?	• Absorbed in some cases by communists, but high RR potential • Ethnic and nationalist right with communist sympathies	• New "populists" may assert themselves: social protectionist + grid/group exclusionary appeals

Ethnicity and radical right

The ethnic composition of post-communist countries provides important clues to radical right parties' demands and partisan opportunities. What matters are the proportion of the largest salient ethnic group relative to smaller groups and the relative status of the group in terms of economic and political resource control. Our argument is based on deterrence logic. Ethno-cultural antagonisms are stoked successfully by radical rightist parties when there is a plausible minority scapegoat and when that scapegoat does not have the capacity to inflict major damage on the titular majority and its political organizations, either because it is too weak in numbers, and/or controls too few economic assets and/or is not needed by one or all of the relevant parties of the largest ethnic group to build a winning governing coalition.

Radical rightist causes in general have the smallest potential in ethnoculturally homogeneous societies. Here it is difficult to find scapegoats, particularly if there are neither plausible indigenous target minorities, nor substantial immigration. Radical right parties may also tend to have limited appeal in highly contested new state formations where the ascending elites must craft broad political alliances and cannot antagonize very substantial ethno-cultural minorities if they want to consolidate their rule, particularly where these minorities were dominant in political-economic terms in the past, as were Russians in Soviet republics that proceeded to become independent states after 1991.[7]

Countries with the greatest potential for radical right mobilization are those with small, entrenched ethnic minorities, as well as those with irredentist claims against their neighbors, whether they are old or new states. Potential grid/group mobilization should be particularly strong where both conditions coincide. Thus, countries such as Hungary and Romania reach out to irredentist Hungarian (Romanian) minorities abroad (such as Hungarians in Slovakia, Romania, Croatia, or Serbia or Romanians in Moldova), but also harbor minorities themselves that can become the object of grid/group antagonisms

---

7   Beissinger's (2008) account of why ethnic pluralism sometimes permits the stabilization of democracy homes in on exactly this configuration in some of the new multi-ethnic countries resulting from the former Soviet Union. Of course, as additional element to nudge a country to inter-ethnic peace by restraining the new non-Russian titular ethnic majority, he correctly mentions the influence of the European Union, for example in the Baltic countries, but also beyond.

in a socially incendiary environment of economic strains (for example, Roma, Jews, Hungarians).[8]

Our theoretical framework associates citizens' preference formation with socio-cultural processes of grid/group identification and trajectories of post-communist political-economic reform. It explains radical right party success through a spatial logic of party competition in which the programmatic positions and strategies of the most important initial partisan players in post-communist democracy—namely those of communist successor parties and their anti-communist challengers—are at least initially not freely chosen by political entrepreneurs, but result from communist "legacies" that endow competing emergent parties with resources, activists' ideologies, and capabilities to solve collective action problems. It is in fact radical right wing parties that are conceptualized as the "free agents" that enter successfully only when other parties for reasons of historical constraint and political-economic reform cannot immediately choose electorally efficient positions that would preempt the entry of new competitors.

The main empirical implications of our theoretical sketch are that the electoral payoffs of radical right parties should vary across post-communist countries over time and across space in systematic fashion related to regime legacies and ethno-cultural configurations. The scope of our theoretical framework is intended to include all post-communist democracies that hold competitive elections. When data were unavailable (as, for instance, in the cases of Bosnia and Herzegovina, Georgia and Moldova), we reduced the scope of empirical testing.

If the theoretical framework we have proposed has a semblance of usefulness, we should detect some characteristic profiles of political appeals of parties in different party systems after national-accommodative or patrimonial communism. In the former, there should be very little space for competition among relevant parties over economic-distributive issues and the organization of the economy, as all major competitors have a reputation to embrace market liberalization. Much of the differentiation, even among "moderate" mainstream parties, should be over socio-cultural conceptions of the polity that relate to group-grid characteristics, at least in the first phase of post-communist political-economic reform. The politicization of quasi-welfare state

---

8   Table 4 disaggregates cases within both the national-accommodative East Central European stream as well as the East European patrimonial legacies to hypothesize where the potential for radical rightist party formation may be particularly likely. Table 4 is available online at: http://www.duke.edu/~lbs11/.

services and insurance systems in the most recent phase of post-communist political-economic reform, however, may enable parties with a right wing grid-group appeal to deliver the feat of ostentatiously associating a defense of the national community with populist lip service against the ills of social policy retrenchment, while simultaneously pursuing a politics of social policy retrenchment in the government executive.

After patrimonial communism, by contrast, polarization over economic policy reform and over socio-cultural grid/group conceptions is less likely to crosscut than to reinforce each other. Economic polarization is alive and well (Frye, 2002). Parties that oppose market liberalization and institution building supplemental to a capitalist economy in order to attract losers of the political-economic reform process may find it easy to reinforce their popularity by exclusionary group and authoritarian group appeals. Particularly in the presence of ethnic minorities and irredentist yearnings this may boost the electoral opportunities of distinctive radical right parties.

Spaces of partisan competition in post-communist democracies: economic distribution and socio-cultural issues

Table 2 reports the position of radical right parties or their closest relevant competitors, measured by parties' position on grid/group issues (group: nationalism, grid: socio-cultural conservatism). But we also present the position of parties on major economic issues, namely the question of spending on social services (versus tax cuts) and the merits of privatizing state-owned companies. We do not report small splinter parties. We have organized the display of data by legacies and conditions of state formation and we report grid-group (socio-cultural and nationalistic) positions and distributive economic policy positions.

In many of the formerly national-accommodative communist regimes, such as Hungary, Poland, Slovakia, Estonia, we find electorally attractive "nearby" parties, in terms of grid-group positions that have nationalist-socially conservative appeals similar to those of the radical right parties. In terms of economics, as expected, none of the parties assumes radical pro-market or anti-market positions after national-accommodative communism.[9]

---

9   The oxooption being the populist Samoobrona in Poland whose electoral support vanished after the 2007 parliamentary elections, partially due to sexual harassment accusations within party leadership.

Table 2.   Radical right parties, *"nearby"* competitors and their policy stances

Legacy	Country	Party labels	RR	Socio-cultural grid-group positions?		Distributive economic policy positions?	
				Natio-nalism	Cul-ture	Spending	Privatiza-tion
B-A	Czech Repub-lic	KSCM (18.5 + 12.8)	n	16.6	6.2	4.4	4.0
		RMS+NS (1.1 + 0.2)	RR	19.2	15.9	11.5	9.3
N-A + H	Hun-gary	MIEP (4.4 + 2.2)	RR	19.8	19.0	7.9	5.9
		Fidesz (35.1 + 42.0)	n	16.2	15.1	9.3	9.1
	Poland	LPR (7.9 + 8.0 + 1.3)	RR	19.0	19.2	8.2	8.5
		PiS (9.5 + 27.0 + 32.1)	n	14.7	15.1	11.5	13.6
		S (10.2 + 11.4 + 1.3)	n	16.1	13.1	5.2	4.4
	Slove-nia	SNS (4.4 + 6.3)	RR	17.1	11.7	10.1	9.3
		Nsi (8.6 + 90.09)	n	15.1	17.3	13.0	14.7
N-A + E/I	Croatia	HSP (6.4 + 3.5)	RR	19.0	15.0	9.7	7.7
		HDZ (33.9 + 36.6)	n	15.7	14.2	8.8	11.8
	Lithua-nia	LKD (3.1 + 0.3)	RR	15.9	18.0	9.1	10.2
		LKDS (3.1 + 0)	n	11.0	19.0	13.0	14.0
		TS (8.6 + 14.6)	n	14.8	15.8	12.6	15.4
	Slova-kia	SNS (3.3 + 11.7)	RR	19.4	16.1	10.4	10.3
		KDH (8.3 + 8.3)	n	15.7	19.7	14.4	15.4
		HZDS (19.5 + 8.8)	n	13.8	9.5	10.2	12.2
N-A + E	Estonia	ISAMAA (7.3 + merged 2007 – 17.9%)	n	19.1	14.6	12.8	16.2
		RL (13.0 + 7.1)	n	17.6	16.0	11.8	8.0
	Latvia	TB/LNNK (5.4 + 6.9)	n	19.3	14.5	12.9	13.9
		NONE	RR	No data	No data	No data	No data

Notes: Legacy: legacy and state formation; Party labels: % support around 2000-3 + later; RR: RR or "nearby" competitor? Nearby competitor is labeled as "n"; Nationalism: strong nationalism = 20; Culture: socio-cultural conservatism (strong =20); Spending: spending cuts and tax cuts (= 20) or raise taxes to increase public services (=1); Privatization: merits of privatization high (=20) or low (=1); B-A: bureaucratic-authoritarian regime; N-A + H: national-accommodative regime + ethnically homogenous; N-A + E/I: national-accommodative regime + minorities/ irredentism; N-A + E: national accommodative regime + ethno-politically contested state building;

Legacy	Country	Party labels	RR	Socio-cultural grid-group positions? Nationalism	Culture	Distributive economic policy positions? Spending	Privatization
P + H	Albania	PBK (~2.5 + 2.5)	RR	No data	No data	No data	No data
		PLL (4.0 + 0)	n	19.0	14.0	16.0	17.5
P + E/I	Bulgaria	National Union Attack (0 + 8.9)	RR	No data	No data	No data	No data
		VMRO (1.3 + 5.7 in coalition)	n	18.6	13.5	11.2	12.0
	Romania	PRM (19.5 + 12.9)	RR	19.6	18.7	5.6	4.7
		PUR (1.4 + then moderate)	n	12.9	13.1	9.7	12.1
		PNG (after 2004/2005)	RR	No data	No data	No data	No data
	Russia	LDPR (11.5 + 8.1)	RR	17.5	14.1	9.4	7.8
		KPRF (12.6 + 11.6)	n	16.3	14.3	3.5	3.7
		SRS (27.7 + 28.6)	RR	18.7	16.8	6.5	11.0
	Serbia	SPO (7.7 + 3.33)	n	13.5	13.8	11.3	14.8
	Macedonia	VMRO-DPMNE (2002: 20.8 + large coalition 2007: 32.5) VMRO-NPNDP (2007: 6.1)	n	17.5	17.3	11.8	16.1
		None	RR	No data	No data	No data	No data
P + E	Bosnia and Herzegovina	Not applicable due to the number of RR parties	n				
		SDA, SDS, HDZ (46 total + 53 total)	RR	19; 20; 20	18; 18.5; 19	14; 11; 14.5	14.5; 15; 17.5
	Moldova	PPCD (9.7 + 9.07)	n	13.4	10.4	8.5	11.7
		None	RR	No data	No data	No data	No data
	Ukraine	NU (23.6 + 13.95)	n	17.0	11.8	9.4	13.5
		KUN	RR	No data	No data	No data	No data

Notes: P + H: patrimonial regime + ethnically homogenous; P + E/I: patrimonial regime + minorities or irredentism; P + E: patrimonial regime + ethno-politically contested state building; Bosnia: the vote shares are from elections to the House of Representatives election in Bosnia–Herzegovina, October 2002 (the vote share are: SDA: 22; HDZ: 10 SDS: 14 in 2002; source: Burwitz, 2004).

Source: Benoit and Laver (2006).

And in all of the national-accommodative post-communist polities, the radical right parties signal slightly more market-skeptical positions than their nearby mainstream conservative counterparts while also endorsing even more extreme nationalist positions that are sometimes paired with equally authoritarian socio-cultural conservatism. It is telling that with the exception of Poland, genuine radical rightist parties have earned very limited success in the formerly national-accommodative communist countries, with the partial exception of countries with substantial minorities and irredentist conflicts. This applies to Croatia, Slovakia, and a borderline case we have here classified as homogeneous, Slovenia.

The electoral weakness of the radical right may have been bought at the price of much larger, more mainstream, "near radical right" parties that command substantial support in most of the formerly national-accommodative communist countries.[10] Hungary's Fidesz/Civic Party became the paradigmatic case for a moderately conservative party with at times radical right-wing grid/group rhetoric.

In the formerly patrimonial communist countries, wherever there are substantial ethnic minorities (but do not constitute a strong counter-balance to the major ethnic group) or constellations of irredentism, genuine radical right parties are electorally highly successful. In Russia, where the misnamed Liberal Democrats as the most clear-cut radical right party, their relatively more muted electoral performance is due to the presence of an intransigent, nationalist communist party (KPRF) and advantages enjoyed by dominant 'parties of power' in electoral competition. In the other three countries—Bulgaria, Romania, and Serbia—the Benoit/Laver expert survey does not permit us to classify the communist successor parties as "near" to the radical right, since their grid/group positions differ quite dramatically from each other and because the former communist parties began to transform themselves into social democratic parties. Only in Russia has the KPRF maintained a hard-line stance against economic market reforms. Radical right parties constitute a pole in party systems with ethnic divisions that separates a populist, social-protectionist and anti-market radical right with strong grid/group appeals from typically more fragmented centrist and market liberal parties that stand for more cosmopolitan and socially tolerant life style choices.

---

10   This pattern would become even clearer if we classified Slovenia as having a minority/irredentism issue.

Our table shows that in none of the formerly patrimonial communist countries without ethnic minority challenges are there substantial radical right parties or even nearby parties that would appeal to radical right themes. In cases such as Moldova and Ukraine, political entrepreneurs will refrain from strong grid/group appeals, given the exigencies of bringing about basic state institutions first in the countries where national independence is a contested innovation.

Let us now consider more general patterns in cross-national comparison that result from a factor-analytical representation of the party alignments in democracies, as calculated by Benoit and Laver (2006: table 5.7.b). In most countries a factor analysis of all the issue positions on which a country's parties were scored yields an economic-distributive and a socio-cultural libertarian/authoritarian factor that characterizes the distribution of parties in the political space in parsimonious, efficient ways. Because the same policies were scored in all countries, it is possible to compare the relative strength of factors depicting different core party appeals, as measured by a factor's eigenvalue. Panel 1 of Table 3 calculates the ratio of the eigenvalues earned by: (1) the factor that represents economic-distributive conflict with (2) that on which the socio-cultural policy questions load most strongly.[11] In all of the formerly patrimonial communist dictatorships, considerations of economic distribution and property rights far surpass the capacity of socio-cultural issues to structure the landscape of party competition.

The same result is driven home by the answer to the question of whether the issue of "nationalism" loads more heavily on the socio-cultural factor or the economic factor. An answer is provided in the middle panel of Table 3. It reveals the pattern one might anticipate from the first panel reported in the same table. After national-accommodative communism, the question of national autonomy loads on the socio-cultural issue dimension, whereas after patrimonial or bureaucratic-authoritarian communism there is much greater weight on polarization over economic issues that also pull the question of nationalism into their vortex.

---

11   In Hungary the factor which assembles a variety of socio-cultural grid and national group related questions is five times as strong as that which configures around economic-distributive issues (Hungary score = 0.20 where: social = 6.62; econ = 1.33; 1.33/6.62 = 0.2).

Table 3. Communist legacies and spaces of partisan competition

		National-accommodative communist legacy	Bureaucratic-authoritarian or patrimonial communist legacy
1. Factors loadings of parties' policy scores	Socio-cultural factor is much stronger than the economic factor (ratio < 0.75)	Hungary 0.20 Croatia 0.25 Slovenia 0.31 Poland 0.58 Lithuania 0.71	Serbia 0.51 Macedonia 0.65
	Socio-cultural and economic factors are equally strong (0.75 < ratio < 1.33)		Moldova 1.13
	Economic factor stronger than the socio-cultural factor (1.33 < ratio < 2.50)	Slovakia 1.60 Estonia 1.79 Latvia 2.16	Albania 1.47 Czech R. 2.28
	Economic factor is much stronger than the socio-cultural factor (ratio > 2.50)		Bulgaria 3.30 Russia 4.21 Romania 4.38 Ukraine 4.53
2. Dominant factor	Socio-cultural	Croatia Estonia Hungary Lithuania Poland Slovenia Slovakia	Macedonia Moldova
	Economic	Latvia	Albania Romania Russia Ukraine
	None		Czech Republic Bulgaria Serbia
3. Dominant coefficient to predict left-right placement	Economic	Estonia Latvia	Albania Czech Republic Bulgaria Macedonia Romania Russia Ukraine
	Both economic and socio-cultural	Lithuania Poland Slovakia Slovenia	Moldova
	Socio-cultural	Croatia Hungary	Serbia

Notes: 1. Factor loadings of parties' policy scores: ratio of factor strength (eigenvalue) on which economic issues load (taxes-spending and privatization) and socio-cultural policy issues ("social"). 2. Dominant factor: on which factor of division among parties does "nationalism" load (on socio-cultural factor, economic factor or on the separate dimension)? 3. Dominant coefficient (coefficient strength) to predict left and right placement: Predicting parties' left-right placements: economic (taxes/spending), socio-cultural (moral code) or environmental. The dominant coefficient is greater two times than the other one.

Source: Benoit and Laver (2006, tables 5.7.b and 6.A2).

Consistent with this message, the third panel shows that knowing parties' positions on socio-cultural issues is a much better predictor of the way experts assign left-right scores to parties in national-accommodative communism than that knowledge delivers in countries after patrimonial communism.

Cross-national empirical implications

What are some additional empirical differences between patrimonial and national-accommodative regimes? Does the claim that radical right-wing parties are stronger in democracies, which follow patrimonial communism show up in the data? What is the effect of the largest minority ethnic group on the mobilization potential of the radical right? Do the regimes differ in their patterns of inequality and social expenditures?

Table 4 outlines several differences in social expenditures and inequality between the two regimes.[12] National-accommodative regimes, on average, spend more than the patrimonial ones do on social expenditures and also tend to have lower levels of economic inequality. The average GINI coefficient of inequality around 1996-1998 in Hungary, Poland and Slovenia was 25.1 compared to 31.6 in Bulgaria, Romania, Russia and Serbia. Similar disparities are also present in total social security expenditures as a percentage of GDP. While the most of the national-accommodative regimes spend over 20% of GDP on social security, patrimonial regime cases often spend less than 15% of GDP (Table 4). Within the national-accommodative regimes, however, ethnically diverse countries, such as the Baltics and Slovakia, spend the least and have the highest level of inequality.

Although it is beyond the scope of this paper to fully investigate the link between redistribution and ethnic diversity in Eastern Europe, multiple studies have shown that ethnic diversity can undermine welfare generosity (Elias and Scotson, 1965; Alesina et al., 1999; Habyarimana et al., 2007). Uncertainty about the distribution of material resources and the ethnic division of labor during crises enables strategic politicians to invoke ethno-regional sentiments (Olzak, 1992).

As far as party competition is concerned, we argue that radical right mobilization is highest in countries with small ethnic groups in peaceful competitive democracies. Contrary to some intuition, we suggest that the potential of the radical right for group mobilization does not linearly increases with the

---

12   Table 4 is available online at: http://www.duke.edu/~lbs11/.

size of the largest minority ethnic group. This finding cuts against predictions, which have associated the size of the ethnic group (or sharp jumps in immigrant inflows) with increased political mobilization of ethnicities (Olzak, 1992, p. 35). The reason for this departure, we argue, is that two distinct mechanisms may be at play when it comes to peaceful democratic competition and political mobilization leading to violence.

If politicians are risk averse when it comes to ethnic violence, they have incentives to comply with the democratic rule of game, for stirring ethnic hatred bears the danger of spiraling out of control and badly damaging the ethno-cultural majority. By contrast, mobilizing against small ethnic groups that cannot monopolize the central administration and the state's resources is largely devoid of the risk that such mobilization will escalate into violence. Only under conditions of intense competitiveness among rival parties drawing their bulk of support from the ethno-cultural majority, have ethnic entrepreneurs a strong incentive to contain inter-ethnic conflict and actually seek alliances with the political representatives of ethno-cultural minority parties. Paradoxically, when the main parties, dominated by the titular nationality, need small ethnic parties to form coalitions in government, this may increase the salience of ethnic cleavages in party competition (Wilkinson, 2004).

Small ethnic parties demand concessions from the main parties in exchange for forming ruling coalitions, and they typically articulate their demands in ethnic and cultural terms. Incorporating ethnic parties has the distinct advantage of channeling ethnic tensions into party competition rather than organized violence. At the same time, it re-focuses party competition towards socio-cultural issues which are of concern to the ethnic minority. Politicians must be able to make potential group losses credible to large electoral constituencies, yet this is implausible in polities that pit large ethno-cultural majorities against minorities.

We, therefore, expect to observe the highest potential for radical right mobilization in countries with relatively small ethnic groups. By contrast, in countries with a large ethnic minority, and with contested state building, the reservoir for the radical right is parched. Examples of such countries with weak radical right parties include Moldova, Ukraine and Macedonia.

Ukraine is an example of a country with a large ethnic minority, a '60-40' split, and possesses a negligible radical right. The extremist Congress of Ukrainian Nationalists ran under the platform of Yushchenko's 'Our Ukraine' and provided security forces to Julia Tymoshenko during the Orange Revolution (Kuzio, 1997).[13] Yushchenko, not surprisingly, caters to the 'nationalist' base of Western Ukraine.[14] 'Our Ukraine' is a nearby competitor to the radical right, and has successfully drained the pool of potential radical right voters.

When Yushchenko regained power in 2006, the 'orange bloc' engaged in the so-called 'war of languages'. According to the Ukrainian constitution, the predominantly Russian-speaking areas are allowed to use Russian as the official language.[15] The 'orange bloc' has attempted to curb the rights of Russian-speaking minorities, yet their efforts have been largely unsuccessful. At the same time, the close competition between the Western Ukrainian party alliance, on the one hand, and the Russo-Ukrainian party, on the other, has made both sides tone down the ethno-cultural base of their disagreement. Moreover, when the Russian speaking authorities realized that the restriction of language rights contradicted the European Charter for Minority and Regional Languages, the policy was revoked, following pressure from the European Union (Medvedev, 2007, p. 205).

Contrast Ukraine with Slovakia, a country with much smaller minority, split 90-10 between Slovaks and Hungarians, and has hosted a vibrant radical right party since the early 1990s, the Slovak National Party, or SNS. SNS is currently a member of a governing coalition, led by Robert Fico and his party SMER. The two small parties in the Slovak political system, the Slovak National Party and liberal-oriented Hungarian party, are locked in a seemingly permanent struggle over Hungarian minority rights in Slovakia. Both are needed to form government coalitions; ironically, they also "need each other for their survival, like inseparable twins," sustaining the salience of the ethnic dimension in Slovak party competition.[16]

At the same time, SNS is in constant danger of having its nationalistic party program absorbed by the more centrist SMER. When asked directly

---

13   The paramilitary units of UNA (another fringe radical right party in Ukraine) provided security for pro-Yushchenko and pro-Tymoshenko forces in 2004 as well. Moreover, between 2002-2006, once elected to Verkhovna Rada for the Lviv district, Andriy Shkil, (UNA leader), joined the Yulia Tymoshenko bloc faction. Sources: Verchovnaya Rada (2009); UNA-UNSO (2009).

14   For example, on October 12, 2007 President Yushchenko awarded the Hero of Ukraine title and the Order of State posthumously to the chief commander of the Ukrainian Insurgent Army of 1942-1950, Gen. Brig. Roman Shukhevych, in a highly symbolic ceremony. In Western Ukraine, the UPA soldiers are viewed as freedom fighters that opposed both the Nazis and the Red Army. The left and pro-Russian parties have accused the UPA of war crimes against civilians. Source: Kyiv Weekly (2007).

15   Source: KUN (2009); Vasovic (2005).

16   Interview with Olga Gyarfasova, IVO, summer, Bratislava, 2007 and 2008.

whether SMER is considering promoting a 'patriotic' agenda in order to lure voters from the SNS, Andrej Kolesik, leader of the SMER parliamentary club, answered unambiguously. Kolesik even outlined the steps that the major Slovak party is taking to appeal to Slovak voters on ethno-cultural basis.[17] SMER's nationalistic appeals are constrained, however, and mild when compared to SNS leader Slota's more virulent style of ethnic appeals. Aside from football hooliganism among both Slovak and Hungarian citizens, however, there has never been a violent confrontation between Slovaks and Hungarian-Slovaks since 1989.

These two brief illustrations serve only to highlight our argument about the relationship of ethnic group size to radical right party success. Large minorities induce fairly moderate behavior among majority parties, whereas smaller minorities create incentives for more aggressive and possibly violent ethnic appeals. Since collective action is easier among smaller ethnic minorities, party formation is facilitated and these parties tend to have focused, narrow agendas. Laitin (1999) has suggested that there may be incentives for sizable minorities to seek accommodation and economic success in new polities, an argument that allows him to explain the surprising peace in the Baltics.

In order to assess the plausibility of our claims about the size of ethnic minority groups and radical right party success, we build on a new measure of ethnic heterogeneity called HET (Siroky, 2009a). The HET measure accounts for relative group sizes, consistent with our theory, and allows us to measure the distance between a theoretical distribution of ethnic composition and the empirical distribution in any given country.[18]

Since HET is flexible in terms of the selection of theoretical priors, we can implement a version of HET with 90-10 priors on the first and second largest ethnic groups, reflecting our theoretical argument that countries with an ethnic minority comprising 10% of the population are most prone to radical right mobilization. Returning to the example of Slovakia, in which 90% are

---

17   Interview with Andrej Kolesik, July 2008, Slovak Parliament, Bratislava.
18   We are noting using a common measure of ethnic fractionalization known as ELF for two major reasons. First, ELF depends on the number of groups and thus is not comparable across countries with different numbers of groups. Second, ELF gives very high values to countries with many tiny groups but our theory posits that ethnic tensions are derived from a relationship between one dominant group and a small minority group. The major advantage of HET is that "it evaluates the relative proportions of the ethnic groups consistent with the theoretical literature, whereas ELF devotes the greatest weight to the most dominant group as a result of squaring the proportions" (Siroky 2009a).

Slovak and 10% are Hungarian, the HET index yields a value close to one. The value of the HET index is close to zero when the empirical distribution of ethnic groups in a given country is roughly 50-50, a situation that is represented in a stylized version of Ukraine.

The middle values of HET are associated with more or less ethnically homogeneous states, such as the Czech Republic or Poland. This implies, counter-intuitively, that homogenous states are somewhat more likely to host strong radical right parties than states with large ethnic minorities. The Czech Republicans, Hungarian MIEP and the League of Polish Families all fit this pattern, whereas Ukraine, Moldova and Macedonia, which all have large ethnic minorities, all lack strong radical right parties.

We now turn to the empirical evaluation of our claims. The big caveat is that we are dealing with a very small number of countries, which constrains our choices of statistical techniques based on the asymptotic properties of large-N samples. For these reasons we first use a non-parametric technique known as Random Forest which does not depend on sample sizes, does not assume linearities in data, and can account for curvilinear relations between variables.

Now we will turn to a method that will allow us to asses the marginal importance of variables that explain variation in vote shares for radical right parties. Fig. 1 depicts a "variable importance plot" produced from a non-parametric ensemble method, called Random Forests, which has proven to be a powerful method for selecting important predictors in the presence of many noise variables (Siroky, 2009b). In this application, the method helps to detect the core variables driving radical party vote shares and then ranks the variables in order of their importance (Breiman, 2001; Siroky, 2009b). The method does not rely on any restrictive assumptions and produces results that are intuitive and consistent with our theoretical expectations. The results show that three variables—ethnic heterogeneity, health expenditures and governance quality—strongly predict vote shares for radical right parties at the aggregate national level, while the majority of other variables can be safely ignored.

The first component of the plot (percentage increase in MSE) can be thought of as a decrease in accuracy of predicting vote shares for the radical right in the 2000s if the variable is removed. The best performing variables, regulatory quality: 'greg', rule of law: 'gruel', government effectiveness: 'gefec' are measures of the quality of governance (World Bank, 2007).[19] This is not surprising since radical right parties campaign on anti-corruption platforms (Bustikova, 2009) and attract dissatisfied constituents. Moreover, quality of governance is a proximate measure for the regime type and welfare provision. First, patrimonial regimes score much lower on all components of quality of governance when compared to national-accommodative regimes. Second, quality of governance is a pre-requisite for infrastructural powers of the states that deal with welfare goods provision. For example, it is difficult to imagine a well functioning universal health care in a country with a weak regulatory capacity. In this first component of the plot, the measures of state capacity trump measures of health and social security expenditure ('eheal', 'esoc').

Aside from the variables associated with quality of governance, our measure of ethnic diversity, 'het9010-61' increases accuracy of the prediction if kept in the analysis. The importance of a variable that captures ethnic diversity is corroborated by the second component of Fig. 1. The second component of the plot captures the increase in node purity and can be thought of as another variable selection procedure (Siroky, 2009b). The algorithm searches for the most important explanatory variables that can partition the variation in the dependent variable (support for the radical right). The top four selected variables in the second component of Fig. 1 are: (1) expenditure on health as percentage of gross domestic product in 2000; (2) measure of ethnic diversity based on our theoretical prior or 90-10; (3) percentage of votes for the nearby (moderate) right wing party which competes for radical right votes; and (4) levels of literacy around 1939 as a legacy proxy for state capacity (Corduneanu-Huci and Bustikova, 2006).

---

19   The governance indicators are average scores: 2003-2006 (WB). Government effectiveness measures the quality of public services, the quality of the civil service and the degree of its independence from political pressures, the quality of policy formulation and implementation, and the credibility of the government's commitment to such policies. Regulatory quality measures the ability of the government to formulate and implement sound policies and regulations that permit and promote private sector development. Rule of law measures the extent to which agents have confidence in and abide by the rules of society, in particular the quality of contract enforcement, the police, and the courts, as well as the likelihood of crime and violence.

Fig. 1.   Variable importance plot. Variables are ordered according to their
            importance from the most to the least important

Variable Selection for RR Vote Shares in 2000s

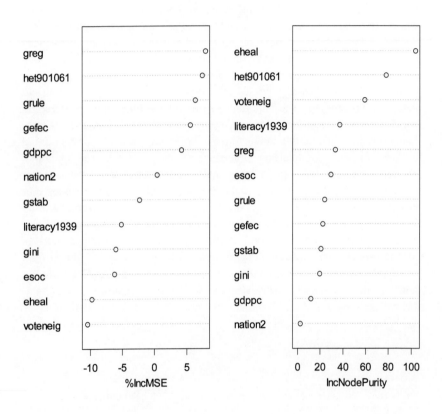

The algorithm does not assume a linear relationship between the radical right vote shares and the independent variables, but considers all possible monotonic transformations. But our theoretical postulates have been made in linear fashions. Is it possible to corroborate results from the data-partitioning algorithm in Fig. 1 with an analysis that would mirror our theoretical expectations about the directionality of the variables? Using our small sample of sixteen countries, we perform a Bayesian linear regression on the square root of vote shares for the radical right in the 2000s with four dependent variables: measures of health expenditure, regulatory quality, ethnic heterogeneity based on a 90-10 prior and a control dummy for the regime type, national-accommodative versus patrimonial (Table 5).[20] The mean (median) of the posterior distribution is a coefficient, or a conditional effect, of a given variable.

Though Bayesian analysis does not depend on the asymptotic properties of large samples, it does not fully overcome the small N problem because the empirical distribution cannot overcome the prior distribution. Table 6 and plots of posterior distributions (Fig. 2 and Table 5) reveal that all our '5%' credible intervals (from 0.025 to 0.975) of posterior distributions contain zero. This means that variables, multiplied by a slope that can be a zero, may have a null effect.

We would nevertheless like to stress that the effect of all three variables of interest points to the direction that is consistent with our theory. The median, (almost identical with the mean): the effect of health expenditures and regulatory quality points to the negative direction (the posterior distribution is shifted to the left of zero in Fig. 1). This suggests that decrease in health expenditure and lower regulatory quality is associated with larger vote shares for the radical right. Het9010 measure of ethnic diversity goes in the opposite direction: its increase goes hand in hand with the increased vote share for the radical right. Thus, if theoretically the country is approaching our distribution of ethnic groups being split between 90-10, we observe higher vote shares for the radical right. We are not suggesting substantive effects, but we are using the analysis to corroborate our theoretical intuitions about the directionality of the variables in a small N setting. These results are in accordance with our theoretical postulates.

---

20   Table 5 is available online at: http://www.duke.edu/~lbs11/.

Fig. 2.   Posterior densities from Bayesian linear regression. Dependent variable: vote shares for the radical right in Eastern Europe, square root. N=16; the model is using standard conjugate non-informative priors. Figure generated using a MCMC package in R (Martin et al., 2009; R)

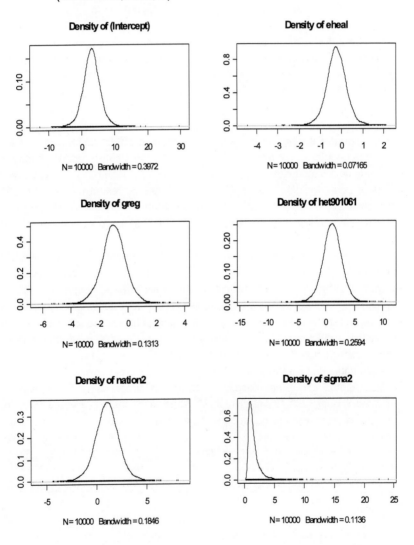

Conclusion

This paper grounds the analysis of the potential for radical right mobilization in the ethnic composition of countries and in the institutional legacies of communist and pre-communist rule. Ethnic endowments predispose countries with small minorities to be susceptible to the radical right appeals. This deep legacy has to be considered in the context of institutional legacies inherited from communism. Since national-accommodative regimes started their transitions with communist parties inclined toward moderation and eagerness in implementing capitalism, major right wing parties had to differentiate their appeals, and they did so on a socio-cultural rather than an economic platform. Patrimonial regimes, by contrast, inherited a polarized political environment and followed a significantly more contested path toward capitalism. The losers of reforms in patrimonial regimes were not cushioned by the relatively generous welfare states that existed in the national regimes. Diverging trajectories of these two regimes became more pronounced due to the fast pace of welfare retrenchment and the sharp rise in inequality, which for instance resulted in a dual-track medical care that benefits the "transitional winners" and creates a pool of dissatisfied voters. However, it is the agency of political parties that translates dissatisfaction with the economy and poor governance into ethno-cultural hostility towards the 'other.'

This article has focused on the demand side of radical right voter appeals. Legacies are static, and change slowly if at all, so they cannot fully account for abrupt changes in vote shares from one election to another. They do nonetheless cast a long shadow over dynamic processes such as democratization and the transition to market economies. Legacies account for the rough patterns of radical right mobilization in the first two decades of post-communism. To provide a more complete account of radical right mobilization, it would be essential to dissect the strategic role of parties in translating economic dissatisfaction into socio-cultural grievances. In such an analysis, legacies would constitute a springboard constraining the strategic moves of parties in the competitive electoral domain.

References

Alesina, A., Baqir, R., Easterly W., 1999. Public goods and ethnic divisions. The Quarterly Journal of Economics 114 (4), 1243-1284.

Beissinger, M., 2008. A new look at ethnicity and democratization. Journal of Democracy 19 (3), 85-97.

Benoit, K., Laver, M., 2006. Party Policy in Modern Democracies. Expert Survey Scores of Policy Positions of Political Parties in 47 Countries, 2004-2005. Routlegde, London.

Breiman, L., 2001. Random Forests. Machine Learning 45, 5-32.

Burwitz, B., 2004. The elections in Bosnia–Herzegovina, October 2002. Electoral Studies June 23 (2), 329-338.

Bustikova, L., 2009. The extreme right in Eastern Europe: EU accession and the quality of governance. Journal of Contemporary European Studies 17 (2), 223-239.

Corduneanu-Huci, C., Bustikova, L., 2006. The Black Box of the Post-communist Past, Post-communist Political Economy and Democratic Politics. Comparative Politics Workshop at Duke University. April 7-8, 2006.

Elias, N., Scotson, J., 1965. The Established and the Outsiders. A Sociological Enquiry into Community Problems. Frank Cass & Co, London.

Frye, T., 2002. The perils of polarization: economic performance in the post-communist world. World Politics 54 (3), 308-337.

Greskovits, B., 1998. The Political Economy of Protest and Patience. East European and Latin American Transformations Compared. Central European University Press, Budapest.

Grzymała-Busse, A., 2007. Rebuilding Leviathan: Party Competition and State Exploitation in Post-Communist Democracies. Cambridge University Press, Cambridge.

Habyarimana, J., Humphreys, M., Posner, D., Weinstein, J., 2007. Why does ethnic diversity undermine public goods provision? American Political Science Review 101 (4), 709-25.

Held, J. (Ed.), 1996. Populism in Eastern Europe. Racism, Nationalism, and Society. East European Monographs, Boulder CO.

Hockenos, P., 1993. Free to Hate: The Rise of the Right in Post-Communist Eastern Europe. Routledge, New York.

Kitschelt, H., McGann, A., 1995. The Radical Right in Western Europe: A Comparative Analysis. University of Michigan Press, Ann Arbor.

Kitschelt, H., Mansfeldova, Z., Markowski, R., Toka, G., 1999. Post-Communist Party Systems: Competition, Representation, and Inter-Party Co-operation. Cambridge University Press, New York.

Kopecky, P., Mudde, C. (Eds.), 2003. Uncivil Society? Contentious Politics in Post-Communist Europe. Routledge, London.

KUN, 2009. Available from: http://cun.org.ua/ukr/content/view/1364/66/.

Kuzio, T., 1997. Radical right parties and civic groups in Belarus and the Ukraine. In: Merkel, P., Weinberg, L. (Eds.), The Revival of Right-Wing Extremism in the Nineties. Frank Cass, London, pp. 203-230.

Kyiv Weekly, 2007. October 15, 2007. Available from: http://www.kyivweekly.com/.

Laitin, D., 1999. Identity in Formation. Cornell University Press, Ithaca, NY.

Martin, A., Quinn, K., Park, J., 2009. Markov chain Monte Carlo (MCMC) package for R.

Medvedev, R., 2007. A splinted Ukraine. Russia in Global Affairs 5 (3), 194-213.

Minkenberg, M., 2002. The radical right in postsocialist Central and Eastern Europe: comparative observations and interpretations. East European Politics and Society 16 (2), 335-362.

Minkenberg, M., 2009. Leninist Beneficiaries? Pre-1989 legacies and the radical right in post-1989 Central and Eastern Europe. Some introductory remarks. Communist and Post-Communist Studies 42 (4), 445-458.

Mudde, C., 2005. Racist Extremism in Central and Eastern Europe. Routledge, London.

Olzak, S., 1992. The Dynamic of Ethnic Competition and Conflict. Stanford University Press, Stanford.

Ost, D., 2005. The Defeat of Solidarity. Anger and Politics in Postcommunist Europe. Cornell University Press.

Pop-Eleches, G., 2007. Historical legacies and post-communist regime change. The Journal of Politics 69 (4), 908-926.

Ramet, S. P. (Ed.), 1999. The Radical Right in Central and Eastern Europe Since 1989. The Pennsylvania State University Press.

Shafir, M., 2008. From historical to "dialectical" populism: the case of post-communist Romania. Canadian Slavonic Papers 50 (3-4), 425-470.

Siroky, D., 2009a. Secession and Survival: Nations, States and Violent Conflict. Ph.D. Dissertation, Duke University.

Siroky, D., 2009b. Navigating Random Forests and related advances in algorithmic modeling. Statistics Surveys 3, 147-163.

UNA-UNSO, 2009. Available from: http://www.una-unso.org/av/mainview.asp?TT_id=16&TX_id=118.

Vachudova, A., 2005. Europe Undivided Democracy, Leverage, and Integration After Communism. Oxford University Press.

Vanhuysse, P., 2006. Divide and Pacify: Strategic Social Policies and Political Protests in Post-Communist Democracies. Central European University Press, Budapest-New York.

Vasovic, A., 2005. Far-right group flexes during Ukraine "revolution". NCSJ/AP, January 1. Available at: http://www.ncsj.org/AuxPages/010105AP_ Ukraine.shtml.

Verchovnaya Rada, 2009. Available from: http://gska2.rada.gov.ua/pls/site/p_ exdeputat?d_id=5412&skl=5.

Wildavsky, A., et al., 1990. Cultural Theory. Westview Press, Boulder CO.

Wilkinson, S., 2004. Votes and Violence. Electoral Competition and Ethnic Riots in India. Cambridge University Press.

World Bank, 2007. World Bank Governance Indicators.

Historical legacies and the size of the red-brown vote in post-communist politics

John Ishiyama

ABSTRACT: In this paper I examine the relatively under investigated topic of how historical legacies shaped the emergence of the "red-brown" political tendency in East-Central Europe and the former Soviet Union — which is sometimes referred to as "National Bolshevism" or "National Communism" or "Strasserism." More specifically I ask the question, how do historical legacies help explain why extreme right wing voters support the successors to the formerly dominant communist parties (or what I refer to as the "red-brown" vote)? I find that the most important legacy variable that affects the red-brown phenomenon is the legacy of the previous communist regime.

Introduction

This paper is not about the extreme right in post-communist Eastern Europe *per se*. Rather, in this paper I examine the relatively under investigated topic of how historical legacies shaped the emergence of the "red-brown" political tendency in East-Central Europe and the former Soviet Union — which is sometimes referred to as "National Bolshevism" or "National Communism" or "Strasserism." This tendency, has given rise to political movements that glorify a national past, are often irredentist or imperialist (particularly in Russia), are intolerant of "aliens" (both anti-immigrant and anti-Semitic), and oppose globalization and Europeanization. On the other hand, proponents and followers of such movements continue to identify with the communist past and positively evaluate the successors to the communist parties (often because of a sense of nostalgia).

More specifically I ask the question, how do historical legacies help explain why extreme right wing voters support the successors to the formerly dominant communist parties (or what I refer to as the "red-brown" vote)? Building upon an earlier work in 1998 in which I investigated the factors that explained communist-nationalist political cooperation at the organizational level (Ishiyama, 1998) this paper examines how both historical legacies of the past shaped the development of a country's national identity and hence affected popular attitudes related to communist-nationalist cooperation. More specifically, I investigate to the extent to which individuals identify with the tendencies associated with the far right (such as extreme national pride, intolerance of foreigners and/or "others", and are extremely skeptical of Europeanization) and who continue to identify with the organizational successors to the communist parties. I test the proposition that previous pre-communist national identities and the legacy of the communist regime itself laid the ground for the emergence of Communist Nationalism, National Bolshevism, and the red-brown political impulse in the post-communist era.

Beyond the contextual effects of historical legacies I also examine how the dynamics of transition and the internal struggles within the ruling communist parties from 1989-1991 shaped the organizational confusion that emerged later. This organizational confusion, particularly the lack of a clearly demarcated left-right ideological spectrum, is likely to lead to greater far right voter support for the communist past and the communist successor parties.

Further, whether extreme right voters were attracted to the communist successor parties also depended on the organizational "draw" of the successor parties themselves. As several scholars have noted (Grzmała-Busse, 2002; Ishiyama, 1997, 1995) some of the successor parties have transformed and portrayed themselves as socialist or social democratic parties, and have overtly rejected the communist past, as in the case of Hungary and Poland, for instance, making them potentially less attractive to red-brown voters.

In this paper, I use as a "dependent variable" the size of the red-brown vote by examining the proportion of voters who express attitudes of high levels of national pride, who are relatively intolerant of aliens and foreigners, and who oppose Europeanization but who, at the same time, continue to vote for the communist successor parties or those parties that were the organizational successors to the formerly dominant communist parties in Eastern Europe and the former Soviet Union. Using data from the *Democratic Consolidation Data Base Wave 2* (1995-2001) and the *Candidate Countries Eurobarometer* from 2002, I examine the extent to which the "red-brown" political tendency is related to the historical legacies of the past (both the pre communist and the communist), the "legacy" of the organizational transition of the communist successor party itself, and cultural, demographic and geographic legacies as well. Examining the extent to which extreme right voters support ostensibly left wing parties provides a valuable measure as to whether parties and party systems have consolidated in post communist politics. If voters vote primarily because of "nostalgia" as opposed to clear political preferences, this reflects the immaturity of the party system. Second, the ideological confusion represented by right wing voters voting for left wing parties indicates potential lines of fracture in the communist successor parties, parties which were so very crucial in the first decade of democratization and marketization in post-communist Eastern and Central Europe. To some extent, the ideological immaturity of voters may help explain the dissolution of several of the successor parties in recent years.

To be sure, there have been other ways in which scholars have thought of red-brown politics in post-communist Europe. Some scholars have focused largely on the organizational cooperation between communist and nationalist parties in post-communist politics (Ishiyama, 1998; Pravda, 1995). Other scholars have examined red and brown voting patterns (Hanson and Kopstein, 1997, 1998; Shenfield, 1998). Tucker (2005, 2006), for instance, examined the phenomenon of red and brown voting separately, testing the Weimar hypothesis that the difficulties of political and economic transition should lead to increased voter support for both extreme left and extreme right. Interestingly, Tucker found support for the notion that economic difficulties are associated with greater support for the communist successor parties, but little or no support for the idea that such difficulties also benefit the extreme right parties (Tucker, 2005). However, Tucker did not differentiate different types of voters, so it may be the case that nationalist, xenophobic, or racist voters who feel disenfranchised by the economic and political changes would turn to the communist successor parties out of a sense of nostalgia for a stable and empowered political past, rather than because of ideological allegiance. Unlike previous studies, in this paper I focus on the seemingly incongruent phenomenon of extreme right voters voting for the communist successor parties.

In my view, the red-brown political impulse was never a permanent phenomenon but rather indicative of the lack of development of clear lines of political cleavage in post communist countries. This admixture of seemingly extreme right support of leftist parties (due either to nostalgia, or the lack of development of political parties, or voter indifference) was a function of the extent to which past historical, institutional and cultural legacies retarded the development of clear lines of political cleavage. I argue that high rates of red-brown voting are the result of the extent to which the previous communist regime had retarded the development of political competition. In previous communist regimes that had experienced some reform and openness prior to the collapse of communist rule, lines of political cleavage and competition had a "head start" over other more patrimonial (and dictatorial) regimes. Thus, in the successor politics of the former type of communist regime, one observes far lower rates of red-brown voting than in the latter type of regime.

Who is an extreme right wing voter?

There has been an extensive literature that has examined the national right in post-communist Eastern Europe and the former Soviet Union. There has also been considerable conceptual confusion on what is exactly meant by "extreme right" in the post-communist context (Ramet, 1999). As Cas Mudde noted very early on (1996) much of the literature on the extreme right resembles a "shopping list" of characteristics rather than a conceptually clear definition that would define a "family" of extreme right parties and their supporters. Generally speaking the extreme right has been characterized as a collection of nationalist, authoritarian, xenophobic, and extremist parties that are defined by the common characteristic of populist ultranationalism (Minkenberg and Perrineau, 2007; Minkenberg, 2000).

For the purposes of this paper I use the definition provided by Michael Minkenberg that right wing radicalism is:

> defined primarily by the ideological criteria of populist and romantic ultranationalism, a myth of a homogenous nation which puts the nation before the individual and his/her civil rights, which, therefore, is directed against liberal and pluralist democracy (though not necessarily in favor of a fascist state), its underlying values of freedom and equality and the related categories of individualism and universalism (Minkenberg, 2000, 2002, pp. 170-181, p. 337; Mudde, 2000, chp. 7).

In particular, there is the emphasis on the nationalistic myth that constructs an exclusive notion of the nation and promotes an image of extreme collective homogeneity (Minkenberg, 2002, p. 337). As Minkenberg notes, the extreme right can be seen as a reaction to the processes of modernization that has led to the "growing autonomy of the individual status mobility and role flexibility and an ongoing functional differentiation of society (segmentation and a growing autonomy of societal subsystems)". In this light, right wing radicalism can be defined as the radical effort to undo such social change. Indeed "the counter-concept to social differentiation is the nationally defined community; the counter-concept individualization is the return to traditional roles and status of the individual in such a community. It is this overemphasis on, or radicalization of social homogeneity, which characterizes extreme right-wing thinking" (Beichelt and Minkenberg 2002, p. 3). It is important to note that right wing radicals are not opposed to democracy—the key is the focus on ultranationalism, and the suspicion of those institutions and individuals that may threaten the unified body politic (Beichelt and Minkenberg, 2002, p. 4).

In addition to these characteristics, several scholars have noted that the extreme right tends to be also characterized by high degrees of Euroscepticism (Hanley, 2004; Taggart and Szczerbiak, 2004). They contend "there does seem to be a stronger tendency for Eurosceptic parties in the Central and Eastern candidate states to be on the right of the spectrum than in Western Europe. One important reason for this is that right wing parties are more ideologically eclectic in post-communist Central and Eastern Europe, and there is a stronger tendency for the right to be more nationalistic than its Western counterparts" (Taggart and Szczerbiak, 2004, p. 14). It makes sense that Beichelt (2004) notes "that strong Euroscepticism fits well into the ideologies of two-party families which rely on the protest against the hardships of post-socialist transformation: nationalist and (unreformed) communist parties."

Thus for the purposes of this paper, the extreme right wing voter in post communist politics is conceptualized as a voter who is highly nationalistic, hostile to minority rights, and highly skeptical regarding European integration.

Historical legacies and the red-brown impulse
The notion of a wedding between communism and nationalism is not a new idea in the history of East-Central Europe and the former Soviet Union. Indeed the peculiar phenomenon of "national bolshevism" "national communism" and "Strasserism" has been studied by many scholars, but largely at the level of organizations and ideology, and not at the individual voter level (Ishiyama, 1998).

From the perspective of the historical literature, the political wedding of communism and nationalism is not entirely surprising, given the early recognition of the political power of nationalism by Marxists in Eastern Europe. For instance, under the influence of the Austro-Marxist Otto Bauer many socialist thinkers melded nationalism with socialism. Bauer had argued that the nation was a culture-based community that had a history going as far back as primitive society. By asserting the continued existence of the nation across different socio-economic formations, Bauer explicitly rejected the orthodox Marxist view that nation was a product of capitalism and would disappear after the overthrow of capitalism (Szporluk, 1988, p. 200). Indeed many socialists in Eastern Europe thought in terms of "national production" and the "development of the nation's productive forces" (Gershenkron, 1979, pp. 217-218). They, like the nationalists, favored "capitalism in one country" and the centrality of the state in the economic process (Szporluk, 1988, p. 202).

Yet there were other reasons why socialism and nationalism became fellow travelers. An important principle socialists and nationalists held in common, especially after the Lenin postponed the 'withering away of the state', was the emphasis on statist solutions to political, social and economic problems. The emphasis on statism was largely due to the lack of the emergence of clear national identities and the historic dominance of the state (Bunce, 2005). Roman Szporluk (1988, p. 206) makes the argument that in cases like Russia where a multinational empire emerged before a modern national identities were formed, there was little in the way of a distinction between state and society, unlike in the West where nation building preceded empire-building, where a distinction between state and society emerged. This was to deny the countries like Russia an identity which was separate from the state (Szporluk, 1988, pp 206-207; Torbakov, 1992). Further, for Pipes (1975) this "reversal of stages left an indelible mark on Russian political culture. It made it difficult for Russians to distinguish between 'Russia proper', that is, their national homeland, and political boundaries of the state. This confusion not only produced a very strong pressure toward statist solutions for both Russian socialists, nationalists and Pan-Slavists, but in turn, made the Russians suspicious of the aspirations of their subject nationalities, which they treated as a threat to the state's integrity and hence a direct threat to the Russian 'nation'" (Pipes, 1975, p. 1). In Eastern Europe, Valerie Bunce notes the legacy of empire blurred the distinction between state and empire and "complicated the formation of the core's national identity" making the core view the national aspirations of the periphery as threatening and hence a threat to the integrity of the state particularly and, unlike the overseas empires of England and France, given the "geographical proximity of the periphery" (Bunce, 2005, p. 418).

In addition to the weakness of national identities during the imperial period another set of explanations highlight the impact of the legacy of communist rule (Racz, 1993; Agh, 1995; Evans and Whitfield, 1995; Waller, 1995). The intellectual legacy of communist rule was as important as that derived from the pre-communist period. Zuzowski (2006) argues that combining nationalism and communism during communist rule in Eastern Europe did provide a new basis for political legitimacy for the regimes in the region; that communism when coupled with the simple, encompassing idea of nationalism, comprehensible and convincing to everybody, became an efficient political force for a while. However, over time, its internal contradiction could not be maintained and resembled a "bottle with a false label: the contents differed from that which the label proclaims." Similarly, Walter Kemp (1999) has pointed to the fundamental contradiction between communism and nationalism in Eastern Europe—indeed when the communist parties of Eastern Europe attempted to shore up their legitimacy by appealing to nationalism, they essentially sowed the seeds of their own dissolution.

> By presenting themselves as being defenders and inheritors of all that was good in the nation, the communist parties of the people's democracies put themselves in a precarious position wherein, on the one hand, representing national interests could win them legitimacy at the expense of local relations with Moscow and fellow bloc members, while on the other hand, fulfilling the obligation of loyal Soviet satellite would be popularly perceived as an abrogation of the commitment to uphold the nation's sovereignty and identity. In effect the communists were in a no-win situation. They need nationalism to hold on to legitimacy, by the more they stressed those national symbols the more they showed themselves to be the antithesis of what those symbols represented (Kemp, 1999, p. 123)

What resulted, then, from this contradiction was an ideological confusion regarding left and right following the collapse of communist rule. Michael Shafir addresses this ideological confusion in post-communist Eastern Europe when he notes that the Leninist legacy left in its wake an array of strange bedfellows. In Romania, he notes, there have been two traditions in the Romanian extreme right—parties of "radical return" and parties of "radical continuity." The former glorifies the heroes of the interwar fascist period the latter combine Leninism with extreme nationalism (Shafir, 1999). The "radical return" parties look to the values associated with the interwar years, emulating figures such as Tiso, Antonescu, Pavelic, Szalasi and Codreanu; the "radical continuity" ones take their "bearings from the communist legacy itself" (p. 213).

Another approach regarding the effects of legacies of the communist period focuses less on the confused intellectual legacy of the communist period and more on the institutional legacy. One of the more influential works on the effects of previous regime legacy on post-communist politics is offered by Herbert Kitschelt (1995, 1997). Kitschelt argued that the extent to which personalist rule was in place (what he called patrimonial communism) had an important effect on the kinds of politics that followed the transition. Such systems relied heavily on hierarchical chains of personal dependence between leaders and followers, with low levels of intra- elite contestation, popular interest articulation and rational-bureaucratic professionalization. Such systems also tolerated little in the way of dissent in the leadership, and emphasized strongly the doctrine of democratic centralism. This stood in contrast to systems such as those in Hungary and Poland, or *national consensus communism*, where levels of contestation and interest articulation were permitted, and there was a degree of bureaucratic professionalization. In essence, the communist elites allowed for a measure of contestation and interest articulation in exchange for compliance with the basic features of the existing system.

Perhaps one of the more prevalent arguments in the literature on democratic transition is that the characteristics of the previous authoritarian regime are a crucial part in explaining what happens in post authoritarian politics (Remmer, 1989; Huntington, 1991a; Bratton and Van de Walle, 1994; for Eastern Europe and the former Soviet Union see Gill, 1994; Welsh, 1994; Agh, 1995; Kitschelt, 1997; 1995; Orttung, 1992). From this perspective, the nature of the previous regime affects the type of transition that occurs, that is, via gradual transformation or more sudden "replacement," which in turn affects the character of politics in the period following the transition (Huntington, 1991b; Snyder, 1992). Welsh (1994) finds such a connection in Eastern Europe, where regime type affected the extent to which bargaining and compromise took place during the transition period; countries which had an extended period of bargaining and compromise were more likely to produce a trained cadre of politicians within the contending political parties; politicians who had learned how to play according to the rules of democratic competition and electoral politics. The more extended the period of transition the greater the likelihood that the parties (and hence the party systems) emerging from communist rule became more institutionalized and structured, thus, mitigating against the development of post-communist-nationalist ties (Agh, 1995; Kitschelt, 1995). In other words, the more structured the parties in a party system are, the more likely a clear left and clear right is to develop; hence the less likely is the emergence of the ideological "aberration" of post-communist-nationalist political cooperation. Thus in Hungary, for instance, the evolution of the HSP as a structured "Europeanized-left" party has assisted in the development of a distinct left and a distinct right, thus precluding the development of post-communist-nationalist cooperation. The evolution of the HSP, in turn, was the product of the historical legacy of the Hungarian communist regime, particularly via the existence of a "large *reform intelligentsia* and also (a) *mass reform movement* a characteristic product of the special Hungarian developments, originating from the most liberal version of state socialism" (italics in original) (Agh, 1995, pp. 492-493).

On the other hand, personalist regimes (or those led by a single person, often associated with a cult of personality) were more likely to produce parties with personalist characteristics and less distinct ideological identities (Vujacic, 2003; Kitschelt, 1995; Bratton and Van de Walle, 1994). For instance, Vujacic argues that personalist regimes in Eastern and Central Europe tended to produce parties that themselves were based on *personal charismatic* or *personal rule* and blurred the ideological differences between left and right (Vujacic, 2003, p. 386). Further, transitions from patrimonial systems tended to be less structured than transitions from national consensus systems as in Hungary and Poland, and relatively more traumatic. As some scholars note, the less structured and more "traumatic" the transition process in terms of economic costs and political turmoil, the more likely that the distinction between left and right breaks down. For instance, Von Beyme notes (1994, pp. 12-14) that the transformation process in Central and Eastern Europe was far deeper and more complex than previous modernization processes in the West. Further as Minkenberg and Beichelt (2001) argue regarding post-communist politics, right wing groups, especially those that combine socialist and nationalist ideas, benefit from an environment of uncertainty that accompanies trauma. Thus political entrepreneurs who offer simple solutions and appeal to "the people" or "nation" as opposed to universalistic ideas have a competitive advantage, particularly in social systems undergoing significant transformation with high levels of social disorientation (2001, p. 5).

Other scholars have pointed to additional legacies, beyond the political, which impact on the character of extreme right politics in post-communist Europe. For instance, Beichelt and Minkenberg (2002) have examined additional types legacies and their impact on the evolution of right wing politics, particularly cultural legacies. For instance, if extreme right wing politics is in part about establishing the criteria for "exclusion" (that is, who is included within the national community and who is not), then historical definitions of citizenship must impact the character of extreme right wing politics. Indeed, one could distinguish between historical national identities based on religious affiliation as opposed to ethnic kinship or linguistic characteristics. In the former, there is at least the possibility that people of other races or ethnicities could be included in the national community, whereas if the identity were rooted in blood, they could not. Thus, we might expect that in countries with a cultural national legacy, there would be less in the way of extreme (and racially intolerant) right wing radicalism, at least when compared to states with a legacy of an ethnic national identity (Beichelt and Minkenberg, 2002).

Finally, one might also see demography and geography as legacies of sorts. Indeed, in countries where there has been historically a large minority population this provides the opportunity for real conflicts over language issues and education (as with the Hungarians in Slovakia and Romania, or Russians in Estonia and Latvia). Such issues provide political fodder for the extreme right, providing issues around which to mobilize. Further, the existence of "external national homelands", or situations where people of the same nation transcend the boundaries of the existing nation state, as with Hungarians in Slovakia or Romania, this provides for mobilization opportunities for ultranationalist and revisionist groups (Beichelt and Minkenberg, 2002). In both cases, one might expect that the existence of both minority issues and external national homelands, at the minimum, would increase the likelihood that voters (especially of the titular nationality) would be attracted to the rhetoric of extreme right groups. How that might affect extreme right voter support of the communist successor parties would depend to a large extent on whether the successor party itself had adapted nationalism as part of its legitimizing ideology or not.

Analysis

In this section I investigate the effects of the legacy factors cited above on the size of the red-brown vote. To measure the "dependent variable" the extent to which extreme right voters support the communist successor, I consider two aspects: the extent to which the communist successor party depends upon the support of the extreme right voters, and the proportion of extreme right voters that the communist successor attracts. As indicated by the above literature, extreme right voters in post communist politics have a very strong sense of national pride, intolerance of those outside of that community (such as foreigners) and deep suspicion of transnational institutions such as the European Union. First to determine who the extreme right wing voters were for the East-Central European countries, excluding Russia, I used three questions from the 2002 Candidate Countries Eurobarometer (2002) and three somewhat parallel questions from the *Consolidation of Democracy in Central and Eastern Europe 1990-2001* data set for Russia (see appendix A).

Table 1.   Total extreme right wing voters in percentage and by country, 2002 (data from Russia is for 1997).

Country	Respondents (2002, Russia: 1997)	Right wing radical respondents (% of total in country-2002, Russia: 1997)
Bulgaria	739	71 (9.6%)
Czech Republic	811	51 (6.3%)
Hungary	820	82 (10.0%)
Lithuania	625	19 (3.0%)
Poland	664	112 (16.9%)
Romania	706	77 (10.9%)
Slovakia	907	112 (12.3%)
Slovenia	676	145 (21.4%)
Russia (1997)	369	78 (21.1%)
Total for East Central European countries (excluding Russia)	10,607	1540 (12.7%)

Sources: 2002 Candidate Countries Eurobarometer and the Consolidation of Democracy in Central and Eastern Europe 1990-2001.

The three questions used for the East-Central European countries asked the respondent about the extent of their trust of the EU, how proud they were of their nation, and whether they found people of other races in their country disturbing. Respondents who did not trust the EU, who were very proud of their nation, and who found people of other races in their country disturbing, were classified as extreme right voters. For Russian voters three questions were used to identify "extreme right voters," and were taken from the *Consolidation of Democracy in Central and Eastern Europe 1990-2001* data for the Russian voters. Respondents who expressed extreme pride as Russians, who strongly agreed that Russia should go its own way, and who strongly agreed that critical foreigners should be expelled from the country were counted as extreme right voters.

To assess the extent to which a red-brown impulse existed among voters, I used the question in which the respondent identified the party they intended to vote in the next election. Table 1 reports the overall percentages of extreme right wing voters in the nine post-communist states, with a high of 21.4% of the respondents identified as extreme right voters in Slovenia, and a low of 6.3% in the Czech Republic, and with and overall percentage of 12.7% for all nine countries. In Table 2, I examine the percentage of extreme right wing voters supporting the communist successor party, and the extent to which the communist successor party is dependent upon extreme right voters for political support.[1] For the purposes of this paper, I use the list of communist successor parties identified by Bozoki and Ishiyama (2002) for the year 2002. The list of parties is included in Table 2 below, as well as the relevant percentages for each communist successor party. As indicated in the table, the Slovak Party of the Democratic Left (SDL) and the Communist Party of the Russian Federation (KPRF) were most dependent on extreme right voters (at 34.0% and 28.1% respectively of their voter support came from extreme right wing voters) and the least dependent were the Hungarian Socialist Party (5.1%) and the Lithuanian Democratic Labor Party (2.0%).

---

1   Generally right wing supporters of communist successor parties were similar to right wing supporters of other parties. However, most right wing supporters of the communist successor parties tended to be older and more likely to be rural voters as opposed to younger and urban voters (who tended to be attracted to other right wing parties). This would strengthen the idea that voters that held extreme right wing political attitudes supported the successor parties for largely nostalgic reasons.

Table 2.   Total extreme right wing voter support for communist successor party in percentages and by country, 2002 (Russia: 1997)

Country	Communist successor party in 2002	Right wing radical supporter (% of successor party supporters)	Right wing radical supporter (% of all extreme right respondents in the country)
Bulgaria	Bulgarian Socialist Party (BSP)	14.5	32.4
Czech Republic	Communist Party of Bohemian and Moravia (KSCM)	8.6	19.6
Hungary	Hungarian Socialist Party (MSzP)	5.1	25.6
Lithuania	Lithuanian Democratic Labor Party (LDDP)	2.0	15.8
Poland	Democratic Left Alliance (SLD)	12.4	23.2
Romania	Party of Social Democracy (PDSR)	11.7	42.9
Slovakia	Party of the Democratic Left (SDL)	34.0	15.2
Slovenia	United List of Social Democrats (ZLSD)	14.9	4.8
Russia*	Communist Party of the Russian Federation (KPRF)	28.1	57.7

* Data for Russia is from 1997. Sources: 2002 Candidate Countries Eurobarometer and the Consolidation of Democracy in Central and Eastern Europe 1990-2001.

On the other hand, in terms of the percentage of extreme right voters the communist successor party attracted, the Communist Party of the Russian Federation (KPRF) attracted the greatest proportion of extreme right voters (57.7%) followed by the Romanian Party of Social Democracy (42.9%) and the Bulgarian Socialist Party (32.4%). The least attractive to extreme right voters were the LDDP (15.8%) the SDL (15.2%) and the Slovenian ZLSD (4.8%). Thus although the SDL relied heavily on extreme right voters, it was not particularly attractive to such voters, which may explain its ultimate demise shortly thereafter, and the reorientation of the Slovak party system). However, it is also interesting to note that the party that not only depended upon, but was very attractive to, extreme right voters was the KPRF in Russia.

Turning to the legacy variables, Table 3 reports the legacies of the past. First, it is important to note that each of the national cases emerged from a multinational empire, the Ottoman, the Austrian, and the Russian (and in the case of Poland, the Habsburg, the Russian and the German)—thus there is little in the way of variation in terms of the emergence of the imperial legacy. Indeed in each of the cases, except for the Russian case, nationalism was of the *Risorgimento* type, in which national identity was juxtaposed to the existing imperial political order and dependent its demise. If there was a difference, it was between Russia and the other Eastern European states, in that in Russia, national identity was more intimately entwined with the imperial nature of the Russian state. Thus in terms of the red-brown impulse, we would expect much greater evidence of that in the Russian case than when compared to other East European cases.

There was of course variation, nonetheless, in terms of the national identities of the Eastern European nations. One way in which to think of the national legacy is to conceptualize the national legacy in terms of the extent to which membership in the national community is thought of as either relatively open or closed. A political nation is one that in which belief in common set of values and institutions defines criteria for membership in the national community. A cultural nation is one in which the belief in cultural, and especially religious characteristics, dominates. An ethnic nation is characterized by the belief that one is born into a community defined by blood relations and belief in the natural biological roots of the nation (Alter, 1985; Brubaker, 1992). As Beichelt and Minkenberg (2002) note, in Eastern Europe the predominant form was an ethnic or cultural nation.

Table 3.   Legacy variables

Country	Empire	Nation type (Beichelt and Minkenberg, 2002)	Strong national minority (over 3% of population) (Beichelt and Minkenberg, 2002)	External homelands (Beichelt and Minkenberg, 2002)	Previous communist regime type (Ishiyama, 1995)	Organizational Transition (who won in transition) (Ishiyama, 1995)
Bulgaria	Ottoman	Culture	Yes	No	Patrimonial	Conservatives
Czech Republic	Austrian	Ethnic	No	No	Bureaucratic	Conservatives/ standpatters
Hungary	Austrian	Ethnic	Yes	Yes	National consensus	Reformists
Lithuania	Russian	Ethnic	Yes	No	National consensus	Reformists
Poland	Russian/ Austrian/ German	Culture	No	No	National consensus	Reformists
Romania	Ottoman	Ethnic	Yes	Yes	Patrimonial	Conservatives
Slovakia	Austrian	Ethnic	Yes	Yes	Bureaucratic	Reformists
Slovenia	Austrian	Ethnic	No	No	National consensus	Reformists
Russia	Russian	Culture	Yes	Yes	Patrimonial	Conservatives/ standpatters

This was due, in a large part, to the fact that national identity emerged in opposition to the great multinational empires of the 19th century, and hence developed an identity apart from an independent state. Yet one would expect a difference between nations with a cultural identity as opposed to an ethnic identity, at least with regards to the emergence of a red-brown voter impulse later. In a cultural nation, there is at least the opportunity to allow for tolerance of other racial and ethnic groups, since the national community is identified by cultural values as opposed to blood, whereas in ethnic nations there would be greater intolerance of such groups, and hence nationalism would include greater degrees of intolerance for racial and ethnic minority groups than would nations that have a cultural identity.

Another critical legacy variable is the legacy of the previous communist regime itself. To measure the differences between regime types in Eastern Europe and the former Soviet Union, Kitschelt (1995) constructed a useful three-part typology of communist regimes: *patrimonial communism, bureaucratic authoritarian communism and national consensus communism.* The first, *patrimonial communism* relied heavily on hierarchical chains of personal dependence between leaders and followers, with low levels of inter elite contestation, popular interest articulation and rational-bureaucratic professionalization. Moreover, these systems were characterized by a heavy emphasis on 'democratic centralism' which fitted well with the hierarchical structure of dependence between leaders and the led. In this category Kitschelt placed Serbia, Romania, Bulgaria, Russia, Ukraine, Belarus and most of the rest of the former Soviet Union. In the second type, *bureaucratic authoritarian communism*, inter elite contestation and interest articulation were circumscribed, but the level of rational-bureaucratic institutionalization was high. In this category Kitschelt placed the former German Democratic Republic, Czech Republic, as well as Slovakia. The third type of system was *national consensus communism*, where levels of contestation and interest articulation were permitted, and there was a degree of bureaucratic professionalization. In essence, the communist elites allowed for a measure of contestation and interest articulation in exchange for compliance with the basic features of the existing system. In this category Kitschelt placed Poland and Hungary, as well as Slovenia and Croatia. Also within this category, as 'borderline' cases, were the three Baltic states, Estonia, Latvia and Lithuania. Although these states had been absorbed by the Soviet Union, there was a remarkable degree of intra-regime contestation and toleration for the demands of the national independence movements, at least far more so than in other parts of the USSR (Kitschelt, 1995).

Another legacy variable relates to the question of who won the inevitable internal battles within the party between different factions within the communist successor parties, such as pro-market reformers, or anti-market conservatives (Ishiyama, 1995). Thus, an argument related to the effects of previous regime type influences the kind of organizational transition that took place for each party. Such organizational transitions may independently affect the kind of party organizations which emerge later. As Ishiyama notes in his analysis of the communist successor parties in Eastern Europe, different parties underwent very different kinds of organizational transformations, defined by the extent to which they followed what Samuel Huntington referred to as "standpatter" "liberal" or "democratic reformist" paths of internal leadership transformation between 1990 and 1993. These three groups, according to Huntington, were defined by their basic attitudes toward democratic transition, the promotion of popular participation and political competition. For Ishiyama, the key to the kind of transition that took place depended heavily on the internal struggle between democratic reformists, liberals and standpatters within the communist party. As mentioned above, successor parties that were captured by democratic reformists were likely to help establish a pattern of party competition early on that clearly distinguished left and right, hence having a reductionist effect on the red-brown impulse.

Table 4. Red-brown vote by nation type

Nation Type	Successor party appeals to $\geq$ 30% of extreme right voters	Successor party appeals to < 30% of extreme right voters
Ethnic	Romania	Czech Republic, Hungary, Lithuania, Slovakia, Slovenia
Cultural	Bulgaria, Russia	Poland

To "test" the relationship between the legacy variables and the extent of the red-brown vote, Tables 4-8 illustrate the results of cross tabulating each of the five legacy variables listed in Table 3 with the proportion of extreme right voters who report their intention to vote for the communist successor party. The "dependent" variable, red-brown vote, lists where at least 30% of the extreme right respondents who report their intention to vote for the communist successor party in 2002. Table 4 cross tabulates the nation type (ethnic versus cultural) with the red-brown vote exceeding 30%. From this table there appears to be little in the way of a relationship between the nation type that emerged from the imperial experience, and the size of the red-brown vote, although unsurprisingly, Russia, given its particular type of imperial legacy scored very high in terms of the size of the red-brown vote.

Table 5.   Red-brown vote by existence of large national minorities

Large national minority (over 3% of population)	Successor party appeals to ≥ 30% of extreme right voters	Successor party appeals to < 30% of extreme right voters
Yes	Romania, Bulgaria, Russia	Hungary, Lithuania, Slovakia
No		Czech Republic, Poland, Slovenia

However, Table 5 indicates an interesting relationship between the presence of a large national minority group (greater than 3% of the population as indicated by Beichelt and Minkenberg, 2002) and the size of the red-brown vote for the communist successor party. In the three cases where the level of extreme right voter support for the communist successor party exceeded 30% there were large national minorities (Romania, Bulgaria, and Russia). The presence of large minority groups, however, did not guarantee a large red-brown vote, as illustrated by the cases of Hungary, Lithuania and Slovakia. Thus, although it may be the case that the demographic legacy of a large minority population may contribute to extreme right voting, whether these voters support the communist successor parties depends on something else. Further the appeal of irredentism appears to be unrelated to the size of the red-brown vote.

Table 6.   Red-brown vote by existence of external national homelands

External national home-lands	Successor party appeals to > 30% of extreme right voters	Successor party appeals to < 30% of extreme right voters
Yes	Romania, Russia	Hungary, Slovakia
No	Bulgaria	Czech Republic, Lithuania, Poland, Slovenia

As illustrated in Table 6 there was clearly no relationship between the level of extreme right support and the existence of external national homelands.

Table 7 cross tabulates the previous communist regime type with the size of the red-brown vote. From Table 4, there appears to be a fairly strong relationship between the patrimonial communist regime type and the red-brown vote. All three of the patrimonial regimes (Bulgaria, Romania, and Russia) had the largest sized red-brown votes, which is consistent with much of the literature that suggests that greater post-communist ideological confusion was likely following transitions from personalistic regimes. On the other hand the bureaucratic and national consensus regimes produced less of a red-brown voter impulse.

Table 7.   Red-brown vote by previous communist regime type

Previous communist regime type	Successor party appeals to > 30% of extreme right voters	Successor party appeals to < 30% of extreme right voters
Patrimonial	Bulgaria, Romania, Russia	
Bureaucratic		Czech Republic, Slovakia
National consensus		Hungary, Lithuania, Poland, Slovenia

Finally, Table 8 illustrates the results of cross tabulation who won the organizational transition in the communist successor party, pitting reformists, against conservatives and standpatters. Although in three cases where the conservatives and standpatters won the internal organizational struggles from1990 to 1992 in the communist successor parties, the level of the red-brown vote was quite high, in one of the cases where the conservatives/standpatters won (in the KSCM in the Czech Republic) the level of red-brown support was relatively low. This may be due in part to the type of communist successor party in the Czech Republic, which is a more orthodox communist party, or Euro communist party, than it is a national communist party, as is the KPRF.

Table 8.   Red-brown vote by successor party organizational transition

Organizational transition (who won in transition)	Successor party appeals to ≥ 30% of extreme right voters	Successor party appeals to < 30% of extreme right voters
Conservatives/ standpatters	Bulgaria, Romania, Russia	Czech Republic
Reformists		Hungary, Lithuania, Poland, Slovakia, Slovenia

Conclusion
The above results suggest that of the various legacies that have been posited to explain the emergence of the extreme right in post-communist politics, the single most important factor in explaining the size of the "red-brown" vote is the institutional legacy of the communist regime itself. This result, coupled with the relationship between the communist successor parties' organizational transition and the size of the red-brown vote, supports the notion that the previous communist regime affected the extent to which a more structured party system emerged. This, in turn, affected the extent to which a relatively clear left and clear right developed. Thus in countries like Hungary, Poland and Lithuania, there was much less of the emergence of the ideological 'aberration' of post communist-nationalist political cooperation. On the other hand, personalist regimes were more likely to produce parties with personalist

characteristics and thus less distinct ideological identities. Hence in countries like Bulgaria, Romania and Russia, which had patrimonial communist legacies, there were far more in the way of a fairly sizeable red-brown votes than there were in the more institutionalized party systems in Hungary, Poland and Lithuania, at least in 2002.

Other historical, demographic and geographic "legacies" appear to be unrelated to the size of red-brown vote. Indeed, the imperial legacy, historical national identities (ethnic versus cultural notions of national community), and demographic and geographic legacies have very little to do with the size of the red-brown vote. Although these factors may explain the size of the extreme right vote, they have little to do with whether extreme right voters vote for the communist successor parties.

What these findings suggest then is that, as far as the size of the red-brown vote is concerned, longer term historical legacies have little impact on the development of political parties in post-communist politics. What is far more important is the impact of the recent regime legacies (particularly the communist) on the evolution of voting patterns and the development of political parties. This supports the arguments made by Kitschelt (1997, 1995) in the post-communist context but also, more broadly, especially by scholars who argue that previous regime legacies are crucial in explaining the processes of democratic transition and consolidation (Bratton and Van de Walle, 1994).

The recent communist legacy also explains some of the Tucker's (2006, 2005) findings that contrary to the "Weimer hypothesis" the difficulties of political and economic transition resulted in support for the communist successor parties, rather than the extreme right parties. Perhaps extremes right orientated voters, or those who were hostile to minority rights, highly skeptical regarding European integration and nationalistic, were attracted to the communist successor parties because the latter, unlike the extreme right parties, could offer organizational resources and a real opportunity to win elections. It is also likely that such voters' own sense of "left" and "right" had been skewed by the "national communist past" and had more to do with "nostalgia" for a lost greatness, or the security and collectivism (and insularity) of the socialist past, rather than a clear understanding of the policy platforms of the previous parties.

This paper has merely suggested a relationship between previous regime legacies and the size of the subsequent red-brown vote. Perhaps, over time, as these systems mature, the red-brown vote will decline in importance. This seems unlikely, given that the red-brown impulse is firmly rooted in the political cultures of many post-communist states. What is more likely is that this impulse de-aligns from the existing set of political parties (particularly the communist successor parties) as voters realize that the reformed successor parties really do not represent their interests, and that the "nostalgia" factor wears off. This is perhaps what may have happened to the SDL in Slovakia as it collapsed shortly after 2002 parliamentary election (Haughton, 2004) and the Polish SLD more recently. However, if a bona fide leftist socialist party were to emerge that vehemently opposed Europeanization, immigration and capitalism, it is likely that this might mobilize the red-brown impulse once again. This may explain the persistence of the KPRF in Russia and the emergence of a resuscitated communist party in Slovakia. Whatever the case, the support of statism, socialism, and nationalism is likely to remain an important part of the political scene in post-communist politics for the foreseeable future.

References

Agh, A., 1995. Partial consolidation of the East-Central European parties: the case of the Hungarian socialist party, Party Politics 1 (3), 491-514.

Alter, P., 1985. Nationalism. Edward Arnold, London.

Beichelt, T., Minkenberg, M., 2002. Explaining the Radical Right in Transition: Theories of Right-wing Radicalism and Opportunity Structures in Post-Socialist Europe. Frankfurt Institute fur Transformatsionstudien. No. 2/3.

Beichelt, T., 2004. Euro-skepticism in the EU accession countries. Comparative European Politics 2 (1), 29–50.

Bozoki, A., Ishiyama, J. (Eds.), 2002. Communist Successor Parties of Central and Eastern Europe. Armonk New York: ME Sharpe.

Bratton, M., Van de Walle, N., 1994. Neopatrimonial regimes and political transitions in Africa. World Politics 46 (4), 453-89.

Brubaker, R., 1992. Citizenship and Nationhood in France and Germany. Harvard University Press, Cambridge.

Bunce, V., 2005. The national idea: imperial legacies and post-communist pathways in Eastern Europe. East European Politics and Societies 19 (3), 406-442.

Evans, G., Whitefield, S., 1995. The Politics and Economics of Democratic Commitment: Support for Democracy in Transition Societies. British Journal of Political Science 25 (4), 485-514.

Gerschenkron, A., 1979. Economic Backwardness in Historical Perspective. Harvard University Press, Cambridge, MA.

Gill, G., 1994. The Collapse of a Single Party System. Cambridge University Press, Cambridge.

Grzymała-Busse, A.M., 2002. Redeeming the Communist Past: The Regeneration of Communist Parties in East-Central Europe. Cambridge University Press, Cambridge.

Hanley, S., 2004. From Neo-Liberalism to national interests: ideology, strategy, and party development in the Euroscepticism of the Czech right. East European Politics and Societies 18 (3), 513-548.

Hanson, S.E., Kopstein, J., 1997. The Weimar/Russia comparison. Post-Soviet Affairs 13 (3), 252-283.

Hanson, S.E., Kopstein, J., 1998. Paths to uncivil societies and anti- liberal states: a reply to Shenfield. Post-Soviet Affairs 14 (4), 369-375.

Haughton, T., 2004. Explaining the limited success of the communist-successor left in Slovakia: the case of the party of the democratic Left (SDL'). Party Politics 10 (2), 177-191.

Huntington, S., 1991a. How countries democratize. Political Science Quarterly 106 (4), 579-616.

Huntington, S., 1991b. The Third Wave: Democratization in the Twentieth Century. University of Oklahoma Press, Norman.

Ishiyama, J., 1995. Communist parties in transition: structures, leaders and processes of democratization in Eastern Europe. Comparative Politics 27 (2), 147-166.

Ishiyama, J., 1997. The sickle or the rose?: previous regime types and the evolution of the ex-communist parties in post-communist societies. Comparative Political Studies 30 (3), 299-330.

Ishiyama, J., 1998. Strange bedfellows: explaining political cooperation between communist-successor parties and nationalists in Eastern Europe. Nations and Nationalism 4 (1), 61-85.

Kemp, W., 1999. Nationalism and Communism in Eastern Europe and the Soviet Union: a Basic Contradiction? St. Martins, New York.

Kitschelt, H., 1995. Formation of party cleavages in post-communist democracies: theoretical propositions. Party Politics 1 (4), 447-472.

Kitschelt, H., 1997. Post-Communist Party Systems: Competition, Representation, and Inner-Party Cooperation. Cambridge University Press, Cambridge.

Minkenberg, M., 2000. The renewal of the radical right: between modernity and anti-modernity. Government and Opposition 35 (2), 170–188.

Minkenberg, M., 2002. The radical right in postsocialist Central and Eastern Europe: comparative observations and interpretations. East European Politics and Societies 16 (2), 335-362.

Minkenberg, M., Perrineau P., 2007. The radical right in the European elections 2004. International Political Science Review 28 (1), 29-55.

Minkenberg, M., Beichelt, T., 2001. Explaining the radical right transition: Theories of right-wing radicalism and opportunity structures in post-socialist Europe. Paper delivered at the annual meeting of the American Political Science Association, San Francisco.

Mudde, C., 2000. The Ideology of the Extreme Right. Manchester University Press, Manchester.

Orttung, R., 1992. The Russian right and the dilemmas of party organization. Soviet Studies 44 (3), 445-478.

Pipes, R., 1975. Introduction: the nationality problem. In Katz, Z. (Ed.), The Handbook of Major Soviet Nationalities. Free Press, New York.

Pravda, A., 1995. Russia and European security: the delicate balance. NATO Review, 19-24 May.

Racz, B., 1993. The socialist left opposition in post-communist Hungary. Europe-Asia Studies 45 (4), 647-670.

Ramet, S. P. (Ed.), 1999. The Radical Right in Eastern Europe Since 1989. Pennsylvania State University Press, University Park.

Remmer, K., 1989. Neopatrimonialism: the politics of military rule in Chile, 1973-1987. Comparative Politics 21 (2), 149-170.

Shafir, M., 1999. The mind of Romania's radical right. In: Ramet, S. (Ed.), The Radical Right in Central and Eastern Europe Since 1989. Pennsylvania State University Press, University Park.

Shenfield, S., 1998. The Weimar/Russia comparison: reflections on Hanson and Kopstein. Post-Soviet Affairs 14 (4), 355-368.

Snyder, R., 1992. Explaining transitions from neopatrimonial dictatorships. Comparative Politics 24 (4), 379-399.

Szporluk, R., 1988. Communism and Nationalism: Karl Marx versus Friedrich List. Oxford University Press, New York.

Taggart, P., Szczerbiak, A., 2004. Contemporary Euroscepticism in the party systems of the European Union candidate states of Central and Eastern Europe. European Journal of Political Research 43 (1), 1–27.

Torbakov, I., 1992. The "statists" and ideology of Russian imperial nationalists. RFE/RL Research Report, 10-16, January.

Tucker, J.A., 2005. Red, Brown, and Regional Economic Voting: Russia, Poland, Hungary, Slovakia, and the Czech Republic, 1990-99. Paper Presented at the Annual Meeting of the Midwest political Science Association, Palmer House Hilton, Chicago, Illinois. Available from http://www.allacademic. com/meta/p84661_index.html.

Tucker, J.A., 2006. Regional Economic Voting: Russia, Poland, Hungary, Slovakia, and the Czech Republic, 1990-99. Cambridge University Press, Cambridge.

von Beyme, K., 1994. Systemwechsel in Osteuropa (Systems Change in Eastern Europe). Suhrkamp-Taschenbuch Wissenschaft, Frankfurt am Main.

Vujacic, V., 2003. From class to nation: left, right, and the ideological and institutional roots of post-communist national socialism. East European Politics and Societies 17 (3), 359–392.

Waller, M., 1995. Adaptation of the former communist parties of East-Central Europe. A case of social democratization? Party Politics 1 (4), 473-490.

Welsh, H., 1994. Political transition processes in Central and Eastern Europe. Comparative Politics 26 (4), 379-391.

Zuzowski, R., 2006. Nationalism and Marxism in Eastern Europe. Politikon 33 (1), 71-80.

Appendix A

List of questions from the 2002 *Candidate Countries Eurobarometer* and the *Consolidation of Democracy in Central and Eastern Europe 1990-2001* used to determine extreme right wing voters.

Questions from the *2002 Candidate Countries Eurobarometer* for Central and Eastern European Countries.

q13_16: Trust: EU
I would like to ask you a question about how much trust you have in certain institutions. For each of the following institutions, please tell me if you tend to trust it or tend not to trust it?

The European Union
1 tend to trust
2 tend not to trust
8 DK /no opinion
9 NA/refusal

q14: National pride
Location:
Width: 1
Question: ZA3978:Q14/ ZA3979:Q14/ ZA3983:Q10/ ZA3986:Q12
Would you say you are very proud, fairly proud, not very proud or not at all proud to be [NATIONALITY – refer to citizenship here]?

1 very proud
2 fairly proud
3 not very proud
4 not at all proud
7 does not feel to be [NATIONALITY] (spontaneous)
8 DK/ no opinion (spontaneous)
9 NA/refusal (spontaneous)

q54_b: Disturbing: People of another race

Location:
Width: 1
Question: Q54
Some people are disturbed by the opinions, customs and way of life of people different from themselves.
B) And do you find the presence of people of another race disturbing?

1 disturbing
2 not disturbing
8 DK /no opinion
9 refusal/NA

Questions from the Consolidation of Democracy in Central and Eastern Europe 1990-2001 (for Russia)

V229: Pride in (country) citizenship
How proud are you to be Russian?
V336: RU – Country has own, different way
Please tell me whether you agree with the following statements or not. Russia should keep going its own way, even though it is different from other countries.
V180: Tolerance of foreigners in (country)
Question: Please tell me for each of the following statements, whether you agree strongly, agree, disagree or disagree strongly: Foreigners who dislike our government and criticize it should not be allowed to stay.

Two variants of the Russian radical right
Imperial and social nationalism

Timm Beichelt[1]

ABSTRACT: The text combines three lines of discussion. First, on the empirical level two Russian political parties – the CPRF and the LDPR – are characterized with regard to their specific profiles of right-wing radicalism. Second, these profiles are attributed to specific variations of the interpretation of
the Russian past. Third, the empirical findings are traced for insights into the
Leninist legacy concept. The main hypothesis on the empirical level is that
Russian ultra-nationalist actors refer to different currents of a common national imagination in order to combine nationalist ideological elements with
other programmatic features. On the conceptual level, the legacy concept is
able to render systematic insights not into the history of a given state but into
varying interpretations of what can be seen as 'useable pasts' from the perspective of various intellectual entrepreneurs.

Introduction

The following study seeks to explore the extent to which history may help to
explain the strength and the character of party right-wing radicalism in Russia. As is the case in other contributions to this volume, it takes up and ex-
tends the concept of Leninist legacies (Jowitt, 1992). Other than in its original
intent, the legacy framework is not used for an explanation of outcomes of
regime transition. Rather, some of the analytic distinctions dormant in Jowitt's
work are resumed in order to illuminate long-term effects of historic developments in the guise of Russian ultra-nationalism.

As has been shown on various occasions, a large part of the Russian
political elite cultivates a strong nationalism by emphasizing the greatness of
the Russian nation, the importance of the Russian state and the uniqueness
of Russian culture and history (Laqueur, 1993; Devlin, 1999; Laruelle, 2007).
Often, the explanation of the Russian inclination to nationalism consists in the
exceptional pace of societal change Russia has gone through several times

---

1   I would like to thank Petra Stykow, Michael Minkenberg, and two anomymous re-
     viewers for valuable comments on earlier versions of this article. Remaining errors
     and inconsistencies should be attributed to the author alone.

throughout the last century. Within few decades after the breakdown of socialism, nearly every part of Russian society underwent a dramatic change. The Russian Revolution of 1917 ended an *ancien régime* in the true sense of the word: religion and the state formed a unity, higher nobility exploited the pauperized peasantry, and public administration was mainly built on the principle of loyalty. The 'great transformation' of the first half of the 20th century consisted of rush electrification, brutal collectivization, and very rapid industrialization. Post-communist transformation and the collapse of the Soviet Union similarly accelerated social change and added exceptional degrees of uncertainty to all facets of society (White et al., 1993). Ultimately, large parts of society were tired of further experiments and looked for familiar patterns of societal interpretation which could be found in the traditional constructions of family, nation, and – to some extent – orthodox beliefs.

Against this background, one of the few political strategies to gain visibility involved the extension of nationalism into a radical direction. Such a development has also taken place in Russian party politics after the end of state socialism (Allensworth, 1998). The tendency has been supported by the fact that the increasingly authoritarian regime has suppressed many other political forces which might have become a danger to the course taken by former President Putin and his camp (Fish, 2005; Mommsen and Nußberger, 2007). In this sense, one of the few opportunity structures to be used by non-regime actors consisted in radicalizing those elements in the depth of Russian national self-reconstruction employed by the *nouveau régime* itself, drawing on a broad anti-liberal consensus among the Russian public (Umland, 2007; Gudkov, 2007; Rykhlin, 2006).

Specifically, two radicalizing interpretation figures concerning the Russian nation can be observed in the political sphere. One consists of community-oriented interpretations based on the demand of the social equality of native Russians; the other in idealizing the imperialist tradition of the Russian state which so many times in previous centuries established Russia as the most important hegemonic power in Eastern Europe, the Caucasus, and Central Asia. The first position can be labelled "social nationalist" and is mainly taken by the Communist Party of the Russian Federation (CPRF). The second position can be called "imperial nationalist" and is embodied in the Liberal-Democratic Party of Russia (LDPR). Accordingly, both will be discussed in a later section of the paper as parties with right-wing radicalist elements.

Similar descriptions have been used before (Williams and Hanson, 1999). What is new in this contribution is the hypothesis that the specific shape of the Russian radical right follows a double pattern. On the one hand, there exists a common denominator to which all ultra-national forces in the country refer. On the other hand, different wings within the nationalist camp draw on those aspects of a "repertoire of usable past[s]" (Kubik, 2003, p. 343) that best correspond to other components of their respective political programs. As will be seen with reference to the Russian case, these contingent reference points should only be hesitantly labelled "Leninist". Indeed most relevant patterns of historic interpretation reach back well before the period preceding Leninism, some of them even before socialism started to exist as an idea. Therefore, the Leninism argument will be used in a more general sense which has been called a perspective on "legacies of the past" (Comisso, 1997), with Leninist elements serving as a set of reference points among others.

The argument will be developed in several steps. In the following section, the relevance of the Leninist legacies concept for the study of the radical right is discussed. The next step then consists of an elaboration of three different legacies to which actors of the Russian radical right regularly refer: the character of the Russian nation, Russian imperialism, and Russian orthodoxy. The paper then goes on to show that Russian radical forces, specifically the CPRF and the LDPR, compose their programs from different combinations of the way these historic experiences are reconstructed in Russian culture. A conclusion completes the paper.

From a systematic perspective, the three mentioned legacies are heavily interwoven as all three can be subsumed under what some authors conceptualize as one "cultural" legacy (Crawford and Lijphart, 1997). Still, their distinction seems plausible if the legacy concept is understood as an inductive approach. Imperialism and Russian orthodoxy can be traced as partly isolated reference frames in Russian nationalism. In that sense, national identity forms a core legacy within which "imperialism" and "orthodoxy" represent specific, and sometimes additional, characteristics.

Before we move on to the discussion of the legacy framework, the concept of right-wing radicalism shall be defined. Actors of the Radical Right are bent on a romanticized version of the nation that stands at the centre of promises to undo two developments of modernization: the growing autonomy of the individual *vis-à-vis* the community and the ongoing functional differentiation of society (Lipset, 1964; Scheuch and Klingemann, 1967; Minkenberg, 1998). Accordingly, right-wing radicalism is based on societal action, and more specifically on a range of counter-positions to rapid economic and cultural change. Ideologically, these counter-positions can be identified by the similarly charged terms of "ultra-nationalism" (Minkenberg, 1998, p. 33) or "nativism". The latter is defined as "an ideology which holds that states should be inhabited exclusively by members of the native group ('the nation') and that non-native elements (persons and ideas) are fundamentally threatening to the homogenous nation-state" (Mudde, 2007, p. 19). According to Mudde's definition and the core of Minkenberg's concept, the notions of ultranationalism and nativism will be used interchangeably throughout the paper.

Useable variations of usable pasts: the legacy approach and the study of right-wing radicalism

In his seminal article which first introduced the term, Jowitt used the "Leninist legacy" argument to give a pessimistic forecast on the outcome of Post-communist transition. In Jowitt's view, the region's history of authoritarian rule and the delegitimization of individual autonomy shaped East European politics more than democrats or capitalists (Jowitt, 1992, p. 300). His main argument concerned the "dichotomic antagonism between the official and private realms" (Jowitt, 1992, p. 287) during the Communist period. The unwillingness of private individuals to identify with public affairs would lead, according to Jowitt, to "suspicion, division, and fragmentation [rather than] coalition and integration" (Jowitt, 1992, p. 298) as predominant factors of political life in Eastern Europe.

To the general study of post-socialist transformation, Jowitt's work has proved useful on two levels. First, it reminds us of the fact that cultural elements – in a broad sense of the term "culture" – play a crucial role in the development of post-socialist societies. Indirectly, this elevates the Leninist legacy argument to a conceptual statement which answers the question "under which conditions and by which mechanisms distinctive components of the cultural legacy affect the outcomes of transformation at different levels" (Bönker and Wielgohs, 2003, p. 65). In short, Jowitt has therefore established a causal link between cultural elements of the past and institutional elements of the present.

From here, the legacy approach proved useful as a second step which systematically distinguished between different types of legacies. Crawford

and Lijphart identified six of them: cultural, social, political, national, institutional, and administrative/economic (Crawford and Lijphart, 1997). These
categories may in themselves be debated. For example, many authors would
probably merge cultural and national legacies as the development of nationhood is often attributed to cultural factors like language, ethnicity, and identity
(Anderson, 1983; Gellner, 1983). Nonetheless, the legacy approach has been
regularly used as a reminder that a balanced analysis of transformation processes needs to take into account both cultural and non-cultural factors and
that both have to be analyzed in systematic ways (Kopstein, 2003).

When using the legacy concept in order to better understand the characteristics of right-wing radicalism, a further adaptation of the traditional legacy approach is necessary. If the dependent variable switches from the out-
put of transformation to the shape of the radical right, we must examine atti-
tudinal factors and their translation into societal or political action. Right-wing
radicalism – if understood as in the definition above – is rooted in an ideology
of ultra-nationalism, which means that values and norms become constitutive
elements of the *explanandum*. In the end then, the consideration of the impact of legacies on right-wing radicalism is reduced to establishing a connection between cultural variables of the past with cultural variables of the present.[2]

At the same time, however, this emphasis on cultural aspects blurs the
distinction between independent and dependent variables. Both are composed of similar factors. The Leninist legacies Jowitt referred to have later
been enumerated as "intolerance, exclusiveness, rejection of all compromise,
extreme personalization of political discourse, and the search for charismatic
leadership" (Tismaneanu, 2007, p. 36). It is not hard to see that these charac-
terizations bear affinity to the radical right. Its actors have been identified "as
Nazis, (...) others as conservatives and traditionalists. There are others who
are simply occultists and mystics, anti-Masonic and conspiracy theorists, religious fanatics, primitive misanthropists, or clinically disturbed" (Gregor, 1998,
pp.12-13). The close relationship between Leninist legacies and the charac-

---

2   For this reason, this paper focuses on ‚cultural" legacies and largely ignores other
    ones, such as social or institutional legacies. Of course, this does not mean that
    other ways of approaching the topic may identify different types of legacies relevant
    to the character and scope of Russian nationalism. In relation to the above men-
    tioned distinction by Crawford/Lijphart (1997), my categorization merges national
    and cultural legacies. This should not be understood as a general critique to the
    work of Crawford and Lijphart, but is due to the focus on right-wing radicalism which
    approaches „culture" via the ‚nation".

teristics of the Russian radical right makes it difficult to judge if ultra-nationalism is an effect or a driving force for the post-Leninist value system we find throughout not only in Russia, but in wide parts of post-socialist Europe. What we can identify beyond this question of causality, however, are close interconnections between the ways nation, autocracy and orthodoxy have been interpreted in Russia then and now.

Before we get to the substance of those legacies relevant for the Russian radical right, we need to remind ourselves of a few prominent points in the debate of the legacy approach. The strongest criticism against Jowitt's work concerned his allegedly too general approach to Eastern Europe.[3] Also Crawford and Lijphart made this point by hinting at the existence of at least two currents within post-socialist Europe, liberalist forces on the one hand and old elites on the other (Crawford and Lijphart, 1997, pp. 8-11). Translated into the geographic dimension, it soon became clear that the different paths of political development in Central and Eastern Europe also need to be attributed to pre-Communist requisites in the field of economic and bureaucratic development (Kitschelt, 2003; Kitschelt et al., 1999; Ash, 1999/2000). Consequently, the explanatory value of Leninism in general remains a matter of debate. If pre-war experiences shape large parts of post-socialist development, one may question the overall-effect of Communist elements (Kopstein, 2003, p. 239). In fact, I will argue in the following section that Leninist elements are mainly relevant as catalysts for traditions which reach back in the time before the Russian revolution.

In this light, Russia presents a special case within the Leninist legacy framework. The Soviet Union served as the motherland of Communism between 1917 and 1941, and after the war it constituted an anchor for the satellite states of Central and South-eastern Europe. If Leninism, or Communism, does not play a role in the explanation of post-Communist outcomes, where else should that be the case? Studying the impact of legacies of the past on the culture of contemporary right-wing radicalism reveals the specific significance of Communism for the understanding of contemporary societal developments in what Jowitt called Eastern Europe, namely not as an isolated period but a historic phase to be seen in context of (case-specific) longer historic lines.

---

3   In fact, Jowitt was well aware of intra-regional differences in Leninism: As "for the necessary genuflection to national differences: they exist. It is clear that different types of fragmentation will predominate in different countries" (Jowitt 1992, pp. 299-300).

Ambiguous references to Russian radicalism: nation, empire, orthodoxy

In general, it is possible to identify a wide range of reference points in Russian nationalist past-oriented discourses. "Russia has always had a surfeit of self-images, and has found it difficult to settle fast to one or other of them" (Hosking, 2002, p. 229). One reason consists in the diversity of cultural entrepreneurs referring to the Russian past: different perspectives, different accesses. Beyond this obvious fact, however, a selective approach to Russian history is fuelled by the particular ambiguity of many historic turning points that affect Russian national self-understanding.

For contemporary legitimization patterns of the radical right, three elements of reference seem to bear special importance – nation, empire, orthodoxy. Before discussing these in detail, a preliminary remark seems necessary that all three of these elements are to a high degree intertwined. The Russian nation rests at the core of nationalist reasoning and should be seen as an embracing mental concept. Within the nation construct, 'empire' and 'orthodoxy' introduce major ambiguities.

Specifically, Russia's status as an empire guarantees visibility and creates a perceived sense of greatness, but at the same time includes foreign elements into Russian nationhood. The ideal of the 'simple' Russian people – as embedded in national orthodox discourses – renders Russian society as 'pure' in its self-image, which at the same time solidifies its backwardness. Further inconsistencies arise with an eye on the brutal, but partially effective processes of modernization during the first decades of the Soviet Union. The nation could well be assigned a leading role in world history but it fought mainly against its own people through the use of social hardship and repression. Russia's orthodox messianism had turned into a pretence that needed to be feared within and outside the country.

Obviously, these inconsistencies should not be attributed to the Russian case alone. In general, nativist references to legacies are from the beginning bent to highlight certain aspects and stifle others. Any investigation into history must take into account these biases. However, the Russian case seems especially instructive because the evident ambiguities serve as an engine for the development of competing images of ultra-nationalism.

National identity

As one consequence of Russia's enormous geographic size, Russian nationalist entrepreneurs did and do face difficulties to identify the 'natural' boundary of belonging (and non-belonging) to Russian nationhood. Nationalists cannot – as is the case for most Central European states – simply externalize neighbouring cultures and therefore turn them into projection fields for national self-understanding. Instead, in order not to question the oppressive character of Russian geopolitical power, nationalist Russians had and have to lead non-natives, foreigners, barbarians – or however you want to label them – "out of oppression into brotherhood", as a historicist of the Soviet period put it (Vähä, 2002). Developing an own national identity, therefore, resembled a "Sisyphean mission": there was (and is) no separate nation state but rather a "'core nation' of the empire" (Piirainen, 2002, p. 151). National identity construction oscillates between ethnic and civic nationalism. When a civic self-image evolves, it undermines visions of the Russian nation in mono-dimensional cultural terms, and leads nationalists to complain about internal "Russophobia" (Horvath, 2005, pp. 150-184).

As a result, concepts of Russian nationhood during its geographic expansion were varied in nature. In cultural terms, the Russian people (*narod*) shared a sense of cultural belonging that was distant from civic aspects. In a well known essay, the religious philosopher Nikolai Berdyaev characterized Russia as the "most stateless, anarchist country in the world. And the Russian people are the most apolitical people (...). Everything thoroughly Russian, our national writers, thinkers, publicists – all of them were stateless persons"- *bezgosudarstvenniki* (Berdyaev, 1992 (1915/18), p. 298).[4] The different conceptions of the Russian nation come under the name *narodnost'*, which signifies faithfulness to traits of Russian national culture. The term was contested between two major camps: Slavophiles on one hand and Westernizers on the other. Both insisted on "narodnost," but defined it differently. The former saw "it in Russia's Orthodox heritage and communal spirit (*sobornost'*); the latter [believed] that the Russian national spirit, having embraced Western civilization, was now in the process of creating its own national version of that civilization" (Oulanoff, 1985, p. 293).

Accordingly, both *narodnost'* camps conceptualized the Russian people as an organic and natural community. The main difference consisted in the

---

4   This and all other statements from Russian texts or internet sites have been translated by the author, T. B.

relation to Western values. The Westernizers – among them the writer Turgenev as well as the intellectuals Vissarion Belinsky and Alexander Herzen (Berlin, 1978 [1948]) – viewed liberal principles like individual autonomy, economic freedom and responsibility as pathways out of the country's backwardness. In contrast, Slavophilism – initiated by intellectuals like Ivan Kireevsky and Aleksei Khomyakov (Gleason, 1985) – formed a multi-faceted intellectual movement that focused around the 'true' way of living among 'simple' Russian people whose best defence against harmful Western influences was to gather around the churches in Russian villages.[5]

The split between Slavophiles and Westernizers continues far into the 20th century. To mention the best known example, the conservative dissident writer and Nobel prize winner Aleksandr Solzhenitsyn is cited with "sweeping diatribe[s] against Western decadence and the individualist heritage of Renaissance humanism" (Horvath, 2005, p. 171). The assaults by Solzhenitsyn and other conservative nationalists indicate a cross-cutting cleavage between ideologies of domestic societal organization and foreign policy orientation. Russian nationalism "was tendentially anti-liberal and anti-Western" (Gregor, 1998, p. 1); the West turned into something "alien and hostile" (Devlin, 1999, p. 9).

From a nationalist's perspective, *perestroika* and other reforms of the late 1980s triggered off two contradictory developments. On the one hand, the destruction of the ailing Soviet state was largely embraced. Again, Solzhenitsyn serves as a handy example for those conservatives who judged Soviet rule as hypocritical and highly repressive. In their eyes, the Soviet regime completely lacked the spiritual dimension as demanded by the Slavophiles. For nationalists, the state had never been supposed to remain Marxist-Leninist, but expected to become "theocratic" and "sacred" (Gregor, 1998, p. 1).

On the other side, the results of Gorbachev's and Yeltsin's reforms were devastating. The great power status was lost, the economic crisis made Russia completely dependent on the West, and inequality rose to unprecedented levels. The break-up not only of the Soviet Union, but of Russian Federation itself turned into a real possibility. None of these developments helped overcome the prejudices many Russians (and all nationalists) cultivated with regard to the West.

---

5   The term *sobornost'* consists of a core that simultaneously leads to *sobor* = cathedral, and to *sobranie* = assembly.

100   MICHAEL MINKENBERG (ED.)

Subsequently, a re-evaluation not only of the Tsarist state, but also of the Soviet regime took place (Devlin, 1999, p. 89). After all, both systems had been able to hold back Western pressure and influence much more effectively than seemed to be possible under Gorbachev and Yeltsin. During the Tsarist and Soviet past, Russia had to be reckoned with as a great European power. After the breakdown of the Soviet Union, authoritarian nationalists increasingly linked their views of the 'right' traditional order to the Soviet Union as well.

Of course, the differences between Tsarist and Soviet power and their relevance for Russian self-understanding were still heavily discussed (Maslin, 1992; Slater, 1998). After all, the October Revolution had thoroughly and cruelly destructed traditional Russia after 1917. Yet, in the worldview of Russian nationalists both regimes are much more reconciled than was the case during Soviet times, when Russian nationalists sooner or later belonged to the dissident camp. Where reconciliation was not complete, various elements of the Russian and Soviet past were singled out as points of reference. The Tsarist heritage was constructed as the unity of worldly and religious power, in Tsarism's personification of state authority and in its valuation of the peasant society. In complementary terms, the communist legacy rests on "a principled hostility to political pluralism and private property and markets in the economic sphere, an emphasis on substantive (social) justice as opposed to formal equality before the law, and the glorification of heroic and military achievements of the previous regime" (Vujačić, 2003, p. 384).

Empire

As already alluded to, a good part of the complexity of Russian nationalism can be traced to Russia's character as an imperial power.[6] Expanding the Russian lands to the South and the East – a development which started in the 16th century – brought power and influence but at the same time required more resources to uphold political control. Most of the time, this was barely managed by the Russians alone, which led to an influx of Western European bureaucrats and military in the 18th and 19th century. On the one hand, state effectiveness and efficiency were achieved at higher levels than could be expected from a peasant society, which Russia was until well into the first decades of the 20th century. On the other hand, a gap of understanding opened

---

6   "Empire" being understood as an authoritarian power relationship exercised on peripheries by a strong centre Bunce (2005).

up not only between gentry and peasantry, but between state and society in general.

Generally, the Russian state managed its extension to Caucasian and Central Asian territories through the partial cooptation of local elites. The practice culminated in the Soviet Union – a pseudo-federal state dominated by Russia(ns) with a multi-ethnic people and semi-loyal peripheral elites (Carrère d'Encausse, 1978). Throughout history then, representatives of the Russian state could not automatically be ascribed ethnic or cultural Russian identities. The peripheral elites' limited command of Russian language was one problem, rendering regional affairs into incomprehensible black boxes from the perspective of the centre. But also the spirit of Russian power was affected, as populations and elites on the periphery usually did not belong to the Orthodox or even the Christian faith. As a consequence, the Russian state was Russian and non-Russian at the same time. Not only the Soviet Union had been built on multi-national principles; Russian expansion had already before included many non-Russian territories, and there were only limited efforts of compelled assimilation.

In this guise, Russian expansion accommodated contradictory tendencies for Russian nationalists. The great power status undermined the purity of the nation in racist terms, the binding force of Christian orthodoxy in religious terms, and its independence from the West as well as from the East and South in territorial terms. Unlike in more Western European national traditions, the barbarians did not come from outside; they were considered alien but also had their given place within the state. Thus a major threat to national purity came from within. The ambiguity of Joseph Stalin – who was of Georgian origin – constituted a paradigmatic object of reference. On the one hand, he defended his home, the 'Soviet nation', in World War II. On the other, millions of Russians (and others) became victims under his rule.

In political terms, many of these ambiguous tendencies were and are rooted in Russia's status as a large-scale empire. Its imperial tradition separates it from all other post-socialist states, with the arguable exception of Serbia (Vujačić, 2003, p. 361). Whereas nationalism and ultra-nationalism in non-imperial post-socialist countries almost inevitably bear an anti-Russian component, the Russian people and their leader do not have clear options of identifying the 'other' which deprives them of an important instrument of self-identification.

Religion: Orthodox Christianity
Alongside the national and imperial elements, orthodoxy should be seen as the third long-term cultural variable that influences contemporary Russian ultra-nationalism. Its relevance is linked to the claimed attribute of Moscow serving as the Third Rome (Krahn, 1963). After the fall of Constantinople in 1453, Moscow considered itself the remaining protector of true Christianity. While church and state went increasingly separate ways in Western Europe, Moscow stood strongly for a unity between the Christian religion and the state. These two elements contributed to Russian self-understanding as a messianic civilization, an interpretation pattern that was encouraged by the fact that Moscow was the only major European capital that had been able to resist Napoleon. In 1848, the writer Fyodor Tyutchev wrote: "Russia is above all the Christian Empire; the Russian people is Christian not only through the orthodoxy of its beliefs but also (...) by that ability of renunciation and sacrifice which forms a basis of its moral nature" (Krahn, 1963, p. 212).

From here, two rhetorical links can be reconstructed. First, the traditional life of the Russian people, notably their passive faith, became a semi-holy entity which defended the last bastion of true orthodoxy in an otherwise schismatic Europe. Second, orthodoxy turned into a stronghold of anti-liberalism. Defendants of the old regime referred to theocratic reasoning. In other words, there was no serious constitutionalism based on civic principles. The state theory of Tsarist Russia, represented by philosophers like Konstantin Leontiev or high officials like Konstantin P. Pobedonostsev, combined church and state in highly reactionary ways (Masaryk, 1992 (1913), section XVII). Its mission consisted in opposing the allegedly catastrophic egalitarian and utilitarian influences from the West, which could only lead to a revolution like the one leading to the Napoleonic wars all over Europe.

When the Russian revolution finally took place in 1917, the Orthodox Church of course lost its status of being synonymous with the Russian state. Under Stalin, attending a church or publicly showing faith constituted a great risk of being identified as counter-revolutionary (which then usually lead to a strong possibility of a fatal prosecution). Later the oppression of churches, monasteries and their abiders loosened somewhat (Dunlop, 1983, pp. 167-200). Still, during Soviet rule, the church almost completely ceded its autonomy to the state by entering into cooperation and collaboration with the KGB (Laqueur, 1993, pp. 231-243). While the official church managed to survive, the consequences for the spread of faith were devastating. By 1991, around only ten percent of the Russian population defined themselves as believers (Laqueur, 1993, p. 222).

Thus during post-socialist transition the Russian orthodoxy was present mainly as a formal institution, without a strong societal support. Due to its weak basis in the population, the church's claims for public moral principles could only have a limited impact. Instead, political leaders, not only those from the radical right, rediscovered Orthodoxy as a legitimation element (Anderson, 1994; Behrens, 2002). Numerous new cathedrals were built and tax exemptions were granted to the church. Patriarch Alexius II, the Patriarch of Moscow and primate of the Russian Orthodox Church, was until his death in 2008 widely respected as a symbol of Russian unity. In that function, he represented the Orthodox Church as an "'empire-saving' institution" (Dunlop, 1995), serving discursive needs of both the political mainstream and extremist segments of society.

Anti-modernist radicalism in the contemporary party system: imperial and social nationalism

In this section I try to demonstrate how all major political parties in Russia have indeed employed the three discussed legacies in different ways. As a result, all contemporary political (parliamentary) parties should be labelled nationalist, and several of them even ultra-nationalist (see below). According to the definition used in the introduction, this ultra-nationalism turns them into parties with program elements of the radical right. However, the label does not necessarily apply to the whole range of the political parties concerned. As Mudde suggests, a true party of the radical right should be identified by a programmatic "populist radical right core ideology (...) without any significant alternative faction(s)" (Mudde, 2007, p. 40). Of course, not all Russian parties can be classified as radical nationalist in the sense of this definition. Still, several authors have concluded that nationalist elements characterize all political parties which have managed to remain relevant despite the growing authoritarianism of the regime (Buhbe and Makarenko, 2007; Glass, 2003; White, 2006).

For the description of the party system, two kinds of data should be taken into consideration. On the one hand, election outcomes and the resulting distribution of parliamentary seats offer information on the electoral success of parties. This information shows us that Russia has undergone a rather thorough restructuring; from a highly fragmented party system with hardly any structure at all in the 1990s to moderate fragmentation and stability during the rule of President Putin (Gel'man, 2006; Stykow, 2008). Currently, four parties are represented in the Duma, the two regime parties "United Russia" (UR) and "Just Russia" (JR), the Communist Party (CPRF) and the National Liberal Party (LDPR).[7]

Of course, this de-fragmentation and de-polarization has come at the price of re-authorization and a considerable degree of repression to opposition forces in Russian society (Fish, 2005; Remington, 2007). Still, a second kind of data reveals that the concentration to a small N party system corresponds to long-term support rates in the electorate. Table 1 reveals that only the different "parties of power" as well as the CPRF and the LDPR have been able to draw on a more or less stable electoral basis throughout the last 15 years of post-Soviet development (see Table 1).

Table 1.   Party preferences, 1995-2008

Political party	1995	1999	2001	2002	2003	2004	2008
Communist party	7	20	18	20	18	8	8
Liberal democrats	8	6	5	6	8	6	8
Union of right forces		1	4	4	3	2	
United Russia			12	13	8	24	58
Women of Russia	5	4	3	4	3		
Yabloko	8	10	5	4	5	2	
Just Russia							3
None/DK	38	38	50	46	48	49	

Source: White (2006, p. 10). The data for 2008 are taken from VCIOM, a public opinion institute.

In the context of competitive authoritarianism (Levitsky and Way, 2002), non-regime parties have limited opportunities to preserve a position in the party system. First, and as a side-condition of authoritarianism, independent parties

---

7   Data is from the Russian Central Electoral Commission, www.izbirkom.ru, downloaded on March 9, 2009.

are restricted to strategies that will not challenge the parties of power exces-sively. Accordingly, their programs may only contradict the ideology of the rul-ing elite to a limited degree. Secondly, within the limits accepted by the re-gime these parties need to develop strategies of visibility in order to match the many advantages the regime parties enjoy during electoral campaigns. It has long been argued that an articulation of ultra-nationalism represents a plausible agenda of evoking attention in the public debate while not funda-mentally challenging the underlying regime (Shlapentokh, 1999).

Therefore, a central element of reference for nationalist parties is the ideology of the party of power. In contemporary Russia, it is represented by the party and the Duma faction of "United Russia" (UR); a party which was founded in 2001 and merged major competing parties of power in a step to signal allegiance to President Putin. In its program for the 2007 Duma elec-tion, the party alluded to various nationalist images of the past, for example by the promise to "further develop Russia as a unique civilization", to defend the "general space of [Russian] culture and language" as well as to "strengthen Russian sovereignty and the capacity to defend the country".[8] Some scholars argue that the programmatic profile of UR is rather low while the party's main function consists in dealing with intra-elite conflicts for the redistribution of national resources (Remington, 2008). While this is certainly true, the party has to compete with other parties during election times in order to keep up the façade of "imitation democracy" (Shevtsova, 2007, p. 41). Even within the authoritarian regime competing parties therefore have to posi-tion themselves *vis-à-vis* the dominant party of the regime. During the 2007 elections notably Vladimir Putin – who headed the party list on the ballot – put special emphasis on aggressive messages with strongly nationalist content (White, 2009).

As Table 1 demonstrates, the only parties in the Russian system which may claim to be permanent competitors to Russia's various parties of power are the CPRF and the LDPR. Both parties claim to be mass member parties and present membership numbers of about 600 000 each (Glass, 2003, pp. 3, 6). Their character as parties with a countrywide basis is also supported by the fact that their parliamentarians have widely been elected in the party list section of the electoral system (Remington, 2001: 179). A further indicator for

---

8   The citations are from the party's homepage, see http://edinros.er.ru/er/rubr.shtml?
     110099, viewed on March 11, 2009.

the parties' homogeneity is their coherent voting pattern in the State Duma (Bremzen et al., 2006, p. 20).

To what extent are the two parties nationalist or nativist, and how can their specific profiles be characterized? The LDPR resembles a strong leader party, in which few decisions are made without the approval of its president Vladimir Zhirinovsky (Oschlies, 1995). The party never again reached the 23% of the party list vote of the 1993 Duma elections, but managed to stay present beyond electoral thresholds in almost all nationwide elections since.[9] The LDPR, and with it Zhirinovsky, is characterized as populist, occasionally anti-Semitic, nativist, and internally autocratic (adaptations from Mudde, 2007). Zhirinovsky became known in the early 1990s with his extreme great power rhetoric, speculating about the need for Russia to create a counter-balance to the immanently instable regions south of the territory of the former Soviet Union. This position, which is laid out in various versions of his notorious book "The Last Surge to the South" from 1993, remains the cornerstone of Zhirinovsky's ideology of "revolutionary expansionism" (Umland, 2006, p. 387). Its nationalism is merged with strong elements of fascism as the would-be pacification of "the south" by imperial means is not only seen as an extension of Russia's external power but also as a means of Russian spiritual rebirth (Umland, 2006).

Beyond Zhirinovsky, the LDPR program has been developed from a tight nationalist agenda and now covers a broad range of political issues. Its core remains radical nationalist when alluding to the "great Russian people, (...) to the re-establishment of the country's territory and to the defence of compatriots abroad".[10] Of course, the last two statements aim at blurring the difference between the Russian Federation and the Soviet Union because only the latter underwent territorial change, namely by dissolution in late 1991. Accordingly, the reference to "compatriots abroad" indicates a post-imperial moment by openly approaching all citizens of the former Soviet Union who may feel discontent with the post-soviet political structure. A hint into the same directions constitutes the LDPR's openness to paganist beliefs (Moroz, 2007, p. 247) which marks the potential inclusiveness of nationalist imperialism.

Whereas the LDPR thus presents a rather clear case for a right-wing radical populist party, the CPRF's programmatic emphasis rests on a different

9   Again, see www.izbirkom.ru, downloaded on March 11, 2009.
10   The party program can be found at http://www.ldpr.ru/partiya/prog/963/, downloaded on March 11, 2009.

mix of socialist and nationalist elements. Even more openly than is the case with regard to the LDPR, the party program calls for a rebirth of a Soviet order which shall be established in a "Fatherland in entirety and independence".[11] According to the program, this can only be reached by a re-foundation of a brotherly union of Soviet peoples. Again, the play on words with the term "Soviet" marks an explicit flabbiness concerning the actual borders of the Russian nation.

The CPRF's heritage – as the successor party of the Communist Party of the Soviet Union (CPSU) – is a direct link to the party's big power ideology and makes its force in Russian society unsurprising. Since the early 1990s the party's leadership openly accepted the three Tsarist state principles of 'autocracy, Orthodoxy, and nationality':

> Russia's modern communists no longer attempted to justify socialism in terms of historical development as conceived by Marx but were (...) indebted to Marx's Russian nationalist and religious opponents. Their vocabulary and ideas were derived (...) from nineteenth-century apologists for Russian autocracy and Russian Orthodox nationalism (Devlin, 1999, p. 168).

Also, the would-be internationalism of the Communist Party has been reinterpreted. Gennady Zyuganov declared that Russia had a "'special historic responsibility' [of resisting an] 'immoral and materialistic West', [which] seeks to extract mineral and cheap labour from the less-developed countries in a process of exploitation" (Gregor, 1998, p. 10).

Altogether, therefore, the nationalist elements of the ideologies of both major nationalist political parties do not differ very much. This does not mean, however, that there are no differences. While the two parties converge in their anti-Western nationalism, their visions of how to embed domestic society into a national vision take different paths. Table 2 presents population views of the three relevant parties in the State Duma after the elections of December 2007 (see Table 2). Given the poor research situation concerning party action in Russia, such data is preferable to official party programs, which are of limited relevance to the content of political action in parliament and in the public (Remington, 2007).

---

11   The quotes are taken from the party program, http://kprf.ru/party/program/, downloaded on March 11, 2009.

Table 2.   Images of parties among population: "How do you evaluate the general political and ideological line of party...?" (2006)

Political/ideological aim	United Russia	KPRF	LDPR
A. [Equality versus freedom]			
Priority of social equality	37	58	24
Priority of individual freedom and personal success	40	14	39
Hard to answer	23	28	37
B. [Position of state in economy]			
Orientation at free market economy	44	14	35
Orientation at strong state regulation in economy	33	56	28
Hard to answer	23	30	37
C. [Openness to societal change]			
Orientation at thorough changes in society	39	22	38
Orientation at stability, refusal at thorough change	36	48	25
Hard to answer	25	30	37
D. [Position towards regime]			
Rather an opposition party	16	48	34
Rather a party that supports the regime ("партия, поддерживающая власть")	65	23	30
Hard to answer	19	29	36

Political/ideological aim	United Russia	KPRF	LDPR
E. [Integration into European structures]			
Integration into European structures and global society	38	13	27
Preservation of Russian independence, its distinct way, independent of the West	40	57	35
Hard to answer	21	30	38

Source: VCIOM: ПОЛИТИЧЕСКИЕ ПАРТИИ: "ИДЕЙНЫЙ ПОРТРЕТ", Пресс-выпуск № 565, 31.10.2006. See http://wciom.ru/arkhiv/tematicheskii-arkhiv/item/ single/3503.html.

According to the data, voters are aware of ideological differences between the two parties on virtually all domestic issues. The CPRF is seen as a party of social protection: it is judged to favour social equality and state regulation of the economy and it combines societal stability with a preference for independence from the West. The LDPR's profile is less pronounced. A relative majority of the population (39%) sees it as a defender of individual freedom and success, but 24% believe the party prioritizes social equality. 35% of voters consider the LDPR as directed towards a free market economy, conversely, 28% judge it to be a force that supports state regulation of the economy. Moreover, 34% see it as an opposition party, 30% as a supporter of the dominant regime. Symptomatically, in the same survey 15% of the population rate the LDPR as being a leftist party, 22% consider it to be rightist. Interestingly, only 12% think the LDPR is a party that prioritises "Russian patriotism".[12] In contrast, the CPRF is clearly identified as a "leftist" party by 56% of the voters, with a policy prioritising "social justice". Similar to the image attrib-

---

12   Again see VCIOM: ПОЛИТИЧЕСКИЕ ПАРТИИ: "ИДЕЙНЫЙ ПОРТРЕТ", Пресс-выпуск № 565, 31.10.2006 (source to Table 2). A further 16% think that the LDPR could be attributed to all three camps (leftist/rightist/patriot) at the same time, 25% find it hard to answer.

uted to the LDPR, only a minority of 10% believes the CPRF is mainly a Russian patriotic party.[13]

The unclear image of the LDPR stems partly from the great ambivalence of its actions. In public, Vladimir Zhirinovsky and his allies present themselves as oppositionist forces, usually by populist reasoning (Tolz, 1997; Williams and Hanson; 1999, Oschlies, 1995). In parliament, however, the LDPR is reported to have supported President Putin in more than 85% of the votes in the Russian Duma in 2000, only slightly topped by Unity (Remington, 2006, p. 18). The CPRF offers a different picture, being non-supportive of the president and his administration most of the time. However, as Table 3 shows, even the CPRF offers legislative cooperation occasionally. While it usually opposes the President in social policy and privatization issues, it partly supported Putin's judicial reform, which consisted in re-subordinating the judiciary under central and vertical power (Hendley, 2007).

Table 3.   Mean presidential support scores by faction, by legislative issue category (2000-2001)

	De-monopolization (n=46)	Judicial policy (n=33)	Social policy (n=18)
Unity	92.8	89.8	87.5
LDPR	94.8	81.1	80.3
CPRF	5.8	60.6	21.4

Source: Remington (2006, p. 19).

The different degree of opposition can be partially traced back to the crucial juncture of the 1993 founding elections. Yeltsin had abolished the CPSU in 1991 and introduced a Voucher privatization in 1992 against fierce Communist resistance. As a result, he could only be treated with great hostility by the newly founded CPRF. The LDPR, however, possessed and used an – albeit limited – coalition potential.[14] A relatively large and disciplined faction with a

---

13   I attribute these low figures to the general nationalist mainstream as discussed above – since all major parties capitalize on national issues, voters do not see the necessity to notice the feature as a distinguishing marker between party profiles.

14   This, of course, is a reference to Sartori's party system approach which measures a party's relevance by its potential to oppose or cooperate with other parties (Sartori 1976).

blurry program could by be used by the Kremlin for temporary coalitions. Zhirinovsky was able to deliver these votes. It should not be overlooked, however, that Putin's takeover in the year 2000 served quite a few of Zhirinovsky's long time political aims. Russian military showed toughness in Chechnya, put an end to the deliberately weak position of the centre in comparison to peripheral regions, and foreign policy switched to a more self-assured and aggressive mode when the West did not reply to Putin's signals of cooperation after September 11, 2001 (Shevtsova, 2007).

These different situations reinforced the programmatic division between radical factions in the Duma. The CPRF was locked in an ideological mix that can best be described as socialist nationalism with community-oriented elements. In a way, Putin's distinct national profile as well as his rather successful economic policy could have served as a starting point for a less fierce confrontation. However, his authoritarian and bureaucratic style of government meant the oligarchic structure of resource exploitation remained in place, and the resulting extreme societal inequality could not be brought into line with the idea of a social community at the heart of the Russian nation. Consequently, the CPRF stayed on oppositionist course. The party had to take into account that its electorate makes up the lowest income quartiles, with more than two thirds of its supporters evaluating economic reform in negative terms (Rose et al., 2001, p. 430).

Zhirinovsky, on the other hand, had less problems of reconciling contradictory goals. For some years, the LDPR has been able to score on the one issue where it presents a structured position: imperial nationalism. With the party's active support, the Duma voiced its support for boycotts of Moldovan and Georgian products, and for an extremely hostile foreign policy against Estonia and Latvia. Also with regard to Serbia and Kosovo, a traditional sphere-of-influence position is voiced. Concerning internal policy, the LDPR shows another imperial characteristic by favouring the assimilation, rather than the expulsion, of non-Russian migrants.[15] In exchange for the regime's translation of imperial nationalist ideology into real world foreign policy, Zhirinovsky was able to exercise what is expected from a nationalist politician – to pay homage to an authoritarian leader by supporting him in parliament. In return, Putin acted generously by decorating Zhirinovsky with two Presidential

---

15   This was one of the LDPR's positions in the most recent Duma election campaign of 2007 (see *Vremya Zhirinovskogo: Moskva*, p. 2 – the campaign newspaper was widely distributed in Moscow in November 2007).

medals, one as a "Merited Lawmaker of the Russian Federation" (2000), another for "Merits for the Fatherland" (2006).[16]

Conclusion: the Russian case and the study of "Leninist legacies"

As discussed above, exploring the relevance of legacies for right-wing radicalism means to link a culture of the past to a culture of the present. With our
results from the Russian case study, we are now able to further specify the
implications of this approach.

First, and most importantly, the different profiles of political actors with
an ultra-nationalist agenda have shown that given symbols may be referred to
in diverging ways. The way political actors place symbols into their actions
and image-making is contingent. While the KPRF and the LDPR – and indeed
other parties from the Russian political mainstream – converge in important
elements of their ultra-nationalism, they have highlighted different elements of
perceived Russian legacies and combined them in original ways. Both parties
help themselves by choosing from a "'tool-kit' of symbols (...) and worldviews", and they have used them "in varying configurations to solve different
kinds of problems" (Kubik, 2003, p. 343).

Specifically, the Communist camp uses the traditional image of the nation as a socially coherent space. It would be an overstatement to say that
something like an industrialized "*sobornost'*" serves as the idealized point of
reference. Still, Zyuganov and others frequently refer to the Russian *narod* as
a non-alienable community (see previous chapter).[17] In turn, the LDPR puts a
stronger emphasis on the imperial dimension of the Russian nation, insisting
on external ethno-political dominance paired with domestic assimilation. Both
the socialist nationalist and the imperial nationalist harmonies are familiar to
all Russian conservatives, and indeed also to the small liberal camp that opposes Russian conservatism.

Second, the investigation has also shown that radical political actors are
not completely free in their choice of "pick[ing]-your-past-and-assert[ing]-its-
relevance-for-the-present" (Kubik, 2003, p. 319). Rather, developing a specific profile depends on context conditions and opportunity structures. In order
to again pick up an example from the Russian radical right, the appearance of
a strong leader in Russia's "super-presidential regime" (Holmes, 1993/1994)

---

16   The information can be found in the Russian version of Wikipedia: Жириновский,
      Владимир Вольфович, retrieved 12.3.2008.
17   These Russian terms have been defined and explained in section 3.1 of the given
      text.

decisively shaped the profile of Vladimir Zhirinovsky's party. Although itself a leading party, its big power ideology needed to cope with the inauguration of the president as the national political leader, and Zhirinovsky's rhetoric adapted accordingly.

Hence, the focus on culture inherent to most legacy research needs to be accompanied by a context of non-cultural elements, such as institutions or social developments. The study of post-socialist legacies has shown that innovation has only taken place if a cleared social space has allowed for a change of established pathways (Ekiert and Hanson, 2003, p. 30). Neither CPRF nor LDPR have the perspective for such an open field of action. They are bent towards conservatism because re-combining patterns of the past with patterns of the present is an option only government forces have. Important actors like Zhirinovsky or Zyuganov are in a position to encourage, influence and shape public discourse. They have managed to extract two distinctive tracks of Russian ultra-nationalism from a broad supply of traditional worldviews. As the situation stands, they will however not be capable of enlarging its supporting camp as long as the regime as a whole reiterates its anti-modernist and anti-Western rhetoric.

Third, it has become clear that dealing with legacies relies on a distinct concept of culture. Culture is neither seen in substantive terms, as is the case in objectivist approaches, nor does it evolve from an intensive rapprochement of an observer trying to interpret observed facts in an anthropological manner (as, for example, in Benedict, 1934). The legacy approach is closer to the latter variant, but offers a second order view. It is an interpretation of interpretations in the sense that worldviews of (political) actors are identified, described, and in the end classified.

The peculiar note of the legacy approach then consists in the difference of intentionality between first order and second order perceptions. While the second order observer's aim is, or should be, to properly make sense of the legacies concerned, the character of the first order observation is characterized by ideological intentions. To state an example of our case, it makes little difference if the perceptions of Russian nationalists concerning Russian imperialism are correct in a historiographic sense. Rather, these and other traditions need to be understood as "symbolic vehicles of meaning" (Swidler, 1986, p. 273). Within Russian society, reference symbols such as the nation or the orthodox church serve as a "grammatical structure" (Dittmer, 1977, p. 555) which lends orientation to intra-societal communication.

Fourth, the orientation of Russian nationalists towards their pasts puts into question the frequent use of the legacy approach as "Leninist". Certainly Jowitt also viewed the communist past as only one period with explanatory relevance among many others (see above). One specific hypothesis in Jowitt's work – that characteristics of the Communist phase might endanger democratic and capitalist transformation – has been transformed into an approach of systematically screening political developments of the present to perceptions of the past. The Leninist label has outgrown its original meaning. In our example of the Russian radical right, the weight of Leninist or Communist elements is indeed rather limited. Most elements of the useable past have their root in pre-socialist times. In that sense, the Leninist period serves as a lens through which even more distant historical periods can be viewed and originally interpreted. In contrast, symbols from the Communist time make little sense to Russian nationalists when taken in an isolated manner. As has been shown, this is largely due to the ambivalent character of many first order interpretations of the Soviet period. Again, Stalin and his ambiguous impact on the morality of the Russian nation can serve as an eminent example.

Do all these explanations lead to a causal link between legacies and right-wing radicalism in Russia? They do, but only in a weak sense (Kitschelt, 2003). Due to a lack of persistent research, it is not possible to more closely identify the concrete mechanisms that transmit the identified cultural patterns. While it is possible to make plausible assumptions "*why* some cultural patterns are replicated and others are not" (Kubik, 2003, p. 319), the current state of affairs does not allow for the identification of *how* they are fed into political life. For this, a much more thorough knowledge of Russian political processes would be needed. Concerning the governing actors, the relevant knowledge is restricted for those outside the government, due to the clandestine character of Kremlin politics. With regard to the Duma and its factions, the knowledge gap stems from the almost exclusive focus of pertinent research on institution building (Remington, 2001; Remington, 2007; Bos et al., 2003). This constitutes a further field of investigation into the relationship between legacies and political party actors that goes far beyond the forces of the radical right.

References

Allensworth, W., 1998. The Russian Question: Nationalism, Modernization, and Post-Communist Russia. Rowman & Littlefield, Lanham.

Anderson, B., 1983. Imagined Communities. Reflections on the Origin and Spread of Nationalism. Verso, London.

Anderson, J., 1994. Religion, State and Politics in the Soviet Union and the Successor States. Cambridge University Press, Cambridge.

Ash, T.G., 1999/2000. Zehn Jahre danach. Transit, 5-16.

Behrens, K., 2002. Die Russische Orthodoxe Kirche. Segen für die "neuen Zaren"? Schöningh, Paderborn.

Benedict, R., 1934. Patterns of Culture. Houghton Mifflin, Boston.

Berlin, I., 1978 (1948). Russian Thinkers. Penguin, Harmondsworth.

Byerdyaew, N., 1992 (1915/18) Duša Rossii. In: Maslin, M.A. (Ed.), Russkaya Ideja. Respublika, Moskva.

Bönker, F., Wielgohs, J., 2003. Does culture matter? Changing views on the cultural legacy of the state-socialist past. In: Minkenberg, M.,Beichelt, T. (Eds.), Cultural Legacies in Post-Socialist Europe. The Role of the Various Pasts in the Current Transformation Process. Frankfurt Institut für Transformationsstudien, Frankfurt/Oder.

Bos, E., Mommsen, M., Steinsdorff, S. V. (Eds.), 2003. Das russische Parlament. Schule der Demokratie? Leske+Budrich, Opladen.

Bremzen, A., Egorov, G., Shakin, D., 2006. Electoral Mandate and Voting Behavior: Evidence from Russian State Duma, Moscow, Working Paper # WP/2006/061 (Российская экономическая школа).

Buhbe, M., Makarenko, B.I., 2007. Das Mehrparteiensystem im neuen Russland. In: Buhbe, M., Gorzka, G. (Eds.), Russland heute. Rezentralisierung des Staates unter Putin. VS Verlag, Wiesbaden.

Bunce, V., 2005. The national idea: imperial legacies and post-communist pathways in Eastern Europe. East European Politics and Society, 19, 406-442.

Carrère d'Encausse, H., 1978. L'empire eclaté. La révolte des nations en URSS. Flammarion, Paris.

Comisso, E., 1997. Legacies of the past or new institutions: the struggle over restitution in Hungary. In: Crawford, B., Lijphart, A. (Eds.), Liberalisation and Leninist Legacies. Comparative Perspectives on Democratic Transitions. University of California Press, Berkeley.

Crawford, B., Lijphart, A., 1997. Old legacies, new institutions. Explaining political and economic trajectories in post-communist regimes. In: Crawford, B., Lijphart, A. (Eds.), Liberalisation and Leninist Legacies. Comparative Perspectives on Democratic Transitions. University of California Press, Berkeley.

Devlin, J., 1999. Slavophiles and Commissars. Enemies of Democracy in Modern Russia. MacMillan, Houndsmills.

Dittmer, L., 1977. Political culture and political symbolism: toward a theoretical synthesis. World Politics 29, 552-583.

Dunlop, J.B., 1983. The Faces of Contemporary Russian Nationalism. Princeton University Press, Princeton.

Dunlop, J.B., 1995. The Russian orthodox church as an "empire-saving" institution. In: Bordeaux, M. (Ed.), The Politics of Religion in Russia and the New States of Eurasia. M.E. Sharpe, New York.

Ekiert, G., Hanson, S.E., 2003. Time, space, and institutional change in Central and Eastern Europe. In Ekiert, G., Hanson, S.E. (Eds.) Capitalism and Democracy in Central and Eastern Europe. Cambridge University Press, Cambridge.

Fish, M.S., 2005. Democracy Derailed in Russia. The Failure of Open Politics. Cambridge University Press, Cambridge.

Gel'man, V., 2006. From "feckless pluralism" to "dominant power politics"? The transformation of Russia's party system. Democratization 13, 545-561.

Gellner, E., 1983. Nations and Nationalism. Cornell University Press, Ithaca.

Glass, M., 2003. Profile der fünf wichtigsten russischen Parteien. Russland-Kurzanalysen, 3-7. http://www.laender-analysen.de/russland/pdf/Russland analysen004.pdf.

Gleason, A., 1985. Slavophilism. In: Terras, V. (Ed.), Handbook of Russian Literature. Yale University Press, New Haven.

Gregor, A.J., 1998. Fascism and the new Russian nationalism. Communist and Post-Communist Studies 31, 1-15.

Gudkov, L., 2007. Rußlands Systemkrise. Negative Mobilisierung und kollektiver Zynismus. Osteuropa, 57, 3-13.

Hendley, K., 2007. Putin and the law. In: Herspring, D. R. (Ed.), Putin's Russia. Past Imperfect, Future Uncertain. Rowman&Littlefield, Lanham.

Holmes, S., 1993/1994. Super presidentialism and its problems. East European Constitutional Review 123-126.

Horvath, R., 2005 The Legacy of Dissent. Dissidents, Democratisation and Radical Nationalism in Russia Routledge Curzon, New York.

Hosking, G., 2002. Imperial identities in Russia: some concluding thoughts. In: Chulos, C. J., Remy, J. (Eds.), Imperial and National Identities in Pre-revolutionary, Soviet, and Post-Soviet Russia. Suomalaisen Kirjallisuuden Seure - Finnish Literature Society, Helsinki.

Jowitt, K., 1992. The Leninist legacy. In: Jowitt, K. (Ed.), New World Disorder: The Leninist Distinction. University of California Press, Berkeley.

Kitschelt, H., 2003. Accounting for postcommunist regime diversity: what counts as a good cause? In: Ekiert, G., Hanson, S.E. (Eds.), Capitalism and Democracy in Central and Eastern Europe. Cambridge University Press, Cambridge.

Kitschelt, H., Mansfeldova, Z., Markowski, R., Tóka, G., 1999. Post-Communist Party Systems. Competition, Representation, and Inter Party Cooperation. Cambridge University Press, Cambridge.

Kopstein, J., 2003. Postcommunist democracy. Legacies and outcomes (review article). Comparative Politics 35, 231-250.

Krahn, C., 1963. Russia: messianism-marxism. Journal of the American Academy of Religion 31, 210-215.

Kubik, J., 2003. Cultural legacies of state socialism: history making and cultural-political entrepreneurship in postcommunist Poland and Russia. In: Ekiert, G., Hanson, S.E. (Eds.), Capitalism and Democracy in Central and Eastern Europe. Cambridge University Press, Cambridge.

Laqueur, W., 1993. Black Hundred. The Rise of the Extreme Right in Russia. Harper Collins, New York.

Laruele, M. (Ed.), 2007. Le rouge et le noir. Extrême droite et nationalisme en Russie. CNRS Editions, Paris.

Levitski, S., Way, L.A., 2002. The rise of competitive authoritarianism. Journal of Democracy 13, 51-65.

Lipset, S.M., 1964. The sources of the radical right. In: Bell, D. (Ed.), The Radical Right. Garden City.

Masaryk, T.G., 1992 (1913). Russische Geistes und Religionsgeschichte. 2 Bände (Originaltitel: Rußland und Europa. Studien über die geistigen Strömungen in Russland). Eichborn, Frankfurt.

Maslin, M.A., 1992. Velikoe Neznanie Rossii. In: Maslin, M.A. (Ed.), Russkaya ideja. Respublika, Moskva.

Minkenberg, M., 1998. Die neue radikale Rechte im Vergleich. USA, Frankreich, Deutschland. Westdeutscher Verlag, Opladen/Wiesbaden.

Mommsen, M., Nußerger, A., 2007. Das System Putin. C.H.Beck, München.

Moroz, E., 2007. Le néo-paganisme, "foi ethnique", contre-culture ou entrisme politique. In: Laruelle, M. (Ed.), Le rouge et le noir. Extrême droite et nationalisme en Russie. CNRS Editions, Paris.

Mudde, C., 2007. Populist Radical Right Parties in Europe. Oxford University Press, Oxford.

Oschlies, W., 1995. Wladimir Schirinowski. Der häßliche Russe und das postkommunistische Osteuropa. Böhlau, Köln.

Oulanoff, H., 1985. Narodnost'. In: Terras, V. (Ed.), Handbook of Russian Literature. Yale University Press, New Haven.

Piirainen, T., 2002. The Sisyphean mission: new national identity in post-communist Russia. In: Chulos, C.J., Remy, J. (Eds.), Imperial and National Identities in Pre-revolutionary, Soviet, and Post-Soviet Russia. Suomalaisen Kirjallisuuden Seure - Finnish Literature Society, Helsinki.

Remington, T.F., 2001. The Russian Parliament. Institutional Evolution in a Transitional Regime, 1989-1999. Yale University Press, New Haven.

Remington, T.F., 2006. Presidential support in the Russian Ssate Duma. Legislative Studies Quarterly 31, 5-32.

Remington, T.F., 2007. Putin, the parliament, and the party system. In: Herspring, D.R. (Ed.), Putin's Russia. Past Imperfect, Future Uncertain. Rowman&Littlefield, Lanham.

Remington, T.F., 2008. Patronage and the party of power: president-parliament relations nnder Vladimir Putin. Europe-Asia Studies 60, 959-987.

Rose, R., Munro, N., White, S., 2001. Voting in a floating party system: the 1999 Duma election. Europe-Asia Studies 53, 419-443.

Rykhlin, M., 2006. Mit dem Recht des Stärkeren. Russische Kultur in Zeiten der "gelenkten Demokratie". Suhrkamp, Frankfurt.

Sartori, G., 1976. Parties and Party Systems. Cambridge University Press, Cambridge.

Scheuch, E., Klingemann, H.-D., 1967. Theorie des Rechtsradikalismus in westlichen Industriegesellschaften. Hamburger Jahrbuch für Wirtschafts- und Gesellschaftspolitik 12, 11-29.

Shevtsova, L., 2007. Russia - Lost in Transition. Carnegie Emdowment for International Peace, Washington, D.C.

Shlapentokh, D., 1999. The illusions and realities of Russian nationalism. The Washington Quarterly 23, 173-186.

Slater, W., 1998. Russia's imagined history: visions of the soviet past and the new 'Russian idea'. Journal of Communist Studies and Transition Politics 14, 69-86.

Stykow, P., 2008. Die Transformation des russischen Parteiensystems: Regimestabilisierung durch personalisierte Institutionalisierung. Zeitschrift für Parlamentsfragen 39, 772-794.

Swidler, A., 1986. Culture in action: symbols and strategies. American Sociological Review 51, 273-286.

Tismaneanu, V., 2007. Leninist legacies, pluralist dilemmas. Journal of Democracy 18, 34-39.

Tolz, V., 1997. The radical right in post-communist Russian politics. In: Merkl, P., Weinberg, L. (Eds.), The Revival of Right-Wing Extremism in the Nineties. Frank Cass, London.

Umland, A., 2006. Neue ideologische Fusionen im russischen Antidemokratismus: Westliche Konzepte, antiwestliche Doktrinen und das postsowjetische politische Spektrum. In: Backes, U., Jesse, E. (Eds.), Gefährdungen der Freiheit: Extremistische Ideologien im Vergleich. Vandenhoeck & Ruprecht, Göttingen.

Umland, A., 2007. Vers une société incivile? Contextualisation du déclin des partis politiques d'extrême droite en Russie post-soviétique. In: Laruelle, M. (Ed.), Le rouge et le noir. Extrême droite et nationalisme en Russie. CNRS Editions, Paris.

Vähä, E., 2002. Out of oppression into brotherhood: the meaning of the October revolution as part of national identity in soviet history textbooks. In: Chulos, C.J., Remy, J. (Eds.), Imperial and National Identities in Pre-revolutionary, Soviet, and Post-Soviet Russia. Suomalaisen Kirjallisuuden Seure - Finnish Literature Society, Helsinki.

Vujačić, V., 2003. From class to nation: left, right, and the ideological and institutional roots of post-communist "national socialism". East European Politics and Societies 17, 359-392.

White, S., 2006. Russians and their party system. Demokratizatsiya, a7-22.

White, S., 2009. The Duma election in Russia, December 2007. Electoral Studies 28, 171-173.

White, S., Gill, G., Slider, D., 1993. The Politics of Transition. Shaping a Post-Soviet Future. Cambridge University Press, Cambridge.

Williams, C., Hanson, S., 1999. National-socialism, left patriotism, or superimperialism? The 'radical right' in Russia. In: Ramet, S. (Ed.), The Radical Right in Central and Eastern Europe since 1989. Penn State Press, University Park, PA.

The League of Polish Families between East and West, past and present

Sarah L. de Lange, Simona Guerra[1]

ABSTRACT: Historical legacies play an important role in the rise of radical right parties in Central and Eastern Europe. This article conducts an in-depth study of the trajectory of a particular radical right party, the League of Polish Families, in a particular Central and East European country, Poland. The central objective of the article is to highlight that, although there are important similarities between the League of Polish Families and other radical right parties in both Central and Eastern Europe and Western Europe, the League of Polish Families differs in some respects, such as the composition of electorate, ideology from these parties. The article shows that the observed differences have their roots in the Polish historical legacy, that on some accounts deviates from the historical legacies present in other Central and East European countries.

Introduction

To explain party success in Central and East European countries many authors have pointed to the way in which historical legacies shape opportunities for party breakthrough and persistence, arguing that experiences with communism and subsequent pathways to transition determine the way in which parties have flourished and faltered. One particular way in which communist and transitional legacies influence present day politics is through the fertile breeding ground they have created for antiliberal alternatives to mainstream parties (Jowitt, 1992). Many Central and East European countries have recently experienced the emergence of radical right parties (RRPs), which have sometimes been remarkably successful. The success of RRPs in Central and East European countries has been linked to historical legacies in two ways. First, it has been interpreted as a consequence of the widespread discontent that has accompanied the transformation of state-led economies to market

1   The authors would like to thank the participants in the conference „The Radical Right in post-1989 Central and Eastern Europe – the Role of Legacies" for their helpful comments on earlier drafts of the article. Sarah de Lange is grateful to the Robert Schuman Centre for Advanced Studies for awarding her a Jean Monnet Fellowship, which enabled her to work on this article.

economies in the post-1989 era (Anastasakis, 2002; Bayer 2002; Beichelt and Minkenberg, 2002; Minkenberg, 2002). In this interpretation the success of RRPs is a reaction to the transformation process, which has stirred anxieties in many ways analogous to those associated with the process of modernization in Western Europe. Second, it has been understood as the result of the renascence of a shared Central and East European culture that focuses on a strong sense of national belonging, that is, as "the result of the re-emergence of deeply, culturally ingrained perception of social belonging, and of the foundations of the polity, in which the social whole is considered prior to the individual, and in which local culture is valued differently from Western culture" (Blokker, 2005, p. 1; Marks, 2006). Hence, in this form continuity exists between pre-war far right movements and present day RRPs, which has been disrupted by the period of communist rule.

Although each historical in nature, the two explanations are markedly different. The first explanation transposes an argument that has been used to explain the success of RRPs in Western Europe to Central and East European. The second explanation underlies the singularity of the Central and East European experience and concentrates on what sets Central and East European countries apart from West European countries. Each of the explanations has its merits and they are not necessarily mutually exclusive. We argue that it is fruitful to combine the two explanations, because in most countries an important degree of continuity exists between different historical and politically relevant periods. To come to a satisfactory explanation of the breakthrough and persistence of RRPs in Central and East European, it is vital to take each of these periods into consideration. We contend that historical legacies, which comprise many events and processes, such as the processes of nation and state formation, the activities of far right movement during the early 20th century and the interbellum, the experience of communist rule, and the subsequent transition to democracy, can hinder or promote the success of RRPs in Central and East European in two ways. First, legacies shape voters' attitudes towards politics in general and towards political issues in particular, determining whether a fertile breeding ground for RRPs exists. In other words, legacies have an impact on the electoral opportunity structure or the *demand* for RRPs. Second, legacies influence the dimensionality of the political space and the positions parties take in this space. In other words, legacies also have an impact on the political opportunity structure or the *supply* of RRPs.

To demonstrate the important role historical legacies play in explaining the success of RRPs we examine the rise and demise of the League of Polish Families (*Liga Polskich Rodzin*: LPR). We argue that the success of this party is explained by the existence of a favourable electoral and political opportunity structure for a RRP in Poland.[2] More specifically, we demonstrate that the Polish historical legacy has created a fertile breeding ground for RRPs in general, and for a party that campaigns on a programme that combines Catholic conservatism and nationalism in particular. The LPR has correctly assessed the existence of this electoral and political niche and positioned itself strategically in the Polish political space. We compare the rise of the LPR to that of other RRPs and conclude that, although our explanation for the success of this party contains certain idiosyncratic elements, it does provide important insights that can be used to understand the success of RRPs in Europe at large.

The Polish historical legacy

Polish history is first and foremost characterized by the prominent role Catholicism has played in shaping Polish politics and society. From one historical period to the next it has been Catholicism that emerges as the common denominator, providing a link between various historical and contemporary political events. The Catholic roots of Poland date back to the ninth century, when the Piast court adopted Latin Christianity as the official cult in the Polish Kingdom. Casanova (2003, pp. 14-15) believes this decision had two strategic objectives. Internally it integrated "the expanding royal domains" and "several Slavic tribal cults", while externally the Papacy granted the same strategic and geopolitical prestige to the kingdom as to its neighbours, most notably the German Holy Roman Empire and Bohemia. Catholicism gained more ground in medieval Poland and served as a basis for mobilization of resistance during the three partitions (in 1772, 1793, and 1795 respectively). To overcome the political annihilation caused by these partitions, the notion of the Polish state was separated from that of the Polish nation. While the former ceased to exist, the latter flourished. Romantic nationalism and a kind of Slavic messianism that promoted the idea of Polish martyrdom seeking to re-

---

2   Although RRPs have been successful in many Central and East European countries, the Polish case is particularly relevant to students of both East European and West European politics. Poland has a crucial position in Central and Eastern Europe (Lewis, 1999; Markowski, 2000) and developments in the country are usually interpreted as "an exception to, or magnifier of" developments elsewhere in the region (Rupnik, 2007, p. 18).

unite nation and state was embedded with many symbols from Catholicism, most importantly the cross and the icon of Our Lady of Częstochowa (Zubrzycki, 2006). Moreover, the partitions were often described in pamphlets, poems, plays and songs that contained religious metaphors and allegories, which enabled the wide dissemination of the idea of Poland as the Christ of nations (*ibid.*, pp. 43-49, Casanova, 2003, p. 17).[3]

These developments had important political repercussions. During the interwar period, Polish politics was strongly influenced by Roman Dmowski's National Democracy (or *endecja*). Dmowski, a seminal ideologist and skilled diplomat, presented a "plebeian" and "integral" nationalism that pictured Jews and Germans as "a direct threat to the cultural identity and economic survival of the Polish petit bourgeoisie and, thus, to the integrity and ethnic cohesion of the Polish nation" (Walicki, 2000, pp. 14-15). Although the nationalism promoted by Dmowski was initially secular – the National Democracy leader at first believed religion belonged to the private sphere – it became more and more inspired by Catholicism as the years went by. In his pamphlet *The Church, the Nation, and the State* Dmowski argued that Catholicism and Polish nationalism could not be seen independently of one another. He declared that "Catholicism is not an appendage to Polishness [...] it is embedded in its essence, and in a large measure it *is* its essence. To attempt to dissociate Catholicism from Polishness, and to separate the Polish nation from its religion and the church, means to destroy the very essence of that nation" (quoted in Walicki, 2000, p. 32). Thus, at the end of the 1920s the notion of the "Polak-Katolik" had taken root in the Polish minds. Polish national identity had invariantly become a Catholic identity, which united a citizenry otherwise divided by class and territory. The "symbiosis between Catholicism and Polishness, and between church and civil society, was achieved through a long process in which national identity was Catholicized and Catholicism was nationalized" (Zubrzycki, 2006, p. 49).

After the Second World War Polish history evolves around the Soviet occupation and the transition to democracy after 1989. Specific to the Polish experience with communism is the fact that the communist regime in Poland never had a totalitarian character (Linz and Stepan, 1996). In fact, Poland probably qualifies as the most liberal and consensus-oriented of the communist regimes that existed between 1945 and 1989 in Central and Eastern

---

3   Officially, Polish Catholics were urged by the Church to stay away from worldly affairs, because the Holy See had recognized the Partitions of Poland (Zubrzycki, 2006, pp. 48-49).

Europe. It is the only country that experienced an authoritarian regime, in contrast to the totalitarian regimes that took over in, for example, Bulgaria and Romania. As Linz and Stepan (1996, p. 255) argue "Polish society resists classification as having ever been a fully installed totalitarian regime". The Polish communist regime tolerated a modest level of dissent and social contestation and, as such, left room for the establishment of a mass democratic opposition movement.

In the 1980s the movement, organized around the trade union federation Solidarity (*Solidarność*), was the first non-communist trade union in a communist country and gradually grew into a broad social movement that united many anti-communist activists on the basis of their shared opposition to the communist regime. The movement played a crucial role in Poland's transition to democracy, as the Roundtable Negotiations between the regime and the Solidarity-led opposition eventually brought about the first semi-free elections in 1989 and made it possible for Solidarity leader Lech Wałęsa to become the first elected president of Poland. As we will demonstrate below, the opposition between communists and anti-communists still persists today, not in the last place as a result of the lasting influence Solidarity has had on Polish politics.

Furthermore, Solidarity represented a national movement bringing together Polish citizens from various backgrounds. They were united by their shared norms and values, which were primarily derived from Catholicism. In fact, during the Soviet occupation communism quickly became identified as yet another episode of foreign occupation and the Catholic Church "took in its 'traditional' role of guardian and defender of the nation against a 'foreign' state" (Zubrzycki, 2006, p. 60; Eberts, 1998).[4] It provided the Solidarity movement with the resources it desperately needed: an infrastructure, as well as financial and moral support from the West. Churches became the place to meet for dissidents and intellectuals across the country and Catholic priests would organize open air masses at Solidarity demonstrations.[5] What is more,

---

4   In 1945 an attempt had been made to reconcile Catholicism and communism by the foundation of Pax, an organization within the Catholic Church approved by the communist regime. However, from 1956 onwards the regime refused to fund the organisation. Moreover, Cardinal Stefan Wyszyński was sent into exile in 1953 and Pax lost its approval from the Vatican. Hence, the plan of the regime to create an organization that could challenge the moral authority and prominent position of the Polish Church failed miserably (Sawicki, 1982, pp. 13-14).

5   We do not disregard the fact that the role of Catholic Church has sometimes been ambiguous. It maintained close ties with the Soviet Union in the 1940s and 1950s,

Solidarity leader Wałęsa presented himself as a religious man, always carrying a badge depicting the Madonna of Częstochowa with him. When the Cardinal of Cracow, Karol Wojtyła, was elected to the papacy in 1978 the position of the Catholic Church was fortified. The subsequent visit of John Paul II to Poland in June 1979 inspired Solidarity to organize a series of strikes in the summer of 1980, which ended in a significant victory for the opposition movement. More importantly, the support of the Church also instilled the kind of moral authority on the Solidarity movement that the communist regime lacked. The link between Solidarity and the Church lifted the symbolic meaning of religion up to a level in which it acquired unique legitimate authority. Eventually the synergy created between Solidarity and the Church transcended into what Linz and Stepan (1996, p. 272) have described as "Poland's pioneering and heroic path to democratic transition via ethical civil society". In sum, the Polish communist experience further accrued the symbolic and ethical presence of Catholicism and the Church, already established earlier in Polish history, and made it an important source of political mobilization.[6]

A fertile breeding ground for radical right parties

The Polish historical legacy has created a fertile ground for antiliberal sentiments and movements that promote nationalism and populism. The transition from communism to democracy has provided Poland with an opportunity to redefine its national identity, while exposure to the processes of globalization and European integration have increased awareness of Poland's 'Polishness'. Both developments have paved the way for the resurgence of nationalist sentiments and the emergence of nationalist movements. Given that communism represented a "cosmopolitan universalist ideology" (Crawford and Lijphart, 1997, p. 22), cultural and ethnic differences were ignored or denied for several decades. Now that cosmopolitan universalism is no longer the only acceptable ideology, Poles rediscover those differences, as well as

---

as it helped to calm down internal revolts in exchange for concessions with regard to the question of religious education in public schools. We believe, however, that in many ways the ambiguous position of the Church reinforced the symbolic power of religion, since it was the only national institution that had sufficient legitimacy to bargain with the communist regime.

6   This has happened in spite of the erosion of Poles' general approval for the Church as an institution that is actively involved in politics since the late 1980s (Jasińska-Kania and Marody, 2004, pp. 109-131). It seems that the Polish population accepts that the Church plays a prominent role in their daily life and the public domain, but wishes to keep the direct influence the Church has on politics to a minimum.

the Polish nationalist heritage of the interwar period.[7] Additionally, immediately after the transition to democracy Poland has sought to join the European Union. Bücker (2007, p. 123) notes in this respect that:

The EU is one external factor that fosters the proliferation of protective nationalism among certain segments of its member states' populations, and this development might indeed be more salient in the new, Eastern European member states than in the old ones, simply because the EU has been much more visible in the new member states since the breakdown of socialism.

Moreover, as a result of communism the relationship between Polish citizens and Polish parties is weak and highly problematic. Decades of communist rule have given negative connotations to the concept of 'the party', which has caused a general mistrust of parties (Szczerbiak, 2006, p. 116). For this reason volatility is high and new parties get a foot in the door. Especially new parties that promote anti-party discourse and present themselves as popular movements rather than traditional political parties are likely to attract sufficient voters to enter parliament. What is more, under communist rule a populist way of thinking has developed among Polish intellectuals, who conceive of Polish society as divided in two homogeneous groups: the morally right non-communist people and the corrupt communist elite (Mudde, 2000). Given that this dichotomy has always been broadly adopted by prominent dissidents, including former opposition leader and President Lech Wałęsa, it has achieved a legitimate status in Polish politics. As the dissidents of the communist era are the right-wing party leaders of today, and they continue to frame political oppositions in antagonistic terms because they think of a transition to democracy as "unfinished business" (Kubik and Linch, 2006, pp. 10-11; Jasiewicz, 2003), populism is an integral part of Polish politics.

It is important to underline the role that Lech Wałęsa and his Solidarity movement have played in fostering populist tendencies in Polish politics. The Solidarity leader fulfilled two distinct roles. On the one hand, he acted as the leader of a popular movement and hence was the embodiment of civil society. On the other hand, he was a political leader who in the post-communist era served as president. The fact that he fulfilled both roles simultaneously blurred the border between ethical civil society and political society. Wałęsa

---

7   At the same time it is important to note that Poland is one of the most ethnically homogeneous countries in Central and Eastern Europe. During the Second World War the Jewish population has by and large been exterminated, and after the war Eastern minorities have been incorporated in the Soviet Union. Today roughly 95% of inhabitants of Poland are ethnic Poles (Zubrzycki, 2006, p. 62).

himself always stated he acted on behalf of Solidarity, which he saw first and foremost as a social movement. Hence, the Solidarity leader derived his legitimacy from his position as representative of civil society, and not from his position as a political actor, or as a representative of the state. In addition, Wałęsa frequently resorted to apolitical, or even antipolitical rhetoric, which made it difficult for Polish voters to re-acquaint themselves with the rhetoric of democratic and pluralist elections. In the first free presidential elections in 1990 he presented himself as a "non-party candidate", which reinforced the idea of a non-partisan or apolitical democracy (Linz and Stepan, 1996, pp. 273-274). In light of the overlap between the communist regime and the system of one party rule, Wałęsa's refusal to define himself as a partisan further reinforced the distinction between 'us,' anti-communists, and 'them,' former communists, embedding the 'us' in the 'moral discourse of "truth" and the existential claim of "living in truth"' (Linz and Stepan, 1996, pp. 270-271). Thus, within the Solidarity movement unity was strengthened by the shared opposition to communism and established politics, which legitimized populism as an ideology.

Polish politics in the post-1989 era

From the inception of the Polish party system in 1989 the communist legacy has shaped the way in which parties and voters think about political divisions. The communist versus anti-communist divide has been one of the most important political phenomenon in Poland in the 1990s and first years of the 21st century and coincides with other value-oriented divisions, such as the one between seculars and Catholics (Jasiewicz, 2007). The opposition between former communists and anti-communists is traceable to the first free elections held 1991. For the persistence of this opposition in the post-1989 era the presidential struggle between Aleksander Kwaśniewski, a member of the former communists, and Lech Wałęsa, leader of the Solidarity movement, in 1995 has been crucial. These elections polarized the Polish electorate on the basis of their attitudes towards the communist past. During the government led by Jerzy Buzek, which was in office from 1997 to 2001, the *Sejm* could still be viewed as divided among those who supported the former communist regime (37%) and those opposing it (35%). The relevance of this distinction has been further increased by the lustration law that came into effect in 2007 (Rupnik, 2007).

Religious divisions largely overlap with the division between former communists and anti-communists. Because of the role played by religion in the communist era, former communist are usually viewed as secular and former anti-communists as religious. To give an indication, of the deputies who belonged to right-wing parties in the 1997-2001 *Sejm* 45% declared that they attended mass every week, and another 16% stated that they go to Church less frequently. Of the deputies that defined themselves as anti-communists 60% also attended mass at least once a week. Among the deputies who belonged to left-wing parties regular Church visits were far less frequent. Of the politicians who belonged to the Democratic Left Alliance (*Sojusz Lewicy Demokratycznej*: SLD) a mere 3% attended mass every week (Castle and Taras, 2002, p. 110-111). The pervasiveness of the religious divide persists even today. According to Markowski (2000, p. 7):

> The salience of the religious dimension derives from the on-going blurring effects of the re-shaping of the social structure. It is the least costly vehicle of transparent communication between elites and masses, in the case of complicated, (still) incomprehensible, social repositioning and the inability of substantial of the populace to correctly identify the relevant representatives of their socio-economic interests.

Together these oppositions make for a political division that is probably most accurately described as that of "secular and libertarian cosmopolitans vs. religious authoritarian nationalists" (Kitschelt et al., 1999, p. 231). The traditional left-right division, that pits those in favour of more intervention in the economy against those that seek to realize a free market economy, has had a far less pervasive effect on Polish politics. As Kitschelt et al. (1999, p. 270) observe the "strong mobilization of anti-communist forces around the Catholic Church and the ability of the former communists to embrace fundamental socio-economic and political reform during and after a negotiated democratic transition suggest that economic issues do not capture the bulk of inter-party divisions". In recent years economic issues have gained more salience in elections, but the overlap with the cosmopolitan-nationalist dimension has been substantial.[8] Consequentially, the gap between secular, liberal, and libertarian cosmopolitans and religious, social, and authoritarian nationalists has widened and polarization has increased.

---

8   Since the 2005 campaigns for parliamentary and presidential elections, for example, the right has framed the elections as a struggle between liberal and social-solidaristic forces (Szczerbiak, 2007).

In sum, the interpretation given to the concepts 'left' and 'right' differs in Poland from the conventional interpretation of these concepts in West European politics. The left-right distinction has a strong moral and cultural connotation, with the left defined in terms of positive attitudes towards the communist past, liberal social values, secularism, and opposition to a significant public role for the church and the right defined in terms of de-communization and attitudes towards the past, conservative social values, high levels of religiosity, and promotion of an active role of the church in public life. Defined as such the left-right division has had a profound impact on inter-party competition in Poland. For more than a decade two distinct camps have competed for voters and governments have been formed on either side of the left-right divide (Szczerbiak, 2001, p. 93). And although party switching has been quite frequent in Poland, cross-overs from the left to the right and *vice versa* have been largely absent. Moreover, attempts to bridge the divide between left and right have consistently failed (Szczerbiak, 2001).

In spite of the dominance of the left-right distinction, the right-wing camp has always been extremely fragmented. It has been united by a shared opposition to communism but at the same time divided by ideological heterogeneity. The right includes currents as diverse as Christian Democracy, clerical-nationalism, and liberalism (Friszke, 1990; Hanley et al., 2007). Moreover, these ideological currents consist of geographically-based subgroups that put different ideological emphases. Consequentially, in the elections held in the immediate post-1989 years many different right-wing parties competed and entered parliament. In 1996 these parties decided to join forces in the broadly organized Solidarity Electoral Action (*Akcja Wyborcza Solidarność*: AWS). The AWS espoused an eclectic mix of "socially conservative trade union-oriented corporatism, Christian Democracy, economically interventionist and liberal forms of Catholic nationalism and less overtly Church-inspired strands of liberal-conservatism" (Hanley et al., 2007, p. 43). As a result of this ideological heterogeneity the electoral coalition dissolved in 2001 and since then several right-wing parties have been represented again in the *Sejm*, the most important being the Civic Platform (*Platforma Obywatelska*: PO) and Law and Justice (*Prawo i Sprawiedliwość*: PiS).[9] The fragmentation of the Polish right has seriously reduced its electoral success. Even though roughly 40% of Polish citizens identified themselves as either 'right' or 'centre-right' at the time of

9   Castle and Taras (2002; see also Szczerbiak, 2004; 2006; Szczerbiak and Hanley, 2004) also point to the weak institutionalisation of the AWS as a reason for the implosion of the electoral coalition in 2001.

the 2001 elections, only 23% of the voters supported parties that qualified as such (Castle and Taras, 2002, p. 132).

The fragmentation of the right also leaves room for the emergence of a party that specifically caters to voters with far right attitudes, most notably voters that identify with Catholic nationalism. Already in the early 1990s voter surveys indicated the existence of a mid-sized reservoir of far right voters in Poland, with over 15% of the population positioned at the far right of the political spectrum.[10] This figure was lower than in the Czech Republic, but higher than in Hungary. For these voters religious questions were especially salient (Kitschelt et al., 1999, p. 290). It appears that the right failed to pick up on the presence of this electoral niche, since none of the right-wing parties represented in the 1990s actively promoted religious issues. On the contrary, many of the right-wing parties campaigned on an economically and culturally liberal programme.

The LPR: breakthrough without persistence

For this reason some scholars predicted the rise of a Polish RRP during the 1990s. Ost (1999, p. 85), for example, hypothesized that "if the former communists in power discredit the left in the mid-1990s the way former Solidarity leaders discredited liberalism in the early-1990s, we might see the emergence of a strong national populist movement". However, a successful RRP did not emerge during this period. Prior to 2001 several populist parties contested elections, but none of these passed the threshold for parliamentary representation. Party 'X' (*Partia 'X'*), for example, rejected both left- and right-wing ideologies and presented itself as a 'third force' that spoke on behalf of the true Poles. The party did not become a durable actor in Polish politics, even though its founder, Stanislaw Tymiński, gained 25.75% of the votes in the second round of the 1990 presidential elections.

In 2001 the fate of RRPs in Poland changed when the LPR gained 7.87% of the votes in the parliamentary elections. Officially founded on 23 June 1999 as a coalition of several splinter movements and parties, most notably Jan Łopuszański's Polish Agreement (*Porozumienie Polskie*: PP), Antoni Macieriewicz's Catholic-National Movement (*Ruch Katolicko-Narodowe*: RKN) and Maciej and Roman Giertych's National Party (*Stronnictwo Naro-*

---

10   In a voter survey conducted in 1992 9.6% of the questioned voters located themselves on position 6 on a left-right scale that ranged from 1 to 7. Another 5.9% of the questioned voters located themselves on position 7. In 1993 these figures had risen to 11.0% and 6.6%, respectively.

dowe: SN), the party capitalized on the widespread opposition to EU accession and Catholic-nationalist sentiments of a portion of Polish voters (Paszkiewicz, 2004, pp. 108-109). Programmatically the emphasis was on "Catholicism, the Nation and Patriotism", whilst the main campaign issues were the renegotiation of the accession treaty and a stop on foreign investment in Poland. The party was supported by Father Tadeusz Rydzyk, who had a fundamental role as initiator of a Catholic and national movement, and the popular radio station *Radio Maryja*. Rydzyk founded the Catholic station in 1991 and was able to create a broad network of listeners who supported "a conservative, nationalistic, and anti-liberal agenda". Although sometimes described as "a strong patriot" and a "guardian of religious values, someone who rallies against corruption and immorality in government and society", Rydzyk is a controversial figure (Eaglin, 2008, p. 3). He has been accused of anti-Semitism and xenophobia and has actively campaigned against Poland's accession to the EU, as he believed that it "would impose a moral behavior on the country" (*ibid*, p. 1). With the support of Father Rydzyk and Radio Maria the LPR was able to reach significant parts of the Polish population and pass the threshold for representation in the 2001 elections (Pankowski and Kornak, 2005, p. 168).

Table 1 documents the electoral rise and demise of the LPR. The electoral breakthrough of the party occurred in 2001, when it gained sufficient support to send 38 deputies to the *Sejm*. The rise of the LPR is best understood in light of the emergence of the EU as a political issue, which was the direct consequence of the immanent accession of Poland to the EU. The electoral growth of the LPR continued in the run up to and aftermath of the Copenhagen Summit, which took place on 13 December 2002. At this summit the final conditions for Poland's accession to the European Union were discussed. Of course, the summit itself, the prospect of accession, and the promise of a referendum on the question of accession heightened the salience of the question of EU integration, but initially the Polish public reacted positively to the content of the accession agreement. Gradually the sentiment changed and a more skeptical attitude towards the EU developed among Poles (CBOS, 2004). However, established parties had their hands tied and could not openly express any opposition to the EU in general, and the accession treaty in particular. Even the Polish Peasant Party (*Polskie Stronnictwo Ludowe*: PSL), traditionally a defender of rural interests, had no choice but to support the agreement since it participated in the government coalition lead by the SLD. This left the LPR as the only party that was overtly critical of the accession agreement. For this reason it was relatively easy for the party to gain more support among Catholic-nationalist and consequentially Eurosceptic parts of the population. In the subsequent accession referendum and elections to the European Parliament the LPR candidates presented themselves as the only ones that could defend Polish values and interest in Brussels. This message struck a cord with Catholic-nationalist voters (Markowski and Tucker, 2005). Although the referendum was lost, the LPR realized an impressive victory in the European elections. The party gained 16% of the votes and sent 10 representatives to the European Parliament. The success of the LPR at a European level created widespread fears of a Eurosceptic backlash in Poland (Gaisbauer, 2007).

In the 2005 elections the LPR nevertheless proved incapable of translating its European success to the national level. The mainstream right parties framed the elections as a battle between "social Poland" and "liberal Poland"; that is, the elections revolved primarily around socio-economic issues (Szczerbiak, 2007). Given that the LPR mainly campaigned on cultural issues, most notably Euroscepticism, the electoral appeal of the party was limited. Consequentially, it did not manage to expand its vote and seat share. With the accession secured and the EU referendum passed, the LPR lost momentum. After accession the levels of support for EU integration increased, particularly after February 2005. A year after Poland joined the EU, the vast majority of Poles thought in favourable terms about the EU and, even though support among potential LPR voters remained lower than that of mainstream parties, 64% of these voters expressed support for the EU (with 39% of the LPR voters opposed to the EU). Over the course of the next years support for the EU amongst Polish voters continued to grow (CBOS, 2005). Consequentially, the LPR was no longer able to capitalize on the issues that had initially promoted the success of the party.

Despite the electoral stagnation in the 2005 elections, the LPR decided to join a PiS-led government coalition in 2006. Previously the party had faithfully supported a single party minority government headed by PiS-leader Kaczyński, but this government proved highly unstable. To enhance the stability of the government it was enlarged with the LPR, on the one, and Self-Defence (*Samoobrona Rzeczpospolitej Polskiej*: SRP), on the other hand

(Jasiewicz and Jasiewicz-Betkiewicz, 2006; 2007).[11] In the government coalition LPR-leader Roman Giertych assumed the position of Deputy Minister and Minister of Education and advocated profound reforms of the Polish educational system.[12] The government participation of the LPR was, however, strongly criticized by the party's electorate, which believed it sold out on its electoral promises. With the salience of the EU issue seriously diminished and the credibility of the party as populist opposition force reduced by its government participation the LPR collapsed in the 2007 parliamentary elections. The support for the party diminished from 8% to a mere 1.2%, well below the 5% threshold for parliamentary representation. Today the LPR is no longer represented in the Polish or European parliament. The party has nevertheless managed to maintain representation at the local and regional level and LPR officials are still in office in a number of the municipalities and provinces.

Table 1.   Support for the LPR in elections from 2001 to 2007

Elections	Year	Votes	%	Seats
Sejm	2001	1,025,148	7.87	38
EP	2004	969,689	15.92	10
Sejm	2005	940,762	7.97	34
Sejm	2007	188,264	1.28	-

Source: Państwowa Komisja Wyborcza (www.pkw.org.pl).

11   The SRP of Andrzej Lepper primarily campaigns against the increasing economic and social inequalities that have resulted from the Polish embracement of free market principles. It defends the interests of farmers and of the north-eastern and western regions, which have been most severely affected by the economic transition. Like the LPR, the SRP opposes EU and NATO membership, but on economic issues the party takes unambiguously left-wing stances (Krok-Paszkowska, 2003).

12   Giertych announced that he wanted to „sanitate" the education system on a four pillar basis: "order, patriotism, prestige, and truth" with no "homosexual influences". His project of "supervising" all the new history textbooks and the introduction of classes on patriotism and religion raised students' discontent at the opening of the school year in September 2006 (Kosc, 2006).

Explaining the success of the LPR

At first sight the rapid rise and demise of the LPR seems closely related to the emergence and disappearance of European integration as a salient political issue. Although this issue certainly played an important role in the ascent and descent of the party, a comprehensive explanation for its success is less easily given. The historical analysis presented in this article already highlighted the existence of a fertile breeding ground for RRPs in Poland. However, despite the existence of a sizable reservoir of potential RRP voters many predecessors of the LPR never passed the electoral threshold. The reasons why the LPR succeeded where other RRPs failed are twofold. First, the LPR correctly assessed the Polish political opportunity structure and skilfully located itself in a quadrant of the Polish political space in which many voters, but no other parties were located. Second, the party campaigned on issues that were highly salient to its potential voters and took up distinct positions on these issues. Hence, the LPR cleverly matched its supply to an already existing demand. Let us elaborate on these two points.

On the basis of a qualitative content analysis of the LPR manifestos (2001, 2005, and 2007) and speeches of prominent LPR politicians three core ideological traits (Catholic conservatism, nationalism, and populism) and two omnibus issues (anti-communism and Euroscepticism) can be identified. The ideological traits each have a clear link to the Polish historical legacy, as demonstrated above, while the omnibus issues represent issues that have a link with each of the ideological traits.

Catholic conservatism features prominently in the ideology of the LPR. The party stresses the importance of Catholic faith for Polish identity and actively promotes a traditionalist moral. It strongly opposed abortion, euthanasia, gay rights, and legalization of soft drugs, while it advocated a prominent position for the Church in public life. Moreover, the LPR vehemently opposes the presence of 'the other', that is, the non-Catholic, in Poland. Although the LPR programmes speak in covert terms about race and nationality, it openly attacks the roles Jews and homosexuals fulfil in Polish society (Jasiewicz, 2008, p. 16). Examples of Catholic conservatism are abundant in LPR manifestos and speeches. In the 2005 manifesto, the party declares that "We [the LPR politicians] treat our political, professional, and social activity as service of God, Poland, and the Nation" (Jasiewicz, 2008, p. 15). In his Heidelberg speech, Roman Giertych has claimed that "we cannot propagate within youth education that the same sex partner relationships are normal, because in objective terms they are a departure from the natural law". To promote Catholicism at the European level the LPR sustained a campaign to include references to the Christian roots of Europe in the preamble of the Constitutional Treaty.

Nationalism also figures prominently in the ideology of the LPR. The party underlines the centrality of Polishness, which it understands in cultural terms. The aforementioned Catholic identity is crucial for the definition of Polishness. The party propagates the survival of the national tradition and culture, as well as the emergence of a public moral standard that reflects Catholic norms and values. The nationalism of the LPR also affects the party's stances on economic issues. It is sceptical of foreign enterprises, investments, and land buy-outs and warns against the dangers of globalization. In this context one should also view repeated warnings against German expansionism and revanchism[13], as well as incidences of anti-Semitism (Lang, 2005, pp. 8-9).[14] Although immigration is only a minor problem in Poland, the LPR does already highlight the potential threat posed by immigration to the Polish identity. Prominent politicians have declared that "migrants weaken the nation" and form a threat the Polish demographic situation and that "Europe will become a continent in which representatives of the Islam world [...] will outnumber us". The latter point relates directly to the LPR's definition of Polishness as Catholic and Europe as Christian.

As regards the populism of the LPR, the party articulates a popular disenchantment with the whole post-1989 political order that it portrays as corrupt and out of touch with the concerns of ordinary Poles. Many of the measures proposed by the LPR reflect a desire to curtail the power of the political elite and give the Polish people more say in politics. Examples include proposals to change the system used for the election of senators and to give the senate more competences, to abolish the current the television and radio system, and to reform of the ministry of finance.

The three ideological characteristics, Catholic conservatism, nationalism, and populism, come together in two omnibus issues on which the LPR

---

13   Throughout Polish history Germanophobia has always been a successful electoral issue. It made a comeback when Poland negotiated its accession to the EU and was promoted mainly by the LPR and PiS.

14   See, for example, the LPR's statements regarding the Jedwabne pogrom. Moreover, one of the LPR's most prominent politicians, Antoni Macierewicz, is the publisher of the anti-Semitic weekly Voice (Głos) (Pankowski and Kornak, 2005, p. 159). The anti-Semitism of the LPR is essentially a rejection of cosmopolitanism and of Western values (Stankiewicz, 2002).

primarily campaigns. The first issue, anti-communism, focuses on the LPR's opposition to the fact that former communists still play a role in Polish politics. The LPR has called for 'decommunisation' for many years and has eventually been one of the main forces behind the new lustration laws passed in the *Sejm* in December 2006. The proposals of the party have been, however, more radical than those included in this law and feature plans to "open and publish all files of the communist security services" and "extend lustration to journalists" and other public figures (Millard, 2006, p. 1018). The LPR's anti-communism links to the party's Catholic conservatism - most former communists are secular -, nationalism – most former communists are cosmopolitan universalists -, and populism - former communists are equated with the corrupt political elite. As Walicki (2000, pp. 39-40) explains "Catholic traditionalists are obsessed with the idea of an essential similarity between communism and liberalism, as equally godless and antinational, and with the alleged Masonic threat to Catholic Poland".

The second omnibus issue, Euroscepticism, forms the core of the LPR campaign and the party's success between 2001 and 2007. According to the LPR the EU poses a multifaceted threat to Poland. First, the LPR perceives the EU as a secular institution and as such endangers Poland's identity as a Catholic nation (Lewis, 2005). Second, the LPR claims that the EU has an erosive effect on national sovereignty and therefore calls to "say no to a programme of resignation from the sovereignty of the Polish state". In a way, the transfer of sovereignty to the EU recalls for the LPR the kind of political annihilation Poland experienced during the Partitions and the German and Soviet occupations. Moreover the party also believes that the EU forces its members to expand minority rights and hence poses a threat to Poland's cultural homogeneity. Third, the EU is presented as a project of political elites and not of the European people. Catholic conservatism, nationalism, and populism thus each resurface in the LPR stance on the question of European integration. As Rupnik (2007, p. 22) notes "the EU is a very convenient target for populist resentment since it is a liberal project – supported by the economic and political elites in charge of the recent transition – and implies a redefinition of national sovereignty and identity".

The combination of Catholic conservative, nationalist, and populist elements in the ideology of the party makes unambiguously located at the far right end of the cultural dimension, where Kitschelt et al. (1999) position the religious authoritarian nationalists. A more systematic analysis of the LPR's position on 11 policy dimensions confirms this assessment (see Fig. 1).[15] To get a better understanding of the position of the LPR in the Polish space, however, it is necessary to also gauge the party's position on the socio-economic dimension. Fig. 1 demonstrates that LPR takes a middle-of-the-road position on this dimension. The party leans slightly to the right of the socio-economic dimension, towards a free market economy, but its position on this dimension is far less outspoken than on the cultural dimension.[16]

The figure also demonstrates that the LPR has found an electoral niche in the Polish political space. The position of the party is markedly different from that of other Polish parties. Compared to other right-wing parties, like the AWS and the PiS, the LPR takes a more extreme position on the cultural dimension. As such it clearly distinguishes itself from its right-wing competitors. Compared to other populist parties, most notably the SRP, the LPR also takes a distinct position. Although SRP takes a position on the cultural dimension that is only slightly less extreme than that of the LPR, the two parties take very different positions on the socio-economic dimension. While the SRP is economically left-wing, the LPR is economically right-wing. As a consequence the LPR also clearly distinguishes itself from its main populist competitor and ally in the PiS-led government. In sum, it appears that the LPR has found an electoral niche in the Polish political space and occupies a position that was previously vacant. An analysis of the attitudes of LPR voters confirms this proposition.

---

15   The configuration of parties in Fig. 3 is based on the expert survey administered by Benoit and Laver (2006) and incorporates parties' positions 11 policy dimensions. These policy dimensions are (1) EU joining; (2) taxes vs. spending; (3) decentralization; (4) privatization; (5) media freedom; (6) foreign land ownership; (7) religion; (8) social; (9) nationalism; (10) urban-rural; and (11) former communists. A factor analysis (varimax rotation) reduces these 11 dimensions to two dimensions. The first policy dimension incorporates the issues 1, 5, 6, 7, 8, 9, and 11 and is best interpreted as the cultural dimension previously discussed in this article. The second policy dimension includes the issues 2, 3, 4, and 10 and is best interpreted as the socio-economic dimension, which was discussed earlier on in this article as well. The first dimension accounts for 50% of the variation in the scores of parties in the 11 policy dimensions, whereas the second dimension accounts for another 41%.

16   When the Polish political space is constructed on the basis of voters' perceptions of party positions, the difference between the LPR's position on the cultural dimension and the socio-economic dimension is even more striking. According to Polish voters, the LPR takes an outspoken religious-fundamentalist position on the cultural dimension (considerably more outspoken than the PiS), while it takes a centrist position on the socio-economic dimension (Markowski, 2006, p. 817).

Figure 1.   A two-dimensional representation of the Polish political space

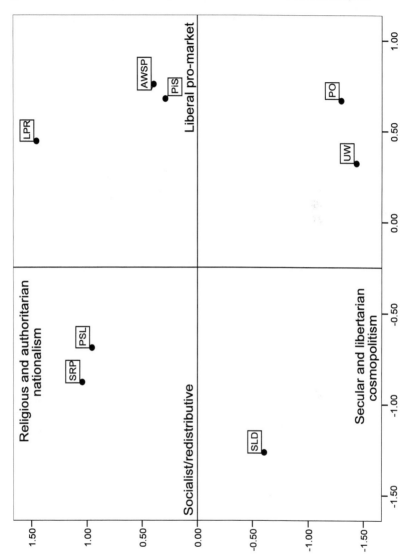

Source: Benoit and Laver (2006)

Table 2 below demonstrates that LPR voters attach greater importance to Catholic conservative and nationalist issues than the average Polish voter.[17] Especially the issues 'abortion', 'low birth rate', 'role of Church', and 'settlement of foreigners in Poland' strike a chord with LPR voters. They also attach greater importance to one of the omnibus issues on which the LPR campaigns, namely 'clearing accounts with communist past'. Interestingly, the EU issue was less salient for LPR voters than for the average voter in the 2001 elections. In 2005 the salience of this issue increased considerably for LPR voters, but it did not surpass that for the average Polish voter.[18] When it comes to economic issues LPR voters do not differ that much from the average Polish voter. They are very important to Polish voters and not less so to LPR voters. The importance attributed to economic issues is notably higher than that attributed to Catholic conservative or nationalist issues, even for LPR voters.

---

17   The analyses are based on the Polish National Election Study (PNES) 2001 and 2005. The 2001 PNES, conducted by the Institute of Political Studies of the Polish Academy of Science, is sponsored by the Polish State Committee for Scientific Research under grant No. 5 H02E 02120; and co-sponsored by the Economic and Social Research Council and Warsaw School of Social Psychology. The 2005 PNES, also conducted by the Institute of Political Studies of the Polish Academy of Sciences, is sponsored by the Polish Ministry of Science and Information under grant No. 5 1 H02E 060 28; and co-sponsored by the Stefan Batory Foundation, the Public Opinion Research Center, the Institute of Philosophy and Sociology of the Polish Academy of Sciences and the Department of Politics & Department of Central and East European Studies of the University of Glasgow. The authors gratefully acknowledge Prof. Radosław Markowski, Prof. Mikołaj Cześnik, and Dr Clare McManus-Czubińska for the access granted to these data. The percentage of LPR voters is 6.8% in the 2001 PNES and 3.7% in the 2005 PNES. The latter percentage is significantly lower than the percentage of votes the LPR received in the 2005 elections (8.0%). Due to the small number of LPR voters in the 2005 PNES it is impossible to conduct a logistic regression analysis that establishes which factors determine the vote for the LPR. Analyses of the socio-demographic composition of the LPR electorate (not reported here) confirm the conclusions of previous studies that it is predominantly female, lower educated, rural and strongly religious (Szczerbiak, 2003).

18   Part of the explanation for this counterintuitive observation lies in the fact that LPR voters do not attach particular importance to the relationship between Poland and the EU, because they reject the latter outright. They opposed Poland's accession to the EU and refuse to deal with the institution now that Poland has become a member.

Table 2.   Salience LPF voters attribute to thirteen political issues

	2001		2005	
	LPR voters	*Polish voters*	*LPR voters*	*Polish voters*
Catholic conservative issues				
Abortion			**6.91**	5.59
Crime	9.08	8.92	8.89	8.77
Low birth rate and decreasing population			**8.07**	7.06
Role of Church	**6.77**	4.59	**6.67**	5.33
Economic issues				
Privatization	5.38	4.94	6.34	5.84
State social responsibility	8.33	7.78	8.37	8.15
State subsidies to agriculture	8.25	7.48	7.82	7.04
Tax policy	8.49	8.25	8.26	8.27
Unemployment	9.86	9.69	9.78	9.64
Nationalist issues				
Foreign capital in Poland	4.95	5.35	6.62	6.48
Settlement of foreigners in Poland			**5.50**	4.50
Omnibus issues				
Clearing accounts with Communist past[a]	**4.75**	3.29	**6.43**	5.16
Polish policy towards EU[b]	**4.96**	6.10	7.25	7.30

Note: Figures in bold represent issues on which LPR score notably higher (-1 or +1) than the average voter.

---

a   In the 2001 PNES labelled „Communist nomenclatura problem".
b   In the 2001 PNES labelled „Joining the EU".

In terms of positions the picture is not much different (see Table 3). LPR voters take different positions than the average Polish voter on Catholic conservative and nationalist issues, but not on economic issues. On Catholic conservative and nationalist issues LPR voters lean more to the right than the average Polish voter. The differences are particularly noteworthy on the issues 'abortion', 'role of Church' and 'settlement of foreigners in Poland'. Surprisingly, LPR voters do not take markedly different positions from the average voter on the question 'clearing accounts with communist past', while they do take more right leaning positions on the question of 'Polish policy towards EU'.

In short, what sets LPR voters apart from other Polish voters is their support for Catholic conservatism and nationalism, as well as their opposition to former communists and the EU. This suggests that the vote for the LPR is first and foremost an ideological vote, and not a protest vote. LPR voters support the party, because they identify themselves with the issues and positions on which the party campaigns. This identification stems partly from the socio-demographic characteristics that shape these voters attitudes (it should come as no surprise that very religious voters attach more importance to Catholic conservative issues than secular voters), but also partly from the successful way in which the LPR has managed to link specific political issues to broader ideological debates and has put these issues on the political agenda at the appropriate time.

The existence of a favorable electoral and political opportunity structure explains the rise of the LPR in 2001, when many voters where dissatisfied with the way in which the AWS had governed during the previous legislative period. Especially the AWS' neglect of cultural issues and positive stance towards European accession had disappointed many Catholic voters who had supported the party in absence of a RRP alternative. The LPR capitalized on this disappointment and proposed a programme different from that of the AWS, one that did not embrace European integration unconditionally and that emphasized cultural issues (Jasiewicz and Jasiewicz-Betkiewicz, 2002). It also explain the demise of the LPR in 2007, when the European question no longer featured very prominently on the political agenda and the PiS had co-opted many of the LPR's Catholic conservative and nationalist stances, thus closing in on the LPR in the political space. Because of these programmatic changes the LPR also lost the support of the influential Father Rydzyk and Radio Maryja, who backed the PiS in the 2007 elections.

Table 3.   Positions of LPR voters on thirteen political issues

	2001		2005	
	LPR voters	*Polish voters*	*LPR voters*	*Polish voters*
Catholic conservative issues				
Abortion			**6.85**	4.36
Crime	4.37	3.58	3.86	4.43
Low birth rate and decreasing population			**2.18**	3.22
Role of Church	**5.22**	2.10	**4.88**	2.65
Economic issues				
Privatization	7.44	6.88	**8.51**	7.29
State social responsibility	2.21	2.66	**2.39**	3.45
State subsidies to agriculture	1.36	1.84	0.90	1.89
Tax policy	2.96	3.07	2.78	3.66
Unemployment	1.88	1.75	**1.36**	2.43
Nationalist issues				
Foreign capital in Poland	5.28	5.10	5.23	4.37
Settlement of foreigners in Poland			**6.93**	5.64
Omnibus issues				
Clearing accounts with Communist past	**3.20**	5.08	3.27	3.51
Polish policy towards EU	**6.85**	5.01	**7.60**	5.75

Note: Figures in bold represent issues on which LPR score notably higher (-1 or +1) than the average voter.

Our explanation for the brief success of the LPR relies heavily on Poland's historical legacy. First, different aspects of the Polish historical legacy (the way in which the idea of the Polish nation has been constructed, as well as the notion of the Catholic Church as defender of Polish identity and independence throughout history) have made the electoral and political opportunity structure very favourable to a Catholic conservative and nationalist party. The Polish historical legacy has instilled strong Catholic conservative and nationalism attitudes in a certain segment of the Polish population, which makes it likely that it will vote for a RRP that appeals to the both attitudes. The legacy has also shaped the dimensionality of the political space and influenced the positions left- and right-wing parties have taken up. It has, for example, promoted the establishment of the AWS, which has always taken a moderate position on the cultural dimension. As a result the religious authoritarian nationalist quadrant of the Polish political space has been virtually empty, creating a niche for a Catholic conservative and nationalist RRP. Moreover, to construct a coherent Catholic conservative and nationalist ideology the LPR could rely on the ideological heritage of previous far right movements, most notably that of Dmowski's interwar movement *Endecja*.

A comparative perspective

Does the importance of Poland's history for the success of the LPR make that it is not comparable to that of other RRPs? This question can be answered in two ways. On the one hand, it is clear that as a result of the particular nature of Polish history prior, during, and after communism the explanation for the success of the LPR contains idiosyncratic elements. On the other hand, the theory behind this explanation, namely that historical legacies structure the demand and opportunities for RRPs, is not only relevant to the Polish case. It can explain the success of RRPs, regardless of their location in Central and Eastern Europe or Western Europe. Let us elaborate each of these points.

First, few countries in Europe have a history of nation- and state-building in which Catholicism and the Catholic Church plays such a crucial role. Hence, in most European countries the demand for RRPs is not determined by voters' religious background, nor is the ideology of these parties characterized by a combination of Catholic conservatism and nationalism. In Central and East European countries like the Czech Republic, Hungary and Romania the Church has never had the central position it has acquired in Poland. From this it follows that the content of the cultural dimension in these countries is less defined by religion and more by ethnicity (Jasiewicz, 2007, p. 28) and that the RRPs that have emerged in these countries define themselves first and foremost in ethnic terms. For this reason, these parties primarily oppose minority groups, such as the Roma. Some RRPs occasionally do make reference to religion, most notably the ones that have been successful in Croatia, Russia, Serbia and Slovakia (Bakić 2009; Beichelt in this volume; Mudde, 2007, pp. 85-86), but these references do not have the same importance as in the Polish case and ties with the Catholic or Orthodox church are much loser in these countries.[19] In most West European countries the role of religion in politics has declined over the past decades and oppositions on the cultural dimension are no longer exclusively structured by parties and voters religious backgrounds.[20] Some scholars have observed 'a growing relevance of Christian motifs and themes' in the programmes of West European RRPs, but it appears that the renewed interest of these parties in Christianity is primarily a reaction to the perceived threat of Islam (Zúquete, 2008, p. 324). However, West European RRPs generally refer to the Judeo-Christian roots of Europe at large, rather than the more narrowly defined Catholic heritage the LPR invokes. Although conservatism is part of most West European RRPs' ideologies, it does not have the same prominence or prevalent Catholic character as that of the LPR. Radical right parties in West-

---

19   Although there is at the time of writing no successful RRP in Lithuania the country is nevertheless interesting from a comparative point of view. It shares part of its history with Poland (see the period of the Polish-Lithuanian Commonwealth). As the oldest surviving institution in Lithuania, the Catholic Church played a prominent role in the development of Lithuanian civil society. Like in the Polish case, the Church acted as a defender of the Lithuanian national identity during the Partitions and the Soviet Occupation. In 1918 the Church encouraged the democratic aspirations of the newly founded Lithuania republic and in the 1930s it heavily criticized the authoritarian regime of Antanas Smetona. During the Soviet occupation, the Church supported the Lithuanian resistance movement in the same way as the Polish Church supported the Solidarity movement. It provided a safe haven for dissidents and acted as a mediator between the communist rulers and the opposition (Vardys, 1978). This leaves room for the breakthrough of a RRP that has a similar ideology as the LPR.

20   In the few West European countries in which religion and the Catholic Church do play a significant role in politics, such as Ireland and Spain, no successful RRPs exist (O'Malley, 2008; Davis, 1998). Italy is the only West European country in which religion and the Catholic Church do have a prominent position in politics and in which a successful RRP exists. However, the National Alliance (*Alleanza Nazionale*: AN) initially adhered to a form of civil religiosity and only converted to Catholic conservatism after the transformation of the Italian party system in the 1990s. According to Tarchi (2003, p. 148), "the AN instigated a strategy aiming to appeal to the many moderates who had been disappointed by the disgrace which beset the Christian Democrats after Tangentopoli. This strategy involved presenting the new party as the custodian of religious values, declaring itself inspired by Catholic thought". Moreover, it has been demonstrated that religious voters are less likely to vote for the AN than non-religious voters (Arzheimer and Carter, 2009, p. 1002).

ern Europe do include some conservative proposals in their programmes, such as abolition of abortion and euthanasia, but explicit references to religion are usually limited. Consequentially, religiosity also does not have an independent effect on the vote for RRPs (Arzheimer and Carter, 2009).

What sets the LPR apart from other RRPs is the fact that the party's definition of the Polish identity relies extensively on the perception of Poland as a religious nation, and that it thus combines Catholic conservatism with nationalism. Whereas other RRPs define the nation in opposition to minority groups (Central Eastern Europe) or immigrants (Western Europe), the LPR defines itself against the secular Polish political elite and the secular West, most notably the European Union. The ideological differences between the LPR and other RRPs are underlined by that fact that the Polish party never was a member of Identity, Tradition, and Sovereignty (ITS), the European party federation in which National Union Attack (*Natsionalen Săyuz Ataka*: Ataka), the National Front (*Front National*: FN), Greater Romania Party (*Partidul România Mare*: PRM), and Flemish Interest (*Vlaams Belang*: VB) used to cooperate.

Second, the differences in content and structure of political spaces, ideologies, and compositions of electorates do not make our general explanation for the success of RRPs irrelevant. On the contrary, the mechanisms through which these parties have secured the support of voters are very similar across countries, and across the East-West divide. Successful RRPs have understood how national identities have been constructed in the countries in which they operate and have identified contemporary threats to this identity. In their programmes they make reference to the crucial years of nation and state formation, to previously successful far right movements, and, in the case of RRPs in Central and Eastern Europe, to the communist period and the subsequent transition to democracy. This argument is best illustrated with an example. At first sight, the efforts of the Dutch List Pim Fortuyn (*Lijst Pim Fortuyn*: LPF) to protect gay rights from Islam, which its leader called a "backward religion", conflict with the LPR's efforts to curtail the rights of gay and lesbians in Poland. A closer look at the ideology of these two parties demonstrates, however, that the positions they take follow directly from the historical legacies that shape the discourse about national identity in their respective countries. In the Netherlands this historical legacy comprises a process of nation building centred on cultural liberalism, whereas in Poland this process took Catholicism as it main source of inspiration.

Conclusion

This article shows that there is an unmistakable link between the electoral success of the LPR and the particularities of the Polish historical legacy. The LPR has successfully capitalized on Catholic conservative and nationalist sentiments, which have been revived after communism promoted cosmopolitan universalism for many decades. As such, the LPR has profited from the two main components of historical legacies identified by Blokker as essential for the success of RRPs.

Although these two components have created the fertile soil from which the success of the LPR could grow in the 2001 and 2005 elections, the eventual timing and extent of the success of the party is explained by the way in which it has connected Catholic conservative, nationalist, and populist sentiments, on the one hand, and salient political issues like decommunization and European integration, on the other. Consequentially, the LPR has been the only RRP that has been able to profit from the opportunities created by the Polish historical legacy. Other nationalist and populist parties have failed in their quest for success, because they have not campaigned on contemporary issues that strike a cord with Catholic-nationalist voters.

Our conclusion resembles that of many other students of Central and East European politics. Although historical-structural explanations that focus on legacies accurately describe opportunities for parties, they are unable to explain the success of individual parties. Instead, actor- and competition-oriented explanations are better placed to explain the timing and extent of the success of particular parties, radical right or other. An exclusive focus on legacies would lead to deterministic and static conclusions that cannot adequately explain why parties emerge at specific points in time and why parties subsequently vanish. One has to take into account "the relative autonomy of political dynamics and actors' strategic choices" (Hanley et al., 2007, p. 24) to come to satisfactory explanations of party success.

For this reason it also makes sense to compare the LPR to other RRPs, both in Central and Eastern Europe and Western Europe. Although the Polish historical legacy is in some ways unique, general explanations for the success of RRPs do account for much of the success of the LPR. The issues on which the party has capitalized show important resemblances to those that have inspired the success of prominent RRPs in other countries in the region and in many West European countries. As such the LPR finds itself between East and West, past and present.

References

Anastasakis, O., 2002. The politics of extremism in Eastern Europe; a reaction to transition. Papales del Este 3, 1-15.

Arzheimer, K., Carter, E., 2009. Christian religiosity and voting for West European radical right parties. West European Politics 32 (5), 986-1011.

Bakić, J., 2009. Extreme-right ideology, practice and supporters: case study of the Serbian radical right party. Journal of Contemporary European Studies 17 (2), 193-207.

Bayer, J., 2002. Rechtspopulismus und Rechtsextremismus in Ostmitteleuropa. Österreichischen Zeitschrift für Politikwissenschaft 31 (3), 265-280.

Beichelt, T., Minkenberg, M., 2002. Radikalismus in Transformationsgesellschaften. Osteuropa 52 (3), 247-262.

Benoit, K., Laver, M., 2006. Party Policy in Modern Democracies. Routledge, London.

Blokker, P., 2005. Populist nationalism, anti-Europeanism, post-nationalism, and the East-West distinction. German Law Journal 6 (2), 1-18.

Bücker, N., 2007. Protective nationalism in today's Poland. Theoretical considerations and empirical findings. In: Karolewski, I.P., Suszycki, A.M. (Eds.), Nationalism and European Integration. The Need for New Theoretical and Empirical Insights. Continuum, New York, pp. 117-133.

Casanova, J., 2003. Religion, European Secular Identities, and European Integration, Paper presented at the Mellon Sawyer seminar at Cornell University on October 7.

Castle, M., Taras, R., 2002. Democracy in Poland. Second edn. Westview Press, Boulder.

CBOS, 2004. The End of Optimism in Thinking about the Effects of the European Integration. Polish Public Opinion, March 2004.

CBOS, 2005. Deterioration of the Opinion about the Functioning of the European Union Institutions. Research Report, November 2005.

Crawford, B., Lijphart, A., 1997. Old legacies, new institutions: explaining political and economic trajectories in post-communist regimes. In: Crawford, B., Lijphart, A. (Eds.), Liberalization and Leninist Legacies: Comparative Perspectives on Democratic Transition. University of California Press, Berkeley, pp. 1-39.

Eaglin A., 2008. Poison from the Pulpit. Transition Online, October 2008.

Eberts, M.W., 1998. The Roman Catholic Church and democracy in Poland. Europe-Asia Studies 50 (5), 817-842.

Friszke, A., 1990. The Polish political scene. East European Politics and Societies 4 (2), 305-341.

Gaisbauer, H.P., 2007. The EP Elections 2004 as a Polish Eurosceptical backlash? Considerations on public and party-based Euroscepticism. In:

Gatnar, L., Lane, D. (Eds.), Popular Opposition and Support for Different Types of the EU. Tribun EU, Brno, pp. 87-110.

Hanley, S., Szczerbiak, A., Haughton, T., Fowler, B., 2007. Explaining the Success of Centre-right Parties in Post-communist East Central Europe: A Comparative Analysis, SEI Working Paper No. 94. University of Sussex, Falmer, Brighton.

Jasiewicz, K., 2003. 'Pocketbook or Rosary? Economic and Identity Voting in 2000-2001 Elections in Poland', Studies in Public Policy No. 379. University of Strathclyde, Glasgow.

Jasiewicz, K., 2007. The political-party landscape. Journal of Democracy 18 (4), 26-33.

Jasiewicz, K., 2008. The new populism in Poland, the usual suspects? Problems of Post-Communism 55 (3), 7-25.

Jasiewicz, K., Jasiewicz-Betkiewicz, A., 2002. Poland, European Journal of Political Research 41, 1057-1067.

Jasiewicz, K., Jasiewicz-Betkiewicz, A., 2006. Poland, European Journal of Political Research 41, 1231-1246.

Jasiewicz, K., Jasiewicz-Betkiewicz, A., 2007. Poland, European Journal of Political Research 41, 1063-1074.

Jasińska-Kania, A., Marody, M. (Eds.), 2004. Poles among Europeans. Wydawnictwo Naukowe Scholar, Warsaw.

Jowitt, K., 1992. New World Disorder: The Leninist Extinction. University of California Press, Berkeley.

Kitschelt, H., Mansfeldova, Z., Markowski, R., Toka, G., 1999. Post Communist Party Systems: Competition, Representation, and Inter-party Cooperation. Cambridge University Press, Cambridge.

Kosc, W., 2006. Class Divisions, Transition Online, September 2006.

Krok-Paszkowska, A., 2003. Samoobrona, the Polish self-defence movement. In: Kopecky, P., Mudde, C. (Eds.), Uncivil Society? Contentious Politics in Post-Communist Europe. Routledge, London, pp. 114-133.

Kubik, J., Linch, A., 2006. The original sin of Poland's Third Republic: discounting "Solidarity" and its consequences for political reconciliation. Polish Sociological Review 1 (153), 9-38.

Lang, K.-O., 2005. Populism in Central and Eastern Europe – a threat to democracy or just political folklore? Slovak Foreign Policy Affairs 3 (1), 6-16.

Lewis, P.G., 1999. Parties and Parliaments in east Central Europe. Poland as Trendsetter, Paper Presented at the Conference Ten Years After: Transition and Consolidation in East Central Europe. Budapest, 17-20 June 1999.

Lewis, P.G., 2005. EU enlargement and party systems in CE. Journal of Communist Studies and Transition Politics 21 (2), 171-199.

Linz, J., Stepan, A., 1996. Problems of Democratic Transition and Consolidation: Southern Europe, South America and Postcommunist Europe. Johns Hopkins University Press, London.

Markowski, R., 2000. Party System Institutionalization: Poland - a Trendsetter with no Followers, Paper Presented at the Conference Rethinking Democracy in the New Millenium. Houston, 16-19 February 2001.

Markowski, R., 2006. The Polish elections of 2005: pure chaos or a restructuring of the party system? West European Politics 29 (4), 814-832.

Markowski, R., Tucker, J.A., 2005. Pocketbooks, politics, and parties: the 2003 Polish referendum on EU membership. Electoral Studies 24 (3), 209-433.

Marks, B., 2006. Radicals in Central Europe. Real danger or a passing fad. Polish Sociological Review 154 (2), 209-230.

Millard, F., 2006. Poland's politics and the travails of transition after 2001: the 2005 elections. Europe-Asia Studies 58 (7), 1007-1031.

Minkenberg, M., 2002. The radical right in postsocialist Central and Eastern Europe: comparative observations and interpretations. East European Politics and Societies 16 (2), 335-362.

Mudde, C., 2000. Extreme-right parties in Eastern Europe. Patterns of Prejudice 34 (1), 5-27.

Mudde, C., 2007. Populist Radical Right Parties in Europe. Cambridge University Press, Cambridge.

O'Malley, E., 2008. Why is there no radical right parties in Ireland? West European Politics 31 (5), 960-977.

Ost, D., 1999. The radical right in Poland: rationality of the irrational. In: Ramet, S. (Ed.), The Radical Right in Central and Eastern Europe since 1989. The Pennsylvania State University Press, University Park, pp. 85-107.

Pankowski, R., Kornak, M., 2005. Poland. In: Mudde, C. (Ed.), Racist Extremism in Central and Eastern Europe. Routledge, London, pp. 156-183.

Paszkiewicz, K.A., 2004. Partie i Koalicje Polityczne III Rzeczypospolitej. Wydawnictwo Uniwersytetu Wrocławskiego, Wrocław.

Rupnik, J., 2007. From democracy fatigue to populist backlash. Journal of Democracy 18 (4), 17-25.

Sawicki, S.J., 1982. Embattled Poland: An Historical Reflection: Reflections on an Ethnic Journey. Victoria University Press, Wellington.

Stankiewicz, K., 2002. Die "neuen Dmowskis" – eine alte Ideologie im neuen Gewand? Der Nationalismus der Zwischenkriegszeit als ideologische Leitlinie der radikalen Rechten in Polen. Osteuropa 1 (3), 263-279.

Szczerbiak, A., 2001. Polish politics in the new millennium. In: Blazyca, G., Rapacki, R. (Eds.), Poland into the 1990s: Economy and Society in Transition. Pinter, London, pp. 91-104.

Szczerbiak, A., 2003. Old and new divisions in Polish politics: Polish parties' electoral strategies and bases of support. Europe-Asia Studies 55 (5), 729-746.

Szczerbiak, A., 2004. The Polish centre-right's (last?) best hope: the rise and fall of Solidarity Electoral Action. Journal of Communist Studies and Transition Politics 20 (3), 55-79.

Szczerbiak, A., 2006. Power without love? Patterns of party politics in post-1989 Poland. In: Jungerstam-Mulders, S. (Ed.), Post-Communist EU Member States. Parties and Party Systems. Ashgate, Aldershot, pp. 91-123.

Szczerbiak, A., 2007. 'Social Poland' defeats 'Liberal Poland'? The September-October 2005 Polish parliamentary and presidential elections. Journal of Communist Studies and Transition Politics 23 (2), 203-232.

Szczerbiak, A., Hanley, S., 2004. Introduction: understanding the politics of the right in contemporary East-Central Europe. Journal of Communist Studies and Transition Politics 20 (3), 1-8.

Tarchi, M., 2003. The political culture of the Alleanza nazionale: an analysis of the party's programmatic documents (1995-2002). Journal of Modern Italian Studies 8 (2): 135-181.

Vardys, V.S., 1978. The Catholic Church, Dissent and Nationality in Soviet Lithuania. Columbia University Press, Irvington.

Walicki, A., 2000. The troubling legacy of Roman Dmowski. East European Politics and Societies 14 (1), 12-46.

Zubrzycki, G., 2006. The Crosses of Auschwitz: Nationalism and Religion in Post-Communist Poland. The University of Chicago Press, Chicago.

Zúquete, J.P., 2008. The European extreme-right and Islam: new directions? Journal of Political Ideologies 13 (3), 321-344.

Interwar fascism and the post-1989 radical right
Ideology, opportunism and historical legacy in
Bulgaria and Romania

James Frusetta, Anca Glont

*ABSTRACT: Do contemporary Bulgarian and Romanian radical right move-
ments represent a legacy of interwar fascism? We argue that the key element
is not that interwar movements provided legacies (of structures, ideologies, or
organizations) but rather a symbolic "heritage" that contemporary movements
can draw upon. The crucial legacy is, rather, the Socialist era, which in asserting its own definitions of interwar fascism created a "useable past" for
populist movements. The Peoples' Republics created a flawed historical consciousness whereby demonized interwar rightist movements could be mobi-
lized after 1989 as historical expressions of "anti-Communist" — and, ergo,
positive symbols among those of anti-Communist sentiment. Although radical
right parties in both countries may cast themselves as "heirs" to interwar fascism, they share little in common in terms of ideology. Their claims to a fascist legacy is, rather, a factor of how their respective Socialist states characterized the past.*

Introduction
The emergence of radical right parties in Bulgaria and Romania, as elsewhere in Eastern Europe, has raised domestic and international concern regarding these states' transition to democratic, multiparty governance after
1989. Part of this concern reflects worries that such groups may achieve sufficient political power to "make good" on their expressed agendas: a radical
break with liberal democracy to defend the homogenous nation (Minkenberg,
2002). If they represent a return to indigenous fascist movements of the
interwar period, as is commonly expressed in the domestic media in both
countries, this would raise grave doubts about the region's successful transition to democracy or, even worse, fears of the possibility of political violence
— from the Western perspective, a specter ascribed to Eastern Europe in
common given the precedent of the Wars of Yugoslav Secession (Todorova,
1997).

There is no question that the Bulgarian *Natsionalen Suioz Ataka* (National Union Attack, hereafter, Ataka) and *Partidul România Mare* (Greater Romania Party, or PRM) have enjoyed relative electoral success. The PRM received roughly 14 percent of the popular vote in the 2004 parliamentary elections, and party leader Corneliu Vadim Tudor 12.6 percent of the presidential vote that same year (although down from 33 percent in the second round in 2000). The PRM subsequently failed to reach the electoral threshold of 5 percent in the 2008 Romanian elections, although it continued to win seats in Romania's European Parliament delegation. Ataka took 8.1 percent in the 2005 parliamentary election, 9.3 percent in the 2009 parliamentary election, and Volen Siderov himself 24 percent in the second round of the 2006 presidential election. Although far-right success is not limited to these countries, the slow (and, in the Romanian case, sporadically violent) transition to democratic governance has encouraged particular critique.

Both parties engage in extremist rhetoric: xenophobic, ultra-nationalist in the sense that not only should the state be synonymous with the nation but that only members of the nation should have rights within the state, specifically anti-Semitic in reference to Jewish conspiracies, and critical of globalization and aspects of the capitalist transition. At their most extreme, both parties engage in rhetoric that indeed evokes the worst aspects of interwar fascism. In 1998, Tudor called for the "isolation [of Roma] in specially designed colonies, where they will want for nothing, but they can steal and beat each other..." while in the 2005 Siderov called for the creation of Roma "labor camps." In terms of their suspicion of minorities, calls for a strong state, flirtation with border revisionism, and demands for dramatic political, social, and economic reforms, both groups comfortably fit Cas Mudde's "conceptual framework" in defining the contemporary radical right in Central and Eastern Europe (Mudde, 2007).

Ataka and the PRM are not the most extreme of the new "far right" parties in Bulgaria and Romania. George ("Gigi") Becali, leader of the Romanian *Partidul Noua Generație* (New Generation Party, or PNG) has closely adopted the style and symbols of the interwar Legion of the Archangel Michael. The *Bulgarski Natsionalen Suioz* (Bulgarian National Alliance, or BNS) marches annually to commemorate the death of General Hristo Lukov, a prominent Bulgarian interwar fascist leader. In the summer of 2007, the group attempted to form a brown-shirted "national guard" to confront accused Roma criminals, while adopting uniforms reminiscent of those of the *Sturmabteilung.*

Do these groups represent a continuation of fascism from the interwar era? If so, do they represent a legacy or a heritage from the fascist past? We posit two scholarly dilemmas in asking these questions. The first relates to the problems of definition: there remains no commonly accepted definition for "generic fascism," let alone for the "radical right" or "conservatism." These definitions are complicated by the fact that significant "cross-pollination" occurred between such groups, who frequently borrowed forms, ideas, and expressions from each other, and, in the case of fascism, drew upon socialism as well. Factions within movements often expressed distinctly different positions: for example, the "left-wing" of the National Socialist Workers Party of Germany led by Otto and Gregor Strassers. Despite strong arguments that the categories of conservatism, radical right, and fascism chiefly represent different elements of "organized intolerance" (Ramet, 1999) or of exclusionary nationalism (Minkenberg, 2002), we argue that there are ideological divisions that defined the historic phenomena of fascism from other contemporary elements of the right. Conservative parties of interwar Europe sought to defend existing political, social, and economic interests but avoided sharp discontinuities with existing legal forms of the state. Radical- right parties were more amenable to the destruction of liberal democratic practices and radical revision of the state, but did not seek a more general social revolution. Fascists, so much as a generic fascist ideology can be ascribed, ideologically posited the need for a radical, cross-class social, economic and political revolution to achieve the palingenetic rebirth of the nation and to exclude groups outside the nation, particularly (but not universally) excluding Jews (Blinkhorn, 1990; Payne, 1995; Griffin, 1996). While drawn together by their common perceptions of problems and challenges to the nation, these categories represented different proposed responses.

The second question also is in reference to a definition: that of legacy. Do contemporary "radical right" groups draw on, or are directly shaped by, the legacies — the social, cultural, and ideological structures — of inter-war indigenous fascism, in the way that scholars suggest that a "Leninist legacy" continues to shape transition after 1989 (Jowitt, 1991; Crawford and Lijphart, 1997)? Or do they rely on heritage: not the continuation of the structures and ideas of interwar fascism, but rather the symbolic use of indigenous fascism as part of a "useable past" in the discourse of contemporary politics: in other words, a perceived (but not real) legacy of the past (Boia, 2001; Iordachi and Trecsényi, 2003; Todorova, 1997)?

This distinction is not merely a semantic one. Although many post-1989 political groups in Eastern Europe have been ascribed, or self-ascribed, as fascist, there is a legitimate question to be raised whether such groups are ideological heirs to historic movements or if they use the symbolic trappings and styles of fascism to clothe a dissimilar hodgepodge of populist positions (Ghodsee, 2008) — complicated by the fact that fascism itself is not easily ascribed to a "left-right" political spectrum. While acknowledging that other scholars have cautioned against drawing too close a comparison between historic fascist movements and contemporary radical right parties (Minkenberg, 2000), we argue that the ideological dimensions and comparison between contemporary and historical groups remains largely unexplored in the existing literature. This article provides a substantial historical background to Romanian and Bulgarian fascism as a prerequisite for considering the legacy of fascism on contemporary political groups.

The PRM and Ataka have adopted individual elements or symbols of earlier movements; the BNS and PNG have made rather more overt attempts to draw upon fascist symbols, uniforms, statements, and hero cults in establishing their political platforms. This does not mean that they share fascist ideological thought in much the same way as German National Socialism has become an important symbolic source for the American white power movement, yet the ultimate motives of both groups are distinctly different (Griffin, 2006). In this sense, we draw a difference in terms of a "useable past" in which historical symbols of fascism can readily be used by post-1989 political groups, and a "legacy" in which historical ideologies and structures of fascism are continuing and constraining factors on contemporary politics.

Such use has been possible both because of the dominance of the Socialist era's historical master narrative and its subsequent, widespread post-1989 rejection — an aspect of what Ken Jowitt has termed the "Leninist legacy" of the region. The Communist parties of Bulgaria and Romania were not just political monopolies; they sought absolute control over the public past. As Jowitt has noted and Katherine Verdery explored in detail, Communist control over intellectual discourse never realized absolutist goals, and many pre-1944 intellectual traditions and debates were adopted or re-emerged, for example, Dacianism in Romania in the Socialist era (Jowitt, 1992; Verdery, 1995). But fascism was different: as a past ideological enemy, particularly for Communist Parties in a close relationship with the Soviet Union, it remained a public taboo. In this sense, we argue, the crucial legacy is that of the Socialist era, which created conditions for a mutable memory of fascism: the rejection of Socialist-era historical memory allowed for the substitution and revival of new, often inaccurate, memories of fascism. This problem is, moreover, not limited to Bulgaria and Romania; the history of interwar fascist movements, or wartime collaborationist regimes, is a common one in Central and Eastern Europe, and the "ideological vacuum" created by Socialism is similarly common in the region (Cohen, 1999; Minkenberg, 2002).

This has created in many respects a mutable history which contemporary political parties across the spectrum can draw upon, the radical right among them. We correspondingly argue for the consideration of the ideological and rhetorical positions of contemporary right-radical groups — and to compare these with those expressed by interwar fascism — in considering the question of legacies.

Historical roots: the interwar discourse of native fascist ideology in Romania and Bulgaria

In Romania, the Legion of the Archangel Michael emerged self-consciously as a part of an interwar European-wide fascist revolution. As Radu Gyr argued: "the new European (man-J.F.), nationalist, spiritualist and energetic, [...] will create a new world, a new ethic" (Gyr, 1935), the desire for a "palingenetic" revolution that would accomplish a rebirth of the nation. The First World War saw Romania on the side of the victors, doubling its territory. But the social and economic integration of the new "Great Romania" created political crises, later exacerbated by the machinations of King Carol II. The Legion, under the leadership of Corneliu Codreanu, offered an alternative route to modernization to solve this crisis (Livezeanu, 1995).

At its core, the Legion was, unusually for fascist movements, a professedly religious movement that looked at Orthodoxy for validation of its beliefs, palingenetic but expressed through religious mysticism. Its ideology centered on the construction of the " new man" whose purpose was to embody Orthodox morality and spread such in society through example and missionary work. The focus of state rituals and propaganda in National Socialist Germany and Fascist Italy were based on profane elements: race and state. The Nazi goal of *Volksgemeinschaft* was ultimately a racial goal; the Italian Fascist goal of empire stressed the territorial expansion of the state through conquest and the extension of the power of the party and state into the lives of its inhabitants.

The Legion of the Archangel Michael's definition of the organic nation centered itself along theological terms: the "new order" the Legion envisaged was not a racial or imperial utopia, but a Christian one. Codreanu's avowed goal was to bring about true Orthodox life in Romania, through a transcendental revolution, although his sincerity has been debated by scholars (Iordachi, 2004; Ioanid, 2004). As such, the movement "does not aim solely at the earthly accomplishment of the Romanian nation, but at guiding it on its path to salvation [...] not only a national rebirth, but a rebirth of Christian life." (Polihroniade, 1937).

Codreanu was *Omul Nou* (The New Man): the quintessential embodiment of the Legion's revolutionary promise (Protopopescu, 1937). The image of the *Capitan* in the press can be traced to the performative aspects of Legionary ideology, an *Imitatio Christi*, focused on *Theologia Crucis* rather than *Theologia Gloriae*. From thence emerges the New Man's emphasis on faith, sacrifice and obedience: as Codreanu instructs in the 1933 *Cărticica Șefului de Cuib* [The Nest Leader's Handbook] "all share one thought: the Fatherland, one flag, one commander, one king, one God, one will: that of serving faithfully unto death." (Codreanu, 1933) The Captain was likened to a monk, embracing "ascension in spirit and the closeness to the purity of asceticism." Similarly, the Captain is indispensable as a vessel of salvation, leading the "cell of shining light, which [...] will save of its own accord" (Moța, 1936). Codreanu appears either as the avatar of salvation, or, as he suggests in the core text of the movement, *Pentru Legionari* [For My Legionaries], directly empowered by the Archangel Michael (Codreanu, 1936).

The Legionaries who died in the Spanish Civil War were perceived as saints: "for the salvation of our nation God had to accept the sacrifice of Moța, the same way he accepted the sacrifice of the lamb for the salvation of humankind" (Ionescu, 1937). The Legion created its own pantheon of martyrs: not simply secular analogies, but martyrs that were worshipped in a similar fashion as Orthodox saint; their sacrifice made in the name of the movement and leader – and, for the Legion, in the name of God.

> I am joyful, and I die happy with my contentment for having been able to feel your call, to understand and to serve you. [...] I did not do enough for the Legion these past years, but I believed and believe in you, and I never sinned against this belief not even in the most hidden fold of my soul. (Moța, 1936)

Some of the lower clergy shared the belief that Codreanu's actions were a manifestation of God's direct intervention in Romania. One priest related how he became a Legionary after witnessing Codreanu praying, realizing that he "transformed his mind into a *liturghisitor* [the ordained celebrant of the liturgical and sacramental life of the community] and his soul into an altar to God" (Palaghita, 1993). The symbolism of transforming the new man's mind into a container for the liturgy is powerful; in Orthodoxy the liturgy is the bond that keeps the heavenly and the earthly Church indissolubly connected. Although the Legion was leery of seeking to usurp the Church, it confidently proclaimed "God is a Fascist!"

The implication of this union, as directly stated in Moța's quote above, is that to transgress against Legionary ideology is "to sin." The Legion cast matters in terms of good and evil, and Moța construes disobedience as outright evil. Thus, failure to protect the nation is transformed from treason into sin; and the Legion recast the "political class" of Romania from secular revivals into the tormentors of the modern Messiah: Codreanu's image and political struggle were defined in Christian terms, an axis where the Legion represented good and its opponents evil.

In this nexus, the Legion refined the extant and widespread religious anti-Semitism common in Romania (Brustein and King, 2004). Notably, the Legionary ideologue Moța had previously translated *The Protocols of the Elders of Zion* into Romanian in the early 1920s. Jews were now cast as the "ultimate evil," the most extreme extension of the secular, foreign corruption poisoning Romania. The Jewish minority was given the status of the Antichrist and the future of Romania was defined as a battle against an apocalyptic Bolshevik-Judaic conspiracy. Codreanu's successor after his death, Horia Sima, believed that the book contained "the concrete plans of Jews for realizing their dream of conquering the world." Jews and Freemasons were the protagonists of Guardist conspiracy theories, their socio-economic domination and occult abilities to influence politics rendering them especially dangerous (Iordachi, 2004). Communism, in particular, was viewed as the "work of Lucifer," a "new attempt to destroy the kingdom of god." Even after the Legion's defeat and expulsion in a *coup* by General Ion Antonescu and the Romanian Army in January 1941, the Legionary movement (led by Sima) continued to preserve the Legion's ideology in exile (first in Germany, then in Spain) and prepare for the coming political rapture. The Legion represents an extreme, mystic formulation of fascism's palingenetic revolution, one that that merged popular Orthodox religious traditions with an intellectual belief in the unique spiritual and historical nature of Romania. It was, moreover, by popular participation one of the largest fascist movements in Europe.

In contrast, a Bulgarian national fascist ideology was never clearly articulated. There were at least seven fascist-leaning groups in interwar Bulgaria: the Popular Social Movement (*Narodno Sotsialno Dvizhenie*), the Union of Bulgarian National Legions *(Suioz na bulgarskite natsionalni legioni,* or *Legionari)*, the Bulgarian Motherland Defense (*Bulgarska Rodna Zashita*), the Bulgarian Horde *(Bulgarska Orda)*, the Warriors for the Advancement of the Bulgarian National Spirit (*Ratnichestvo za napreduk na bulgarshtinata,* or "*Ratnik*s"), the Defenders ("*Brannik*s") and the All-Bulgarian Union "Father Paisii" (*Vsebulgarskite suioz "Otets Paisii"*). This plurality represented less the strength of fascist ideology as much as it did the fragmentation of the political far right, which was kept clearly in check by the *Zveno* ("Link") and Royalist dictatorships following their respective *coup d'etats* in 1934 and 1935.

Bulgarian fascists perceived the nation to be in crisis, possibly an understatement in interwar Bulgaria. The "national catastrophes" of the Balkan Wars and First World War meant extensive territorial losses and hostile regimes in Greece, Romania and the Kingdom of Yugoslavia. Domestically, the state was sapped by political infighting stemming from the coup in 1923 against the post-war Agrarian regime, the Communist uprising of 1923, and the spread of Macedonian émigré terrorism. The Turkish minority was seen as a possible "fifth column," with efforts made to limit its ties to Kemal Atatürk's revolutionary state. The Great Depression crippled the country's agricultural economy and deepened the sense of crisis, leading to a new coup in 1934, and in 1935, the establishment of a "royal dictatorship."

Bulgarian fascists sought a national revolution to address this crisis — albeit a limited revolution in the sense of a transformation of government, the economy and social values to serve the goals of an idealized and unified nation. The concept of *bulgarnost* ("bulgarianness") dominated fascists' visions of Bulgaria, but it retained the existing ethnographic definition of the nation, and sought the realization of an existing nation-building project rather than the transformation of the nation. The various Bulgarian fascist groups offered little that was new in terms of defining the nation, despite flirtation with non-Slavic origins (an Aryan fusion between ancient Thracians and the proto-Bulgars of the early medieval era). True, these groups agreed on the need to reaffirm and "perfect" Bulgarian national consciousness, and to create a unified national spirit in which "separate — personal and class — interests [must be subordinated to]... the interests of a vaster community" (Mutafchiev, 1935).

To achieve this, Bulgarian fascist groups demanded shifts in state policy. A revisionist and aggressive foreign policy would secure for Bulgaria "what used to be and has to be ours:" the territory lost in the Balkan and First World Wars. An interventionist economic policy would moderate capitalism and force it to "serve the people and their interests." The Bulgarian Legionaries favored a corporatist economy influenced by Italian Fascism; Alexander Tsankov's *Narodno Sotsialno Dvizhenie* (Popular Social Movement) stressed "harmonious and organized cooperation." Every group called for the state to create social justice and support a "healthy national spirit" and "unified way of life." "The ideals of Bulgarian youth must be: a spiritually revived, nationally-unified and a strong Bulgaria." The church, traditional culture, the Bulgarian language and national history were all to be protected and strengthened against foreign influence and corruption (Tsankov, 1938; Legion, 1938).

Such fascist calls to defend the nation are difficult to separate neatly from similar calls by nearly all non-Communist political groups in Bulgaria between the wars. Fascist goals were not dissimilar to previous nation- and state-building efforts in Bulgaria. Most parties favored revision of the Treaty of Neuilly, state economic intervention, and a focus on "cultural politics" to strengthen the nation (and continue nineteenth century nation-building). The coup of 1934, led by the *Zveno* circle (a technocratic and ostensibly "non-political" group backed by elements of the army) pre-empted fascists by declaring that they aimed to "direct the spiritual and intellectual life of the country towards union and renovation for the benefit of the nation and of the state" and would "organiz[e] the citizens into an ideologically homogenous national group." When *Zveno* was replaced by the "royal dictatorship" of Tsar Boris III in 1935, potential support for fascism was expropriated by the regime (much as elsewhere in Southeastern Europe, where, in Greece, Hungary, Romania, and Yugoslavia, traditional conservative parties were successful in pre-empting revolutionary fascist challenges.

The national programs outlined by the Bulgarian Legionaries in *Nashata Borba* (Our Struggle) and by Tsankov as leader of the NSD in *Moiata Programa* (My Program) were, overall, quite similar to the *Ideologiia i programa na upravlenieto v Bulgariia* (Ideology and Program of the Government of Bulgaria) published in 1942 under an authoritarian and conservative — but non-fascist — wartime government. As elsewhere in interwar Europe, fascists, the radical right and conservatives shared similar concerns — and the latter not infrequently pre-empted rivals on the right by borrowing or modifying proposed solutions to national crises (Blinkhorn, 1990).

This highlights the problem that the ideological differences between Bulgarian interwar conservatism and fascism are not always clear. The revolutionary aspects of fascist movements in Italy, Germany or Romania were weakly expressed in Bulgaria: there was little call for the radical overthrow of democratic governance, for government based on the leadership principle or the creation of a "new man" and reorganization of society. Granted, fascist and pro-fascist articles argued that parliamentary democracy was weak and in need of reform, but did not call for outright rebellion:

> Many political parties are a known evil. They bring death for
> the parliamentary rule, because they give diversity of com-
> position to parliament, incapable of erasing the homogeny
> and strong government (Vladikin, 1943).

The absence of revolutionary rhetoric might have been intended as reassurance for Tsar Boris III and his government. But the discourse of the far right (in journals like *Otets Paisii*), suggested that the dilemma of interwar Bulgarian democracy was not a problem of parliaments *per se*, but of distinct conditions that could be remedied. Parliamentary rule under the monarchy could be transformed, raised above issues of class and turned into an instrument of the nation.

The fact that fascists drew from existing conservative ideas reflects the crosspollination among groups on the right. But Bulgarian fascists may well have sought a different goal from groups elsewhere: the continuation of the national project. Roger Griffin argues that fascist parties sought a palingenetic revolution that would recast and recreate the nation to "free" or "redeem" the nation from its state of crisis brought about by perceived flaws in modernization (Griffin, 2004; Sternhell, 1986). In the Bulgarian context, however, modernization was perceived as still under way. The Bulgarian nation had already been reborn after "five centuries of Ottoman slavery" (Lukov, 1942). What Bulgarian fascists sought now was the completion of this rebirth. Fascist discourse embraced the idea of the nation's continued development and the optimistic prospect of overcoming the crisis posed by the Treaty of Neuilly and

Bulgaria's unfavorable economic and political position. Bulgaria's fascist groups were not only weak, divided and lacking a well-articulated ideology, but their relatively positive worldview differed considerably from that of Fascism and Nazism.

Romania and Bulgaria's defeat in the Second World War and the subsequent rise of Communist-led "popular front" governments shattered fascist movements in both states. Although individuals might be rehabilitated (particularly in Romania, where thousands of Iron Guardists subsequently joined the Communist Party), the movements were decisively crushed. And yet, ironically, Communist regimes in both states preserved the memory of fascism from 1944 to 1989.

Fascism in Marxist discourse, 1944-1989

Marxism established a systematic approach to fascism that was extensively popularized during the years of Socialist rule, and this has provided a convenient foil for post-1989 radical right parties. Marxists were among the first to analyze fascism given its direct and immediate threat. Early definitions recognized the revolutionary nature of fascism, the attraction it could exercise over the proletariat, and its international potential. By the Thirteenth Plenum of the Enlarged Executive of the Communist International in 1933, the definition of fascism had been recast as "open, terrorist dictatorship of the most reactionary, most chauvinist and most imperialist elements of finance capital" (Griffin, 1995) Instead of providing a discriminating critique, the Stalinist definition created a continuum where fascism was a "catch-all" category at the opposite end of the spectrum from Communism (Cioflanca, 2004). This continued after the war, when Communists sought to monopolize the experience of both resistance to, and suffering under, fascism (Furet, 1999).

Initial post-war Romanian and Bulgarian Marxist approaches accorded fascism more complexity. Lucretiu Patrascanu's *Fundamental Problems of Romania* was published in 1944; while narrowly defined fascism in economic terms, Patrascanu ascribed mass support to the fascists (he included Antonescu among them), highlighted the massacre of Romanian Jews and recognized the indigenous roots of the Holocaust: "Anti-Semitism remains a Romanian phenomenon." Similarly, People's Court Session VII in Sofia, Bulgaria in March 1945 tried 64 government officials for their role in the "fascist" royal dictatorship, including the Commissariat for Jewish Affairs and the use of forced labor battalions. These approaches were soon modified. Patrascanu was arrested in 1948, executed in 1954, and his work remained censored past his 1968 rehabilitation. In Bulgaria, as Steven Sage argues, Session VII was soon dropped from the historical narrative, a Stalinist definition of bourgeois fascism was substituted that included every government from 1923 through 1944. Antonescu and the Iron Guard in Romania, Bulgarian fascism, the interwar conservatives and Boris' dictatorship ("monarcho-fascism") were textbook cases of "blind historical forces" bound to failure under the onslaught of victorious Communism (Cioflanca, 2004; Radulov, 1967). A focus on fascist anti-Communism eclipsed the complex way that Romanian and Bulgarian fascist ideology viewed minorities (Shafir, 2004; Chary, 1972; Memishev, 1977).

By definition, fascism was an "evil other" that had opposed the interests of the nation championed by the Communist Party. Jewish victims were displaced by the idea of Romania and Bulgaria as victims. In Romania, Mihail Roller's 1947 *History of Romania* is a key example of this trend, fascism embodying "monopoly capital" controlled and created by the Nazis for the economic exploitation of Romania. Through "cruel acts, the Legionary-Antonescu dictatorship proved its affinity with the crimes committed by the German Hitlerites" (Roller et al., 1947). The victims of the Holocaust were the Communists, and would remain so in school textbooks even as the menace of fascism was kept alive domestically and rhetorically: "The liquidation of all of the fascist remains and the isolation of reactionary circles is a condition of a durable peace!" (Gheorghiu-Dej, 1945). One of the charges against former Bulgarian foreign minister Traicho Kostov in 1949 was conspiracy with Titoists, American agents and "Hitlerite" fascists. During the 1961 plenum of the central committee, Gheorghiu-Dej denounced the Pauker-Luca-Georgescu and Chisinevschi-Constantinescu factions as "having used their powerful positions in 1944-1948 to admit (and even invite) former Iron Guard members into the party" (Tismaneanu, 2003).

More subtle scholarly approaches emerged during the 1970s and 1980s, distinguishing between the conservative opportunism of Antonescu and Boris III and the ideological views of fascists (Cioflanca, 2004; Zhelev, 1990; Poppetrov, 2008). This represented, in part, the turn of both Bulgaria and Romania to nationalist strains of Communism. By redeeming elements of the "nationalist past," both regimes sought to cast themselves as the representation of not just historical "class" progress, but historical national progress. Ceausescu's endorsement of a Romano-Dacian identity for the Romanian nation (dating its genesis to the mid-third century AD), or Zhivkova's celebration of "1300 hundred years of the Bulgarian nation" were expressions of this trend (Boia, 2001; Verdery, 2003; Crampton, 2007). This was a particular problem in Romania; although the Bulgarian Communist Party could inflate a reasonably substantial legacy, in Romania the Party faced the dilemma that, in the interwar period, it had been perceived as a tool of the Soviet Union and substantially composed of ethnic minorities.

In this regard, it made good sense to maintain a political discourse in which the category of fascism in Romania was not limited to the Iron Guard, nor in Bulgaria limited to the specific fascist groups noted above. Rather "fascism" continued to include a range of varied movements, such as the Romanian Orthodox traditionalists from *Gandirea* and the entire traditionalist current from the interwar debate with the modernizers, or elements in Bulgaria of *Zveno* and Tsankov's early government of 1923. Texts for popular dissemination thus remained rhetorically strident: fascism was "imposed from abroad" and widely hated locally, being supported only by "bandits," "hooligans," "murderers," "terrorists," and the "fifth column of Hitlerism" (Fatu and Spalatelu, 1980). This helped to serve a claim that the Communist parties were expressions of national sentiment and aims. But it also embraced the sometimes comically blatant misuse of the past, such as museum exhibits to "Vlad Tepeş, Socialist Ruler of Romania." The Socialist-era not only created a "straw man" memory of fascism that would be widely rejected after 1989; part of the Communist legacy is arguably the frequent misuse and miscategorization of historical symbols, a tradition that has continued well into transition (Boia, 2001).

"The radical right:" Ataka and the Greater Romanian Party

Fascism was "alive and well" in Communist discourse; but this was a nebulous and diffuse concept of fascism that spanned much of the conservative and nationalist spectrum and diluted the racial, revolutionary, nationalist and violent characteristics of the movement (Judt, 2000). Moreover, Communism's categorization of fascism created a certain symmetry: for many, fascism's chief characteristic was its "anti-Communist" approach. With the revolutions of 1989 and the end of a monopolistic discourse on public history, fascist symbols were a strong symbol of opposition to the past regime. They were not, of course, the only symbol, and renewed reverence for anti-Communist authoritarian figures such as Marshal Ion Antonescu and Tsar

Boris III has been much more visible. In the 1990s the opportunity emerged to "explore" a fascist past that many in both countries saw as a more indigenous part of their national past than Communism. Both Ataka and the Greater Romania Party would experiment with drawing on the fascist heritage. But a consideration of the ideology expressed by both groups in publications, speeches, and television programs reveals sharp continuities with historic fascist ideology.

The *Natsionalen suioz Ataka* emerged as a coalition in the 2005 elections created by (and some argue, an extension of) former journalist, aspiring politician and television personality Volen Siderov. The party's surprising success in elections made it the fourth largest party in the country, reinforced by Siderov's second place in the 2006 presidential elections. The party's consistent popularity in polls by Angus Reid has since dismissed expectations that it would soon fade from politics.

Siderov sets the tone for Ataka in his speeches, "Attack!" show on the private SKAT cable television channel, *Ataka* newspaper, and in three books written before the formation of Ataka. His books detail his accusations regarding Jewish and Masonic plots to use global finance (and the world wars) to weaken and destroy Orthodox Christian Slavs in general and Bulgaria in particular (Siderov, 2003, 2004). Communism, for example, "was not Russian but Jewish," and was assisted to power by the United States (Siderov, 2002). In his books, Siderov sees American influence, the CIA, NATO, globalization, and Zionism (which he equates with the United States) as the latest such plots to rule Bulgaria. Although the most flamboyant part of Siderov's political personality, this has little in common with Bulgarian fascism, which focused little on anti-Semitism (with the later exception of the *Ratnik*s). Although the grand scope of this work parallels elements of Aleksandr Dugin's Eurasianism in seeking a "new order" to oppose American hegemony, unlike Dugin, Siderov is clearly comfortable calling for a xenophobic solution (Laruelle, 2008). Siderov's anti-Semitism is particularly striking, given that anti-Semitism was not a powerful political force in interwar Bulgaria and is largely (if not exclusively) a post-1989 phenomenon (Brustein and King, 2004). Similarly, Siderov draws on Orthodox mysticism not to lay claim to a sense of pan-Slavism but on the Bulgarian Orthodox Church as a national symbol of tradition and strength.

Siderov sets the tone for Ataka's political agenda, much of which is displayed in the party newspaper, *Vestnik Ataka* (Ataka Newspaper), and a weekly television show on the *SKAT* television network. To prevent the weakening the state and the economic victimization of ordinary Bulgarians, the group opposes those it sees as the villains responsible: Roma, ethnic Turks, "queers," corrupt politicians, the economic problems of ordinary Bulgarians, unfair aspects of EU accession and American domination. In establishing this position, Ataka has embraced certain aspects of Bulgarian skinhead culture and interwar fascism — such as the common use of the phrase *"Bulgaria nad vsichko"* (Bulgarians above all).

Arguing that minorities are a danger to an ethnic Bulgarian state by "stealing" social services and undermining the state, Ataka has framed its position in ethnic and national terms that draw on the symbology of interwar fascism to create a healthy national spirit. Siderov has equally drawn on Communist precedents: in calling for ethnic Turks to Bulgarianize their names, he evoked the 1980s campaign by the Communist Party to "assimilate" Turks. This plays well to popular concern of a declining ethnic Bulgarian birthrate in the face of an increasing Muslim Turkish and Roma population, stereotypes of "gypsy criminals" and accusations that the Turkish-affiliated Movement for Rights and Freedoms is unduly powerful in government. Where Ataka goes beyond the common Bulgarian tropes of "Turkish slavery" and anger over the past is by calling for the "de-Turkification" and "de-Islamicization" of Bulgaria, including banning non-Bulgarian language media. Siderov similarly denounces both the "traitorous blow" of the Neuilly Treaty and the 1915 Bulgaro-Turkish population exchange, calling for reparations for descendants of the latter (Popkostadinova, 2006). Ataka officially calls for Bulgaria to be a "mono-ethnic" state and for the assimilation or emigration of ethnic minorities.

Ataka uses its position in parliament to cast itself as a party defending disadvantaged and victimized ethnic Bulgarians against the crisis of transition, calling for national unity — "Bulgaria for the Bulgarians" — in the face of crisis. Ataka's core "20 points" (published in the party newspaper and on the group's website: http://www.ataka.bg) are a hodge-podge that seeks the intervention of state power in a host of social and economic issues. This is effective in forcing certain issues into the national discourse, and Ataka has taken the lead in criticizing the closure of two Bulgarian nuclear reactors at Kozlodui as a price of EU admission, the privatization of state-owned firms, sending Bulgarian troops abroad to assist US operations in Iraq, allowing American troops basing rights in Bulgaria, and in calling for the reinstitution of the death penalty (often temporarily popular following high-profile murder incidents in Bulgaria, such as in 2008). On these issues and others, Ataka has been notably successful in forcing rival political parties to enter the political fray in their own defense or else risk allowing Ataka to monopolize certain positions — and correspondingly attract "single issue" voters, who make up a considerable number of Ataka's supporters at the polls (Stefanova, 2007).

Yet unlike interwar Bulgarian fascist groups, Ataka has not demanded a political and social revolution to create a "new order" in Bulgarian politics. Even if it replicates certain themes of interwar fascist discourse, Ataka does not seem to seek even the limited revolution envisioned by Bulgarian fascists. Whereas Kristen Ghodsee has ascribed to Ataka a singular ability to pursue both a "far-left" and "far-right" agenda at the same time, this characteristic was far more pronounced in interwar fascist groups that sought cross-class social and economic equality through revolution (Ghodsee, 2008). Ataka demands the defense of the nation, the redressing of various injustices, and the practical exclusion from state citizenship of confessional and ethnic minorities; but the vehicle for these goals is through legal continuity and the ballot box. Indeed, Siderov has consistently denied that Ataka is a fascist party.

The same distinctions are true of the Greater Romania Party, which goes even farther in terms of adopting the symbols and heritage of the past. Like Ataka, the Greater Romania Party is largely centered around one man: chairman Corneliu Vadim Tudor. Tudor has set much of the tone for the PRM's agenda (including columns for the party newspaper, *Romania Mare*), stressing the transition period as a period of crisis, the role of foreign conspiracies abroad and corruption at home, and the need for "unity and strength." During Communism Tudor was a "court poet" of Nicolae Ceauşescu and a supporter of the protochronist approach to national history who flirted with rehabilitating right-wing interwar discourse within a nationalist Communist narrative of history, and in the initial post-Socialist period the PRM's platform included elements of Ceausescu's nationalist-Communist agenda. The journal *România Mare* established his trademark combination of polemic articles and attacks on anyone Tudor considered an enemy of the fatherland. Tudor creates a strange and sometimes contradictory political genealogy which tries to reclaim a great deal of the interwar extreme and conservative right while at the same time maintaining the legacy of nationalist Communism. The result is a curious mixture drawing upon ultra-nationalism, including that of the Legion. Until 2004 the party was a forum for anti-Semites, extreme nationalists, former party *apparatchiks*, and Guardists both old and new. Tudor himself openly approached the French National Front, calling for a "fraternal alliance" and stating that PRM "adheres without hesitation" to the front's programs and ideas, and inviting Jean-Marie Le Pen to visit Romania in 1997.

Although Tudor skirts direct allusions to a Legionary influence on his nationalism, two of his collaborators, Ion Coja and Gheorghe Buzatu (a PRM member and former senator) are openly pro-Legionary (Coja, 2001; Buzatu, 1995). Moreover, while the bulk of his ideology is clearly descended from the populist nationalist rhetoric of the 1980s, Guardist symbols and discursive practices are also in evidence, together with those borrowed from other exponents of the interwar right. The driving force behind these appropriations is political opportunism: Tudor and the PRM have appropriated a diverse set of nationalist symbolism from recent political history that draws on Legionary discourse among others.

This is clearly articulated in the strong anti-Semitic undercurrents of the PRM. Tudor's anti-Semitism (prior to his professed rehabilitation in 2004, when he hired an Israeli public relations agent, Eyal Arad, to reshape his public image) meshes well with that of the interwar Legion. Although anti-Semitism, in the sense of hostility to Jews as a collective group, is a common element in much of Romania's twentieth century political discourse (including during the Communist period), Tudor goes further to accuse Jews of masterminding international anti-Romanian conspiracies, and equates Bolshevism, Stalinism and the post-war Communist terror with Jews. Arguably, Tudor has consciously drawn upon the tropes of Legionary anti-Semitism in phrasing his accusations. According to Tudor, the Jews entered Romania on the tanks of the Red Army; all Bolshevik revolutions (Russia, Hungary and Germany) were "led" by Jews, and, along with Hungarians they dominated the "international" (post-war) party leadership, aided by Roma and the Romanian spouses of Jews. Jewish and Freemason conspiracies have been one of his favorite subjects, and he has insinuated that the Holocaust is a hoax intended to steal the riches of Romania (Tudor, 2001). Such anti-Semitic statements are tied to accusations of economic victimization and corruption, on which the PRM can appeal to populist anger over transition.

Many similarities in the ideals of the PRM and the Legion, however, are due to their common context. The idea of Romania as an "island of Roman descent" besieged in a sea of other peoples is present in both Tudor's discourse and that of the Legion — mainly because it is a trope shared by nearly *all* Romanian nationalists. Irredentism (union with the Republic of Moldova) is another of the leit-motifs of the PRM, backed by considerable effort on behalf of Ilie Ilascu, considered one of the heroes in the struggle against Transdniester separatism. Again, this is shared with the Legion, but also across most of the political spectrum.

In reference to the distinctive element of Legionary ideology, the spiritual framing of crisis and the need for redemption, Tudor and the PRM have heavily appropriated certain ideas – but in limited fashion. The classical ideas of Orthodoxism and the Church as an important part of the Romanian national being and a healer of factional misunderstandings among the leaders are fairly common in Vadim's speeches. Two major elements of Legionary discourse appear beyond these. The first is the conflation of historically inspired leaders, considered to be part of the "political genealogy" of the party, with Jesus Christ. The sacralization of historical figures goes hand in hand with the idea of a Messiah of the Nation and the Legionary saints. Tudor draws upon the Legion in hinting that mysticism and piety will save Romania: "asceticism [is] a supreme price of liberty" (Tudor, 2001).

Ultimately, it would be impossible for the Tudor and the PRM to fully embrace the Legion's brand of religious nationalism. Tudor himself was previously a Baptist (though he later claimed conversion to Romanian Orthodoxy) and would be suspect by Legionary standards. The PRM's engagement in "party politics" would also be suspect. And Tudor fundamentally differs from the Legion on a penultimate point: the Legion's leaders were saviors of the spirit of the nation: Codreanu and Moța's fate as martyrs (as well as the fate of the *Echipele Morții* or "death squads") was one of redemption. The PRM, however, presents its leadership as embodying the spirit of the nation. Although Tudor draws upon Legionary symbolism, his leadership style has much more in common with the national Communism of Ceaușescu. Arguably, too, his radical shift in 2004 repudiating his earlier anti-Semitism speaks more to political opportunism rather than heartfelt, shared belief in the Legion's anti-Semitic views.

Much like Ataka, the PRM has been successful in forcing specific issues onto the national political agenda: privatization, corruption within the government, unification with Moldova. Its success, particularly in 2000, came by mobilizing single issue voters and "protest votes" against rival parties. The party's decline in the 2008 Romanian election (in which it failed to gain representation in parliament for the first time since 1993) reflects both the new electoral laws (parliamentary members are elected directly by district, marginalizing fringe parties) and the remarkably low voter turnout in 2008 (less than 40 percent). It remains uncertain what the impact of the global economic downturn in 2009 will mean for the party.

"In the fascist style:" the New Generation Party and the Bulgarian National Alliance

If Ataka and the PRM draw on common tropes from interwar fascism, then the New Generation Party and Bulgarian National Alliance go a step beyond this, in consciously replicating the "look and feel" of fascism. George Becali's political career as leader of the PNG was from its inception based on Legionary material. As a presidential candidate in the 2004 elections, his slogans were taken almost verbatim from the Legion: "Everything for the Country," his chief slogan, was used by the Legion in 1935. When his advisor, scholar Dan Pavel, was confronted on whether he used his expertise on the Legion for profit, he admitted that "as Becali's consultant he would make more money than he would have made in 10 years as a university professor."

While Gigi Becali identifies himself closely with Legionary discourse and symbolism, his is a Guardism refracted through Communism and prompted by political opportunism. His use of Legionary symbols is often egregious: during a televised interview on Oglinda TV he called for Codreanu's canonization within the Romanian Orthodox Church. Yet his attempt at a messianic cult of the leader is as reminiscent of Ceauşescu's as of the fascist New Man. Gigi allegedly entered politics because "thus I found my way to salvation: fighting for the spiritual elevation of the nation." Where Codreanu constructed himself as the New Man, a Christ-like redeemer planning the eventual spiritual transformation of every Romanian, for Becali the elevation of the country is to be achieved simply through his complete assumption of power: he does not call for a further, spiritual revolution. Becali claims God gave him the wisdom and the strength to lead, but he does not mention a revolution of the Romanian soul. This leader-cult is thus closer to Ceauşescu's role as the "guarantor of social stability and interests of the nation" (Boia, 2001). Becali's stated priorities in government similarly call for a program of legislation that is specific to state powers rather than to spiritualism. Ultimately, it is a graft of legionary language on a different political construct; despite attempts to adopt the ideology of the interwar period, Becali instead adopts their language and "style" in pursuing rather different political goals. While more overt in utilizing the legacy of the Legion, the PNG, like the PRM, does not represent a direct and complete continuity of Legionary goals.

God and the Orthodox Church figure prominently in Becali's speeches, much as in Tudor's, although the disclosure of the latter had been a practicing Baptist allowed Becali to claim greater authenticity as a force for right-wing mysticism (Gallagher, 2005). Becali has accordingly drawn parallels between himself and the Legion, in placing the belief in God (and Orthodox symbolism) as central to his political movement. Yet praxis and theological understanding differ considerably. Where the Legion went in villages to build Orthodox Churches with their own hands, Becali "...made tens of churches, even I don't know their number, I gave tens of thousands of dollars. Sixty- to seventy-thousand [in Bucharest alone]." He apes Legionary political religion in placing the Church and Bible at the center of both his discourse on success as a football team owner and politician. Instead of emphasis on redemption and complex interpretation of dogma, Becali sees belief in God more in terms of cause and effect. Thus, when his football club *Steaua* lost an important match, it was because the players sinned: "they fornicated on Easter!" (This is no trivial point, given that the Becali phenomenon is not dissimilar to Berlusconi's use of AC Milan to promote the *Forza Italia*, albeit less successfully.)

The PNG has actively sought to sap the PRM's support base and symbols; just as the PRM has sought to inject its own agenda into Romanian national politics, the PNG attempts to do the same *and* to criticize the PRM, casting itself as a "true" opposition party. In 2004 Becali attempted to appropriate Ilie Ilascu, the hero of the war in Transdniester and currently an MP of the PRM, in extending the PNG into the Republic of Moldova. Similarly, during the 2005 summer floods Becali personally donated monetary aid to Romanian villagers who had lost their homes, the PNG going on to attack the government for its slow response to the crisis. This has allowed the PNG to maintain itself as a rallying point for protest against conventional politics: polling, for example, as the second most popular party in the country during the 2007 deadlock between President Traian Băsescu and Parliament. Becali's ability to make consistently strong political inroads, however, may be attributed to both his unconventional personality (his cursing of a sports reporter over the phone in his role as *Steaua* owner became a Romanian internet meme, and an embarrassment to the PNG) and perhaps to derision of his "inauthentic" attempts to lay claim to fascist heritage. He notably has quarreled with his political advisor, Dan Pavel, over his negotiations for fusion with

Ion Coja and the neo-legionary New Right party [*Noua Dreapta*]. These agreements allegedly fell through because the old Guardists, who continue to live abroad in exile, disapprove of Becali and the PNG for their failures to properly understand Legionary doctrine. While the PNG deploys the Legion in its political genealogy, and makes extensive use of its discourse (emphasizing struggle, religion, sometimes honesty – if enough time has passed after the last scandal) his borrowings place him on the extremist right without giving him fascist credentials.

The *Bulgarski Natsionalen Suioz* (Bulgarian National Alliance, or BNS) similarly and openly draws upon the heritage of indigenous fascism. Founded in 2001 by Boian Rasate, the group allied with other far-right groups and, in 2005, with Ataka. It broke with the larger movement in 2006 and, although its active membership remains small, it has emerged as the leading party on the extreme radical right, absorbing smaller movements and entering the 2009 parliamentary elections. On its website, the BNS defends itself a nationalist party and insists that the "fascism" is a smear used by Socialists and Communists. Despite such proclamations, the group openly praises certain interwar fascist traditions and claims as its patron General Hristo Lukov, the founder of the interwar Bulgarian Legionaries. The BNS reveres these figures next to a more traditional pantheon of national heroes, such as Vasil Levski and Todor Aleksandrov, the ancient Bulgar khanates, and Bulgaria's past military accomplishment (the group's website lauds, for example, the defense of Sofia from American "terrorist" bombing raids in 1943-44).

Like Ataka, the BNS promises to rescue the nation from the crises of transition. The group's website, online forums, weekly cable television show (on SKAT TV) and speeches by its founder, Boian Rasate, frequently stress the need to reclaim and protect Bulgaria from corrupt politicians, globalization, NATO, the United States, Turks and especially Roma (anti-Semitic statements are less common.) To forestall a future in which "Bulgaria will have three million Bulgarians and three million Gypsies" (http://bg.bgns.net/Aktualno/Statii/) in August 2007 the BNS announced the creation of a brown-shirted paramilitary wing, the *Gvard* (Guard) to combat "gypsy crime," drawing a furor from across the Bulgarian political spectrum. Although popular sentiment in press polls expressed concern at the idea of an armed political militia, the BNS proved successful in raising the (perceived) issue of Roma crime on to the national agenda.

While similar to Ataka in taking broad positions on a number of discrete issues (for example, globalization, American hegemony, international capitalism, and minority issues), the BNS particularly focuses on the flaws of the contemporary Bulgarian government, which it denounces as an oligarchy, corrupt, parasites, perverts, traitors, and full of "democratic bullshit." Here, the BNS goes on to unambiguously call for a new national awakening to liberate Bulgaria and create a "new order" in the midst of the chaos of transition. This new order is not merely "Bulgaria for the Bulgarians" or "Bulgarians above all," but contains the seeds of a palingenetic revolution in Bulgarian society. One example is the flirtation by the group with Tangranism, linking the Bulgarian nation not to Slavic and Orthodox traditions but to an Aryan and pagan proto-Bulgarian identity. The group's symbol is stated as derived from that of the "Clan Dulo" of Bulgar Danubian and Volga Khanates. The statements and program of the BNS fit smoothly the broad discourse of interwar Bulgarian fascism.

Such overt attention to the trappings of fascism, however, conceals an ideological problem: to what degree is the BNS a continuation of interwar Bulgarian fascist thought, and to what degree does it reflect a wider international movement of "third positionism?" The group has actively cooperated in conferences and joint rallies with foreign groups such as the Spanish *La Falange,* Romanian *Noua Dreapta,* Belgian *Vlaams Blok,* German *Deutsches Kolleg* and Dutch *Nationale Alliantie.* Self-professed BNS members are not only active on the movement's online forum (http://forums.gvardia.net/index.php) but on broad Bulgarian radical right forums (http://www.forum.bg-nacionalisti.org) and international forums (http://www.stormfront.org). In this light, is the BNS directly drawing from the fragmented Bulgarian interwar fascist movements or also on the heritage of Italian Fascism or German National Socialism? Intriguingly, although *Mein Kampf* was translated and published in Bulgaria for the first time in 2001, interwar Bulgarian fascist tracts have not been republished in print (although many are available online). The merchandise sold by the movement's electronic store in 2007 included Imperial German naval insignias with the Bulgarian tricolor inset, "88" baseball caps (representing "Heil Hitler"), *Totenkopf* patches (worn, the caption notes, by Bulgarian tankers in 1944), and battle flags of the Confederate States of America. The sale of symbols of "international" fascist groups — rather than of, say, the interwar *Ratniks* or *Branniks* — suggests that there are multiple fascist discourses and heritages that members of the BNS draw upon, not all of them Bulgarian. Such a globalization of historical fascist symbols may represent an emerging, international fascist heritage not constrained to Central and Eastern Europe.

Legacy, heritage, opportunity?

Fascist interwar discourse provides the opportunity for contemporary radical right groups to appropriate symbols and tropes that sound exciting, that reside in an idealized national past and whose ideological underpinnings are no longer clear to people educated in the Socialist-era school system. One of the legacies of Communism in Central and Eastern Europe was to eliminate real discussion or examination of fascism, leaving it only in idealized private memory or as a nationalist caricature (Herf, 1997). There was no "Nuremberg moment" in which indigenous fascist ideology could be exposed and substantially debated; the Communist Parties alone dictated the public discourse on fascism. When freer discussions arose after 1989 regarding falsifications in Communist narratives of the past, fascism re-emerged as a viable part of the "useable past" (Iordachi and Trecsényi, 2003).

In this sense, we argue that the heritage of fascism is not that the radical right in these two countries is guided by a direct and continuous legacy of a fascist past, but that interwar fascist movements provide opportunity and material for "political entrepreneurs" of the radical right. This speaks to Maria Todorova's concerns about using the past to "predestine" a Balkan present (Todorova, 2004). But it also speaks to Lucian Boia's concern regarding the use and abuse of the historical past for contemporary political gain (Boia, 2001). Although the problems raised by contemporary political parties of the radical right and historic fascist movements may be similar, the solutions offered are distinctly different — a factor, we argue, in the different ideological underpinnings of these groups.

Arguably, the appeal of indigenous interwar fascism for the PRM, PNG, Ataka, and the BNS is fascism's credentials as indigenous (and nationalist) traditions untainted by the Socialist past. But this was only one element of fascist ideology (even within the relatively diffuse platforms of the various Bulgarian movements), the tenets of which have largely been rendered vague by the legacy of a Socialist monopoly of the past. This allows for the use of these symbols without the call for a "fascist revival," which is useful, since fascist ideology is not well suited for contemporary political life in Bulgaria and Romania. Moreover, it remains unclear to what degree the use of such symbology actually appeals to the voting public in both countries. Of the four groups examined above, the BNS draws mostly closely on fascist discourse — and, ironically, its adhesion to fascism's distaste for politics has crippled its attempts to contest Ataka dominance. This suggests the need for further research to see if the electoral popularity of contemporary radical right parties resonates with public opinion regarding historical indigenous fascist movements. That, in 2006, Cordreanu was found to be the 22nd in a popular vote for the "100 Greatest Romanians of All Time" by the Televiziunea Română television station, is a typical anecdotal piece of evidence occasionally cited in the domestic or international past — out of context, however, with the fact that Communist leader Nicolae Ceauşescu was ranked 11th despite the poor political fortunes of the current Communist Party (Nepecerişti).

In Bulgaria and Romania, fascist ideology was largely unknown and unknowable for 40 years. When this silence shattered in 1989, it brought into conversation two problematic pasts: the recent Communist one and that of barely-remembered interwar fascism. Contemporary radical right parties, perceiving post-Communist freedom as the freedom to select any aspect of the past (in, arguably, any fashion they wished), have opportunistically married fragments of interwar fascist discourse with conservative and socialist visions of the state and nation. In this sense, the legacy of fascist ideology and Communist is being bridged into an aggressive and populist framework suitable for open elections, if not an open society.

References

Blinkhorn, M., 1990. Fascists and Conservatives: The Radical Right and the Establishment in Twentieth-century Europe. Unwin Hyman, London.

Boia, L., 2001. History and Myth in Romanian Consciousness. Central European University Press, Budapest.

Brustein, W., King, R., 2004. Anti-Semitism as a response to perceived Jewish power: the cases of Bulgaria and Romania before the Holocaust. Social Forces 83 (2), 691-708.

Buzatu, G., 1995. Asa a inceput Holocaustul impotriva Poporului Roman [Thus Started the Holocaust Against the Romanian People]. Editura Majada-honda, Bucharest.

Chary, F., 1972. The Bulgarian Jews and the Final Solution, 1940-1944. University of Pittsburgh Press, Pittsburgh.

Cioflanca, A., 2004. A 'Grammar of Exculpation' in Communist historiography: distortion of the history of the Holocaust under Ceausescu. Romanian Journal of Political Science 4 (2), 29-46.

Codreanu, C.Z., 1933. Cărticica Sefului de Cuib [The Nest Leader's Booklet]. Editura C.S.M.C., Bucharest.

Codreanu, C.Z., 1936. Pentru Legionari [For my Legionaries]. Ed. Totul Pentru Tara, Sibiu.

Cohen, S., 1999. Politics Without a Past: The Absence of History in Post-communist Nationalism.
Duke University Press, Durham.

Coja, I., 2001. Legionarii Nostri [Our Legionaries]. Editura UMC, Bucharest.

Crampton, R., 2007. Bulgaria. Oxford University Press, Oxford.

Crawford, B. and Lijphart, A., 1997. Old legacies, new institutions: explaining political and economic trajectories in post-Communsit regimes. In: Crawford, B., Lijphart, A. (Eds.), Liberalization and Leninist Legacies: Comparative Perspectives on Democratic Transitions. University of California, Berkeley.

Fatu, M., Spalatelu, I., 1980. Garda de Fier, organizatie de tip fascist [The Iron Guard, a Fascist-type Organization], second ed. Editura politica, Bucharest.

Furet, F., 1999. The Passing of an Illusion: The Idea of Communism in the Twentieth Century. University of Chicago Press, Chicago.

182 MICHAEL MINKENBERG (ED.)

Gallagher, T., 2005. Modern Romania: The End of Communism, the Failure of Democratic Reform and the Theft of a Nation. NYU Press, New York.

Gheorghiu-Dej, G., 1945. Raportul Politic al Comitetului Central la Conferinta Nationala a Partidului Comunist Roman [The Political Report of the Central Committee to the National Conference of the Romanian Communist Party]. Scanteia (20 October 1945).

Ghodsee, K., 2008. Left Wing, right wing, everything: xenophobia, neo-totalitarianism, and populist politics in Bulgaria. Problems of Post-Communism 55 (3), 26-39.

Griffin, R., 1995. Fascism. Oxford University Press, Oxford.

Griffin, R., 1996. Staging the nation's rebirth: the politics and aesthetics of performance in the context of fascist studies. In: Berghuas, G. (Ed.), Fascism and Theater. Berghan, Oxford.

Griffin, R., 2004. Introduction: God's counterfeiters? Investigating the triad of fascism, totalitarianism and (political) religion. Totalitarian Movements and Political Religions 5 (3), 291-325.

Griffin, R., 2006. Fascism's new faces (and new facelessness) in the "post-fascist" epoch. In: Griffin, R., et al. (Eds.), Fascism Past and Present, West and East. Ibidem-Verlag, Stuttgart, pp. 29-68.

Gyr, R., 1935. Studenţimea şi idealul spiritual [Youth and the Spiritual Ideal]. IN Copuzeanu, Bucharest.

Herf, J., 1997. Divided Memory: The Nazi Past in the Two Germanies. Harvard University Press, Cambridge.

Ioanid, R., 2004. The sacralized politics of the Romanian Iron Guard. Totalitarian Movements and Political Religions 5 (3), 419-453.

Ionescu, N., 1937. Prefaţa Foreword. In: Marin, V. (Ed.), Crez de Generatie [The Credo of the Generation]. Tipografia Bucovina, Bucharest.

Iordachi, C., 2004. Charisma, Politics and Violence: The Legion of the Archangel Michael in Interwar Romania. Studies on Eastern European Cultures and Societies, Trondheim.

Iordachi, C., Trecsényi, B., 2003. In search of a usable past: the question of national identity in Romanian studies, 1900-2000. East European Politics and Societies 17 (3), 415-453.

Jowitt, K., 1992. New World Disorder: the Leninist Extinction. University of California Press, Berkeley.

Judt, T., 2000. The past is another country: myth and memory in postwar Europe. In Deak, I., et al. (Eds.), The Politics of Retribution in Europe: World War II and its Aftermath. Princeton University Press, Princeton pp. 293-254.

Laruelle, M., 2008. Russian Eurasianism: An Ideology of Empire. John Hopkins Press, Baltimore.

Legion "Ivan Asen II" – Varna, 1938. Natasha Borba [Our Struggle]. Otdel za ideologiia I propaganda, Varna.

Livezeanu, I., 1995. The Cultural Politics of Greater Romania. Cornell University Press, Ithaca.

Lukov, H., 1942. Dve rechi proizneseni ot General Hr. Lukov na 8 Dekemvrii 1942 godina [Two Speeches of General Hr. Lukov on December 8, 1942]. Bulgarska natsiia, Sofia.

Memishev, I., 1977. Uchastieto na Bulgarskite Turtsi v Borbata Protiv Kapitalizma i Fashizma, 1919-1944 g [Participation of the Bulgarian Turks in the Struggle Against Capitalism and Fascism]. Partizdat, Sofia.

Minkenberg, M., 2000. The renewal of the radical right: between modernity and anti-modernity. Government and Opposition 35 (2), 170–188.

Minkenberg, M., 2002. The radical right in postsocialist Central and Eastern Europe: comparative observations and interpretations. East European Politics and Societies 16 (2), 337-339.

Moța, I., 1936. Cranii de Lemn [Wooden Skulls]. Ed. Totul Pentru Tara, Sibiu.

Mudde, C., 2007. Populist Right Radical Parties in Europe. Cambridge University Press, Cambridge.

Mutafchiev, P., 1935. Kum novo vurzrazhdane [Towards a new revival]. Otets Paisii 8 (1).

Palaghita, S., 1993. Istoria Mişcării Legionare Scrisă de un Legionar [The History of the Legionary Movement written by a Legionnaire]. Editura Roza Vânturilor, Budapest.

Payne, S., 1995. A History of Fascism 1914-1945. University of Wisconsin Press, Madison.

Polihroniade, M., 1937. Legiunea şi Biserica Crestină [The Legion and the Christian Church]. Buna Vestire 1 (155).

Popkostadinova, N., 2006. Bulgaria: the Le Pen Syndrome. Transitions Online (Oct. 20, 2006).

Poppetrov, N., 2008. Fashizmut v Bulgariia [Fascism in Bulgaria]. Kama, Sofia.

Protopopescu, D., 1937. Contemporanii lui Isus [The Contemporaries of Christ]. Buna Vestire 1 (1).

Radulov, S., 1967. Za ideologiiata na bulgarskiia fashizum [Towards the ideology of Bulgarian fascism]. Istoricheski Pregled 23, 5.

Ramet, S. P., 1999. Defining the radical right: The values and behaviors of organized intolerance. In: Ramet, S. P. (Ed.), The Radical Right in Central and Eastern Europe Since 1989. University Park, Pennsylvania State University Press, pp. 3-28.

Roller, M., et al., 1947. Istoria României. Manual unic pentru clasa a VIII-a secundara [History of Romania: Manual Specifically for the 8th Form Secondary]. Editura de Stat, Bucharest.

Shafir, M., 2004. Between denial and 'comparative trivialization': holocaust negationism in post-communist East Central Europe. In: Braham, R. (Ed.), The Treatment of Holocaust in Hungary and Romania During the Post-Communist Era. Columbia University Press, New York.

Siderov, V., 2002. Bumerang na zloto [Boomerang of Evil]. Obektiv, Sofia.

Siderov, V., 2003. Bulgarofobiia [Bulgarophobia]. Bumerang BG, Sofia.

Siderov, V., 2004. Vlastta na Mamona: koi i kak ni ograbva [The Power of Mammon: Who and How They Plunder Us]. Bumerang BG, Sofia.

Stefanova, B., 2007. Voting "a la carte": electoral support for the radical right in the 2005 Bulgarian parliamentary elections. Politics in Central Europe 2 (2), 38-70.

Sternhell, Z., 1986. The Birth of Fascist Ideology: From Cultural Rebellion to Political Revolution. Princeton University Press, Princeton.

Tismaneanu, V., 2003. Stalinism for All Seasons: A Political History of Romanian Communism. University of California Press, Berkeley.

Todorova, M., 1997. The Ottoman legacy in the Balkans. In: Brown, L.C. (Ed.), Imperial Legacy: The Ottoman Imprint on the Balkans and the Middle East. Columbia University Press 2004.

Todorova, M., 2004. Learning memory, remembering identity. In: Todorova, M. (Ed.), Balkan Identities: Nation and Memory. NYU Press, New York.

Tsankov, A., 1938. Moiata Programa [My Program]. N.p., Sofia.

Tudor, V.T., 2001. In: Discursuri, Vols. 1 and 2. Editura Fundatiei Romania Mare, Budapest.

Verdery, K., 1995. National Ideology under Socialism: Identity and Cultural Politics in Ceausescu's Romania. University of California Press, Berkeley.

Vladikin, L., 1943. Za Pravoto na Natsiiata [For the Right of the Nation]. Nauchna Biblioteka Nova Evropa, Sofia.

Zhelev, Z., 1990. Fashizmut: totalitarnata durzhava [Fascism: the Totalitarian State]. Izdatelstvo na BZNS, Sofia.

AFTERWORD

Modalities of fear
The radical right in Eastern Europe[1]

Sabrina P. Ramet

The contributors to this volume have endeavored to address three central questions: first, which legacies from the past may be considered to influence the values and behaviors of at least some of the parties we may classify as radical right; second, more specifically, what is the relationship of today's radical right parties to the fascist parties of the interwar era (1918-39) and World War Two; and third, if we were to construct a taxonomy of radical right parties, what factors should guide us in so doing?

In an earlier publication, *Michael Minkenberg* has usefully defined right-wing radicalism as "a political ideology, whose core element is a myth of a homogeneous nation, a romantic and populist ultranationalism directed against the concept of liberal and pluralistic democracy and its underlying principles of individualism and universalism" (Minkenberg, 2002, p. 337). In much the same spirit, I have suggested that radical right politics might be understood as a form of organized intolerance, defining the form as "that segment of the political landscape which arose, historically, as a dimension of cultural 'irrationalism', and is inspired by intolerance (of any defined as 'outsiders'), and hostility to notions of popular sovereignty or popular rule…[and] characterized by ideological and programmatic emphasis on 'restoring' supposedly traditional values of the Nation or community and imposing them on the entire Nation or community" (Ramet, 1999, p. 4). The insistence on homogeneity, stressed by *Minkenberg*, leads directly to an intolerance of heterogeneity, with those defined as "different" being understood also as "enemies".

---

1   The below page numbers in italics refer to the relevant chapters of this volume.

In addressing the first question, the contributors to this volume distinguish among three legacies: that of the pre-communist era (pre-1917 for Russia, but defined in this collection as 1919-49 for the other cases discussed herein); the legacy of the communist era, which ended in 1989/91; and finally, the context of post-communist transformation itself, especially in the initial few years. *Frusetta* and *Glont* offer answers to the first two questions which underpin this volume. In their view, the legacy of interwar and Second World War-era fascism, at least where the parties they consider are concerned, is largely limited to providing a set of symbols, historical "heroes", and rhetorical style, although anti-Semitism, a central impulse in pre-1945 fascism, has also been characteristic of some of the contemporary radical parties, including the Bulgarian *Ataka* party as well as Vadim Tudor's Greater Romania Party (at least until 2004). Still, as they note, George "Gigi" Becali, founder and leader of Romania's New Generation Party, has called for the canonization of Corneliu Zelea Codreanu (1899-1938), founder of the Legion of the Archangel Michael, while the Bulgarian National Alliance has glorified the ancient Bulgar khanates and demanded the creation of a "new order" in the country. But, in spite of this demand, the two authors argue that there is little evidence in the region of demands for a broad social revolution along the lines of what pre-1945 fascists sought and conclude that "the crucial legacy [for the radical right today] is that of the Socialist era, which created conditions for a mutable memory of fascism: the rejection of Socialist-era historical memory allowed for the substitution and revival of new, often inaccurate, memories of fascism" *(pp. 160-161).*

De Lange and *Guerra*, in their chapter on the League of Polish Families, are prepared to concede that historical legacies shape perceptions of and attitudes toward political issues, as well as the political space in which issues are contested. However, they find that, in spite of the appearance of other right-wing extremist parties in Poland, such as Bolesław Tejkowski's Polish Nationalist Union and Andrzej Lepper's *Samoobrona* (Self-Defense), the League is the only radical right party in Poland which "has been able to profit from the opportunities created by the Polish historical legacy" *(p. 149).* The League enjoyed temporary success, in this regard, by tapping into the traditionalist views of a segment of the Catholic electorate in the country. While this establishes a tie with the interwar era (see Walicki, 1999; and Mudde, 2000, p. 10), the authors warn that seeking explanations for contemporary radical right behaviors exclusively through the lens of legacies would result in deterministic analysis.

In a chapter published a decade ago, Michael Shafir proposed that one might usefully distinguish between parties of "radical return" and parties of "radical continuity". By the former, Shafir understood radical right parties which looked back to the values and heritage of fascist parties from the period 1919-45; by the latter, he referred to parties which, even if situating themselves on the extreme right of the political spectrum, nonetheless took their cue from the symbols, style of governance, and legacy of the communist era (Shafir, 1999, p. 215). This distinction reminds us that differences within the radical right may have deep roots.

Ishiyama's contribution to this volume draws upon Shafir's essay, among other sources, focusing on what he calls the "red-brown vote". By this he means voters with right-wing extremist views who support organizational successors to the (old) communist parties. *Ishiyama* believes that this phenomenon reflects "ideological confusion" *(pp. 65, 69, 81)* and notes that J. A. Tucker concluded that economic difficulties were a relevant factor in this connection. *Ishiyama*, for his part, prefers to emphasize that, in his view, high rates of red-brown voting are directly correlated with the degree "to which the previous communist regime had retarded the development of political competition" *(p. 65)*. This analysis leads *Ishiyama* to conclude that it is the communist legacy which is the most important in determining the size of the red-brown vote.

In examining the Russian case, *Beichelt* traces the roots of the contemporary radical right farther back in time, urging that such Leninist features as one may find in the Russian radical right serve primarily as "catalysts for traditions which reach back" to the time before the Bolshevik Revolution of 1917, i.e., to the tsarist era *(p. 96)*. *Beichelt* also distinguishes between the "social nationalist" orientation he identifies with the Communist Party of the Russian Federation (CPRF) and the "imperial nationalist" position adopted by Vladimir Zhirinovsky's Liberal-Democratic Party of Russia. Whereas Gennady Zyuganov's CPRF has embraced tsarist-era concepts of Orthodoxy and Nationality, according to Beichelt, calling on Russia to resist Western materialism, Zhirinovsky's party has gone further, calling for a new surge of territorial expansion in order to restore some version of the Russian empire, by extending Russia's frontiers to the Indian Ocean (Eatwell, 2002, p. 7; see also Mudde, 2000, p. 18).

These imperial pretensions are shared by the International Eurasian Movement, set up by Aleksandr Gelyevich Dugin, a Russian nationalist and fascist, and first registered as the Eurasia Party in June 2002, and the National Bolshevist Portal, set up by Andrei Ignatiev, an admirer of the reactionary monarchist Konstantin Leontiev (1831-1891), in June 2005. Both of these groups reject Western values including liberalism, and call for a program of religious and moral traditionalism. Indeed, at the National Bolshevists' website, one may read:

> We reject the modern cosmopolitan system based on capitalism, liberalism and democracy, 'values' of consumption society and the mass culture. We think that way of development for modern civilization based on satisf[ying] constantly growing requirements of [the] Philistine mass leads to a deadlock. We support the revival of Russia as the Eurasian empire which would be built on autocracy, strict hierarchy (as in the Order) and socialist economic structure. In many aspects the ideal for us is the Soviet Union from [the] thirties to 1953 (National Bolshevist, 2010).

Bustikova and *Kitschelt* take a somewhat different approach to the question of legacies, focusing their attention on the "Leninist legacy" and distinguishing among three alternative Leninist legacies: those of national-accommodative communism, of patrimonial communism, and of bureaucratic communism. They find that the first two of these "Leninist" legacies have their roots in pre-1939 non-democratic regimes. Focusing on these two, they conclude that "[t]he legacy of patrimonial communism" has fueled the radical right *(pp. 30, 37)*, while the legacy of national-accommodative communism has been less favorable to parties on the extreme right.

However, while acknowledging that one or another Leninist legacy may have an impact "on the content and origins of the ideological position held by radical parties in the post-communist setting" *(p. 32)* as well as noting "the important effects of authoritarian pre-communist and religious legacies on the 'return of the radical right'" *(p. 31)*, these authors draw our attention to another variable. In their view, the presence or absence of economic grievances should be considered a critical factor in accounting for the relative success or failure of radical right appeals. Furthermore, striking a deeply pessimistic note, they urge that intolerance of those seen as different should be taken as a "given", i.e., as something stable which can be tapped under certain conditions *(p. 30)*.

On this point, Mihai Varga offers an alternative perspective. Basing his conclusions on an analysis of the radical right in Russia, Varga suggests that specific government actions or failures to act have resulted in creating opportunities for right-wing extremists; among the examples he gives are failure to enforce laws against radical right violence, handing out lenient sentences to perpetrators of such violence, collaboration between government agencies and skinheads, and the Russian government's own ethnocentric actions (Varga, 2008, p. 562, pp. 572-574). At the same time, Varga argues that intolerance may not be as resistant to change as *Bustikova* and *Kitschelt* suggest. On the contrary, citing Seymour Martin Lipset, Varga traces support for extremist views to economic and psychological insecurity, informational isolation, and a low level of education (Varga, 2008, p. 565) – all factors subject to at least partial correction over time.

In regard to the third question stated at the outset – Which factors should guide us if we should wish to construct a taxonomy of radical right parties? – we have already encountered several alternative approaches. For *de Lange* and *Guerra,* a key distinction is between parties which offer primarily nationalist but not religious appeals and those that appeal to the traditional faith of the community. For Shafir, the operative distinction is between parties of "radical return" and parties of "radical continuity". For *Beichelt*, the starting point is to differentiate between parties with a "social-nationalist" orientation and those with an "imperial-nationalist" (i.e., irredentist) program. And for *Bustikova* and *Kitschelt*, a distinction may be made between alternative Leninist legacies which in turn create different contexts in which radical right parties must operate.

What is also clear is that the issues of the 1930s are not identical with the issues of today, just as the challenges associated with the communist era are not identical with the challenges which post-communist societies face today. And this, in turn, translates into both rhetorical and programmatic differences. For example, if one looks at the fascist regimes which functioned during the Second World World War in Croatia and Serbia, and at the Arrow Cross regime which ran Hungary from October 1944 to March 1945, anti-Semitism stands out as the dominant feature (albeit combined with anti-Serbism in Axis Croatia) alongside anti-liberalism and anti-communism. Today, by contrast, in spite of continued anti-Semitism in much of the region

(Minkenberg, 2002, p. 346), including in Serbia and Poland, and persistent anti-liberalism among right-wing extremists, there are other "enemies" which have assumed importance for the region's far right adherents. Roma figure prominently here throughout the Central and Southeast European region while, in Bulgaria, Ivan Georgiev's Bulgarian National Radical Party combined anti-Turkish with anti-Roma rhetoric (Mudde, 2000, p. 22).

The War of Yugoslav Succession (1991-95) and War for Kosovo (1998-99) are also relevant here (see Ramet, 2005). Both wars depended on the prior mobilization, even radicalization, of public opinion in Serbia and had the effect radicalizing public opinion not only among Serbs but also, in reaction, among Croats, Bosniaks, and Kosovar Albanians. The result is high levels of anti-Muslim and anti-Albanian sentiment among Serbs, alongside high levels of anti-Serb sentiment among Croats, Bosniaks, and Kosovar Albanians. The role of the war in this regard is clear from the fact that public opinion polls recorded low levels of ethnic intolerance in socialist Yugoslavia before its breakup in the course of 1989-91, but a tangible increase in ethnic intolerance between 1990 and 1996 – where Croatia is concerned, especially in areas heavily affected by the war (Strabac and Valenta, 2010, pp. 85-86). Indeed, Sekulić, Massey, and Hodson confirm that it was "the events of the war itself and especially elite manipulation of public images of these events [that] are strongly implicated in rising intolerance dring the war" (2006, p. 797, bold face removed). And, as they further note, "the war's residual effect has been slow to dissipate" (Sekulić, Massey, and Hodson, 2006, p. 797; see also Hodson, Sekulić, and Massey, 1994, p. 1535). Interestingly enough, after the death of Croatian President Franjo Tudjman in December 1999 and the removal from power of Serbian President Slobodan Milošević in October 2000, Croatian politics became more moderate, while the Serbian Radical Party, which had already established itself as "the most successful far right party in post-communist Eastern Europe" (Stefanovic, 2008, p. 1195), grew in strength over the next years.

However, while hostile contact contributes to fear and even hatred between the groups affected, survey data from 1989-90 in what was then socialist Yugoslavia found that tolerance was highest in those regions with the greatest national diversity – specifically, Bosnia-Herzegovina and Vojvodina (Hodson, Sekulić, and Massey, 1994, pp. 1535, 1547).

Several of the contributors to this volume have highlighted fear of difference as an operative variable in radical right appeal. Where there is an "enemy", there is fear and, where there is fear, the fearful need a bold protector. As Paul Sum has noted elsewhere,

> [t]he radical right drives wedges between and among citizens, eroding social trust, in an effort to gain support. Through breeding and reinforcing fears of others, radical right leaders establish lines of 'particularized trust' which rely on paternalistic social relations and are uncomfortable, if not fully incompatible, with democratic governance (Sum, 2010, p. 25).

Radical right politics responds, inevitably, to local settings and, depending on the context, may target members of ethnic or racial minorities, religious minorities, or sexual minorities. Where these minorities are relative newcomers to the country – as is the case with Asians working in Siberia or with the roughly 30,000 Vietnamese who live in Poland (Sosin, 2006) – the potential for distance and distrust is increased; and distance and distrust are susceptible to manipulation and conversion into fear.

Today's radical right is, for the most part, not as traditional as that of the 1930s and its relationship to mainstream religion is, with a very few exceptions, quite different. Indeed, the new radical right, while continuing to worry about ethnic mixing, has integrated diverse ideological currents to offer an alternative to both center-right and social democratic parties (Spektorowski, 2002, pp. 177, 182). But, as these societies become ever more fully integrated into the European Union and as the democratic institutions which began to be put into place barely two decades ago continue to be consolidated and routinized, the prospects for a radical right diversion of these societies should become steadily more remote.

References

Eatwell, R., 2002. The Rebirth of Right-Wing Charisma? The Cases of Jean-Marie Le Pen and Vladimir Zhirinovsky. Totalitarian Movements and Political Religions, 3 (3), 1-23.

Hodson, R., Sekulić, D., Massey, G., 1994. National Tolerance in the Former Yugoslavia. The American Journal of Sociology, 99 (6), 1534-1558.

Minkenberg, M., 2002. The Radical Right in Postsocialist Central and Eastern Europe: Comparative Observations and Interpretations. East European Politics and Societies, 16 (2), 335-362.

Mudde, C., 2000. Extreme-right Parties in Eastern Europe. Patterns of Prejudice, 34 (1), 5-27.

National Bolshevist Portal (2010). At http://www.nb-info.ru/mainengl.html [accessed on 8 May 2010].

Ramet, S. P., 1999. Defining the Radical Right: Values and Behaviors of Organized Intolerance in Post-Communist Central and Eastern Europe. In: Ramet, S. P. (Ed.), The Radical Right in Central and Eastern Europe. The Pennsylvania State University Press, University Park, Pa, pp. 3-27.

Ramet, S. P., 2005. Thinking about Yugoslavia: Scholarly Debates about the Yugoslav Breakup and the Wars in Bosnia and Kosovo. Cambridge University Press, Cambridge.

Sekulić, D., Massey, G., Hodson, R., 2006. Ethnic intolerance and ethnic conflict in the dissolution of Yugoslavia. Ethnic and Racial Studies, 29 (5), 797-827.

Shafir, M., 1999. The Mind of Romania's Radical Right. In: Ramet, S. P. (Ed.), The Radical Right in Central and Eastern Europe. The Pennsylvania State University Press, University Park, Pa, pp. 213-232.

Sosin, N., 2006. Disappearing in the crowd: Vietnamese immigrants in Poland. cafébabel.com (14 September), at http://www.cafebabel.co.uk/

article/18039/disappearing-in-the-crowd-vietnamese-immigrants-in-poland.html [accessed on 7 June 2010].

Spektorowski, A., 2002. The Intellectual New Right, the European Radical Right and the Ideological Challenge to Liberal Democracy. International Studies, 39 (2), 165-182.

Strabac, Z., Valenta, M., 2010. Ethnic Intolerance, Voting Preferences, and Political Change in Croatia. Südosteuropa, 58 (1), 83-97.

Sum, P. E., 2010. The radical right in Romania: Political party evolution and the distancing of Romania from Europe. Communist and Post-Communist Studies, 43 (1), 19-29.

Varga, M., 2008. How Political Opportunities Strengthen the Far Right: Understanding the Rise in Far-Right Militancy in Russia. Europe-Asia Studies, 60 (4), 561-579.

Walicki, A., 1999. The Troubling Legacy of Roman Dmowski. East European Politics and Societies, 14 (1), 12-46.

SOVIET AND POST-SOVIET POLITICS AND SOCIETY

Edited by Dr. Andreas Umland

ISSN 1614-3515

Quotes from reviews of SPPS volumes:

On vol. 1 – *The Implementation of the ECHR in Russia*: "Full of examples, experiences and valuable observations which could provide the basis for new strategies."

Diana Schmidt, *Neprikosnovennyi zapas*

On vol. 2 – *Putins Russland*: "Wipperfürth draws attention to little known facts. For instance, the Russians have still more positive feelings towards Germany than to any other non-Slavic country."

Oldag Kaspar, *Süddeutsche Zeitung*

On vol. 3 – *Die Übernahme internationalen Rechts in die russische Rechtsordnung*: "Hussner provides a detailed, focused study dealing with all relevant aspects and containing insights into Russian legal thought."

Herbert Küpper, *Jahrbuch für Ostrecht*

On vol. 5 – *Квадратные метры, определяющие сознание*: "Meerovich provides a study that will be of considerable value to housing specialists and policy analysts."

Christina Varga-Harris, *Slavic Review*

On vol. 6 – *New Directions in Russian International Studies*: "A helpful step in the direction of an overdue dialogue between Western and Russian IR scholarly communities."

Diana Schmidt, *Europe-Asia Studies*

On vol. 8 – *Nation-Building and Minority Politics in Post-Socialist States:* "Galbreath's book is an admirable and craftsmanlike piece of work, and should be read by all specialists interested in the Baltic area."

Andrejs Plakans, *Slavic Review*

On vol. 9 – *Народы Кавказа в Вооружённых силах СССР*: "In this superb book, Bezugolnyi skillfully fashions a candid record of how the Soviet Union employed ethnic groups in its World War II effort."

David J. Glantz, *Journal of Slavic Military Studies*

On vol. 10 – *Русское Национальное Единство*: "A work that is likely to remain the definitive study of the Russian National Unity for a very long time."

Mischa Gabowitsch, *e-Extreme*

On vol. 14 – *Aleksandr Solzhenitsyn and the Modern Russo-Jewish Question*: "Larson has written a well-balanced survey of Solzhenitsyn's writings on Russian-Jewish relations."

Nikolai Butkevich, *e-Extreme*

On vol. 16 – *Der russische "Sonderweg"?*: "Luks's remarkable knowledge of Russian history gives his observations a particular sharpness and his judgements exceptional weight."

Peter Krupnikow, *Mitteilungen aus dem baltischen Leben*

On vol. 17 – *История «Мёртвой воды»*: "Moroz provides one of the best available surveys of Russian neo-paganism."

Mischa Gabowitsch, *e-Extreme*

On vol. 18 – *Этническая и религиозная интолерантность в российских СМИ*: "A constructive contribution to a crucial debate about media-endorsed intolerance which has once again flared up in Russia."

Mischa Gabowitsch, *e-Extreme*

On vol. 25 – *The Ghosts in Our Classroom*: "Inan-Freyberg's well-researched and incisive monograph should be required reading for those Eurocrats who have shaped Romanian spending priorities since 2000."

Tom Gallagher, *Slavic Review*

On vol. 26 – *The 2002 Dubrovka and 2004 Beslan Hostage Crises:* "Dunlop's analysis will help to draw Western attention to the plight of those who have suffered by these terrorist acts, and the importance, for all Russians, of uncovering the truth of about what happened."

Amy Knight, *Times Literary Supplement*

On vol. 29 – *Zivilgesellschaftliche Einflüsse auf die Orange Revolution*: "Strasser's study constitutes an outstanding empirical analysis and well-grounded location of the subject within theory."

Heiko Pleines, *Osteuropa*

On vol. 33 – *Cleft Countries*: "Katchanovski succeeds in crafting a convincing, well-supported set of arguments. His research constitutes a step forward in dealing with the notoriously thorny concept of political culture."

Thomas E. Rotnem, *Political Studies Review*

On vol. 34 – *Postsowjetische Feiern*: "Mühlfried's book contains not only a solid ethnographic study, but also points at some problems emerging from Georgia's prevalent understanding of culture."

Godula Kosack, *Anthropos*

On vol. 35 – *Fascism Past and Present, West and East*: "Committed students will find much of interest in these sometimes barbed exchanges."

Robert Paxton, *Journal of Global History*

On vol. 37 – *Political Anti-Semitism in Post-Soviet Russia*: "Likhachev's book serves as a reliable compendium and a good starting point for future research on post-Soviet xenophobia and ultra-nationalist politics."

Kathleen Mikkelson, *Demokratizatsiya*

On vol. 39 – *Российский консерватизм и реформа 1907-1914*: "Luk'ianov's work is a well-researched, informative and valuable addition, and enhances our understanding of politics in late imperial Russia."

Matthew Rendle, *Revolutionary Russia*

On vol. 43 – *Verflechtungen der deutschen und russischen Zeitgeschichte:* "Khavkin's book should be of interest to everybody studying German-Soviet relations and highlights new aspects in that field."

Wiebke Bachmann, *Osteuropa*

On vol. 50 – *Современные интерпретации русского национализма*: "This thought-provoking and enlightening set of works offers valuable insights for anyone interested in understanding Russian nationalism."

Andrew Konitzer, *The Russian Review*

On vol. 57 – *Russland und seine GUS-Nachbarn*: "Wipperfürth's enlightening and objective analysis documents detailed background knowledge and understanding of complex relationships. "

Julia Schatte, *Eurasisches Magazin*

On vol. 59 – *Das sakrale eurasische Imperium des Aleksandr Dugin*: "Höllwerth's outstanding 700-page dissertation is certainly the, so far, most ambitious attempt to decipher Dugin's body of thought."

Tanja Fichtner, *Osteuropa*

On vols 63-68 – *Aspects of the Orange Revolution I-VI:* "These 45 papers and supplemental election reports provide an excellent overview of the Ukrainian 2004 events, as well as their historical and political context."

Uwe Dathe, *Osteuropa*

On vol. 80 – *Nation, Region and History in Post-Communist Transition*: "Rodgers provides with his analysis an important contribution to a specific view on Ukraine."

Marinke Gindullis, *Zeitschrift für Politikwissenschaft*

Series Subscription

Please enter my subscription to the series *Soviet and Post-Soviet Politics and Society*, ISSN 1614-3515, as follows:

❑ complete series   OR   ❑ English-language titles
                                                ❑ German-language titles
                                                ❑ Russian-language titles

starting with
❑ volume # 1
❑ volume # ___
     ❑ please also include the following volumes: #___, ___, ___, ___, ___, ___, ___
❑ the next volume being published
     ❑ please also include the following volumes: #___, ___, ___, ___, ___, ___, ___

❑ 1 copy per volume   OR   ❑ ___ copies per volume

Subscription within Germany:

You will receive every volume at 1st publication at the regular bookseller's price – incl. s & h and VAT.
Payment:
❑ Please bill me for every volume.
❑ Lastschriftverfahren: Ich/wir ermächtige(n) Sie hiermit widerruflich, den Rechnungsbetrag je Band von meinem/unserem folgendem Konto einzuziehen.

Kontoinhaber: _____Kreditinstitut: _____

Kontonummer: _____Bankleitzahl:_____

International Subscription:

Payment (incl. s & h and VAT) in advance for
❑ 10 volumes/copies (€ 319.80)   ❑ 20 volumes/copies (€ 599.80)
❑ 40 volumes/copies (€ 1,099.80)
Please send my books to:

NAME_____DEPARTMENT_____

ADDRESS _____

POST/ZIP CODE_____COUNTRY _____

TELEPHONE _____EMAIL_____

date/signature_____

A hint for librarians in the former Soviet Union: Your academic library might be eligible to receive free-of-cost scholarly literature from Germany via the German Research Foundation. For Russian-language information on this program, see
     http://www.dfg.de/forschungsfoerderung/formulare/download/12_54.pdf.

Please fax to: **0511 / 262 2201 (+49 511 262 2201)**
or mail to: *ibidem*-Verlag, Julius-Leber-Weg 11, D-30457 Hannover, Germany
or send an e-mail: ibidem@ibidem-verlag.de

ibidem-Verlag

Melchiorstr. 15

D-70439 Stuttgart

info@ibidem-verlag.de

www.ibidem-verlag.de
www.ibidem.eu
www.edition-noema.de
www.autorenbetreuung.de